AMC'S BEST DAY HIKES IN
VERMONT

Four-Season Guide to 60 of the Best Trails in the Green Mountain State

3rd Edition // Jen Lamphere Roberts and Tara Schatz

Appalachian Mountain Club Books // Boston, Massachusetts

T0124485

AMC is a nonprofit organization, and sales of AMC Books fund our mission of protecting the Northeast outdoors. If you appreciate our efforts and would like to become a member or make a donation to AMC, visit outdoors.org, call 800-372-1758, or contact us at Appalachian Mountain Club, 10 City Square, Boston, MA 02129.

outdoors.org/books-maps

Distributed by National Book Network.

Front cover photograph of a hiker on Killington Peak © Tara Schatz
Back cover photograph of hikers on Stowe Pinnacle © Tara Schatz
Title page photograph of the Appalachian Trail in Woodford, Vermont © Tara Schatz
Interior photographs by Tara Schatz or Jen Lamphere Roberts, unless otherwise noted
Maps by Ken Dumas © Appalachian Mountain Club
Cover design by Jon Lavalley
Text design by Abigail Coyle

Library of Congress Cataloging-in-Publication Data
Names: Roberts, Jennifer Lamphere, author. | Schatz, Tara, author.
Title: AMC's best day hikes in Vermont : four-season guide to 60 of the best trails in the Green Mountain State / Jen Lamphere Roberts, Tara Schatz
Other titles: Appalachain Mountain Club's best day hikes in Vermont
Description: 3rd edition. | Boston : Appalachian Mountain Club Books, 2023. | Includes index. | Summary: "A guide to the best day hikes in the state of Vermont, for hikers of all level of experience and ability"--Provided by publisher.
Identifiers: LCCN 2023001246 (print) | LCCN 2023001247 (ebook) | ISBN 9781628421606 (trade paperback) | ISBN 9781628421613 (epub) | ISBN 9781628421620 (mobi)
Subjects: LCSH: Hiking--Vermont--Guidebooks. | Walking--Vermont--Guidebooks. | Trails--Vermont--Guidebooks. | Vermont--Guidebooks.
Classification: LCC GV199.42.V4 L35 2023 (print) | LCC GV199.42.V4 (ebook) | DDC 796.5109743--dc23/eng/20230202
LC record available at https://lccn.loc.gov/2023001246
LC ebook record available at https://lccn.loc.gov/2023001247

The paper used in this publication meets the minimum requirements of the American National Standard for Information Sciences-Permanence of Paper for Printed Library Materials, ANSI Z39.48-1984. ∞

Interior pages and cover are printed on responsibly harvested paper stock certified by The Forest Stewardship Council®, an independent auditor of responsible forestry practices.

Printed in the United States of America, using vegetable-based inks.

5 4 3 2 1   23 24 25 26

FSC
www.fsc.org

MIX
Paper from responsible sources
FSC® C005010

Dedicated with love to
Gary Webb Lamphere
—J. L. R.

Dedicated to my favorite hiking companions,
both human and canine: Eric, Flynn, and Malinda
—T. S.

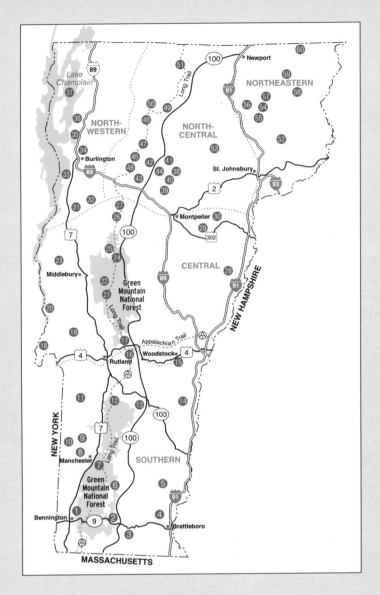

KEY TO ICONS

Alpine zone (an ecological zone characterized by the lack of trees; ground cover and plants are typical of arctic environments)

Exposed ledges (trail crosses an exposed ledge—a consideration in severe weather or in wet or icy conditions; hikes that end at a scenic ledge but do not cross an exposed ledge en route are not marked with this icon)

Steep or difficult terrain

Good for kids

Dog-friendly

Accessible

Waterfall

Pond, stream, spring, or other water feature

Snowshoeing

Cross-country skiing

Shelter

Designated tentsite

Scenic views

Wilderness area (federally designated areas of restricted human activity, with specific rules and regulations)

Swimming

Picnic area

Visitor center

Fee

Fishing

Horseback riding

Fire Tower

CONTENTS

5 // NORTHEASTERN VERMONT 218

NATURE AND HISTORY ESSAYS

AT-A-GLANCE TRIP PLANNER

Trip number	Trip name and location	Difficulty rating	Round-trip distance	Elevation gain	Estimated time
SECTION 1 // SOUTHERN VERMONT					
1	Bald Mountain (Bennington/Woodford) *Bennington and Woodford, VT*	Moderate	5.6 mi	2,099 ft	4.5 hrs
2	Haystack Mountain (Wilmington) *Wilmington, VT*	Moderate	4.2 mi	1,025 ft	3 hrs
3	Mount Olga *Wilmington, VT*	Easy–Moderate	1.8 mi	520 ft	1.5 hrs
4	Black Mountain *Dummerston, VT*	Moderate	3 mi	875 ft	2.5 hrs
5	Putney Mountain *Putney, VT*	Easy	1.2 mi	140 ft	1 hr
6	Grout Pond and Somerset Reservoir *Stratton, VT*	Easy	4.6 mi	250 ft	2.5 hrs
7	Lye Brook Falls *Manchester, VT*	Moderate	4.4 mi	740 ft	3 hrs
8	Mount Equinox *Manchester, VT*	Strenuous	6 mi	2,805 ft	4.5 hrs
9	Gettysburg Quarry and Owl's Head *Dorset, VT*	Moderate	5.1 mi	1,545 ft	3.5 hrs
10	Mount Antone *Rupert, VT*	Moderate	5.8 mi	800 ft	4 hrs
11	Haystack Mountain (North Pawlet) *Pawlet, VT*	Moderate	4 mi	770 ft	3 hrs
12	White Rocks Ice Beds *Wallingford, VT*	Easy	1.8 mi	336 ft	1.5 hrs
13	Okemo Mountain *Mount Holly, VT*	Moderate–Strenuous	6 mi	1,950 ft	4 hrs
14	Mount Ascutney *Windsor, VT*	Strenuous	5.2 mi	2,450 ft	4 hrs
15	Mount Tom's South Peak and the Pogue *Woodstock, VT*	Easy–Moderate	5.5 mi	700 ft	2.5 hrs
16	Killington Peak *Mendon, VT*	Strenuous	7.4 mi	2,335 ft	4.5 hrs

Trip highlights	Trip features
Unusual cobble fields and white sands on summit ridge, views of southern Vermont	🚶 🐕 🔍 ❄ 🌲
Views of Haystack Pond	🚶 🐎 💧 🔍 ❄
Loop hike, varied forests, fire tower	🚶 🐕 🔍 🎿 ⛰ $ 🗼
Rare forest on ridge with blueberries	🚶 🔍
Easy ridgeline walk, grassy summit	🚶 🐕 🔍 🎿 ❄
Swimming in two lakes, easy hiking and camping	🚶 🐎 💧 🔍 🎿 ⛰ 🏊 ⛲
125-foot waterfall in steep wilderness valley	🚶 🐕 🌊 🔍 🎿 🌲
Views from pretty ridge trail on highest Taconic peak	🥾 🐕 🔍 ❄ 🏔
Abandoned marble quarry and views of the Taconic Mountains	🚶 🐎 💧 🔍 ❄
Educational farm, parklike mature hardwood forests	🚶 🐎 🔍 🎿 ⬋ ❄ 🏔 🐴
Panoramic views and biodiverse forests	🚶 🔍 ❄
Open hemlock forest, microclimate at rock slide	🚶 🐕 🔍 ❄ ⛲
Fire tower with views across southern Vermont	🐕 🔍 ❄ 🗼
Waterfall, multiple viewpoints, fire tower	🥾 🐕 🌊 🔍 ⬋ ❄ 🗼
Scenic woodland, pond, views of Woodstock	🚶 🐎 💧 🔍 🎿 ❄ 🏔 🐴
Waterfall, 360-degree views	🥾 🏃 🌊 💧 🔍 🎿 ⬋ ❄

Trip number	Trip name and location	Difficulty rating	Round-trip distance	Elevation gain	Estimated time
SECTION 2 // CENTRAL VERMONT					
17	Deer Leap *Killington, VT*	Easy–Moderate	2 mi	430 ft	1.5 hrs
18	Helen W. Buckner Memorial Preserve at Bald Mountain *West Haven, VT*	Moderate	2.6 mi	240 ft	2.5 hrs
19	Mount Zion Major and Minor *Hubbardton, VT*	Moderate	1.8 mi	326 ft	1 hr
20	Mount Independence *Orwell, VT*	Easy–Moderate	3 mi	200 ft	2 hrs
21	Mount Horrid's Great Cliff *Goshen, VT*	Moderate	1.6 mi	620 ft	1.5 hrs
22	Robert Frost Interpretive Trail *Ripton, VT*	Easy	1 mi	17 ft	45 mins
23	Snake Mountain *Addison, VT*	Moderate	3.6 mi	900 ft	2 hrs
24	Sunset Ledge *Lincoln, VT*	Easy	2.2 mi	387 ft	1.5 hrs
25	Mount Abraham *Lincoln, VT*	Strenuous	5.2 mi	1,589 ft	3.5 hrs
26	Burnt Rock Mountain *Fayston, VT*	Strenuous	5.2 mi	2,090 ft	3.5 hrs
27	Camel's Hump (East and West Sides) *Duxbury and Huntington, VT*	Strenuous	7 mi east side; 5.3 mi west side	2,585 ft east side; 2,230 ft west side	6 hrs east side; 5.5 hrs west side
28	Bald Top Mountain *Fairlee, VT*	Moderate–Strenuous	6.8 mi	1,320 ft	4.5 hrs
29	Spruce Mountain *Plainfield, VT*	Moderate	4.4 mi	1,300 ft	3.5 hrs
30	Owl's Head *Peacham, VT*	Easy–Moderate	3.8 mi	370 ft	2 hrs
SECTION 3 // NORTHWESTERN VERMONT					
31	Mount Philo *Charlotte, VT*	Moderate	2.4 mi	580 ft	1.5 hrs
32	Raven Ridge *Monkton, VT*	Moderate	2.7 mi	410 ft	1.5 hrs
33	Allen Hill *Shelburne, VT*	Easy	1.9 mi	120 ft	1.5 hrs
34	Colchester Pond *Colchester, VT*	Easy–Moderate	3.2 mi	150 ft	2 hrs
35	Niquette Bay *Colchester, VT*	Moderate	3.8 mi	480 ft	2.5 hrs

Trip highlights	Trip features
Rock outcrop, views	
Rare wildlife, open hickory forest	
Japanese garden, views	
Historic site, Lake Champlain views	
Rare plants, wide vistas	
Frost poems throughout fields, woods, and swamp	
Mature hardwood forest, clifftop views	
Ridgeline walk, views of Adirondacks	
Rare, above-treeline tundra plants, 360-degree views	
Boreal ridge, fun rock scrambles, views	
Iconic Vermont peak with rare tundra plants, views	
Grassy summit, views of White Mountains	
Fire tower, views	
Open fern meadows, rocky outcrop with views	
Scenic hike beneath cliff, views on top	
Wetlands, rocky ridge with views, geological oddity	
Lake Champlain views, swimming	
Pondside fields, woods, swimming, birdwatching	
Wildflowers, swimming, lake views	

Trip number	Trip name and location	Difficulty rating	Round-trip distance	Elevation gain	Estimated time
36	Eagle Mountain *Milton, VT*	Easy	2.1 mi	200 ft	1 hr
37	Burton Island *Saint Albans, VT*	Easy	2.8 mi	Minimal	2 hrs
SECTION 4 // NORTH-CENTRAL VERMONT					
38	Worcester Range Skyline *Worcester and Middlesex, VT*	Strenuous	10.5 mi	3,350 ft	8 hrs
39	White Rock Mountain *Middlesex, VT*	Moderate–Strenuous	4.6 mi	1,558 ft	3.5 hrs
40	Mount Hunger *Waterbury Center, VT*	Moderate–Strenuous	4 mi	2,290 ft	3.5 hrs
41	Elmore Mountain *Lake Elmore, VT*	Moderate	4.5 mi	1,145 ft	3 hrs
42	Wiessner Woods *Stowe, VT*	Easy	1.5 mi	100 ft	1 hr
43	Barnes Camp Loop *Stowe, VT*	Moderate	1.5 mi	390 ft	1 hr
44	Stowe Pinnacle *Stowe, VT*	Moderate	2.8 mi	1,520 ft	2.5 hrs
45	Mount Mansfield's Chin *Underhill, VT*	Strenuous	6.2 mi	2,543 ft	4.5 hrs
46	Mount Mansfield's Forehead *Underhill and Stowe, VT*	Strenuous	5.2 mi	2,520 ft	4.5 hrs
47	Sterling Pond *Cambridge, VT*	Moderate	3.3 mi	1,320 ft	3 hrs
48	Prospect Rock *Johnson, VT*	Easy–Moderate	3 mi	540 ft	2 hrs
49	Devil's Gulch and Big Muddy Pond *Eden, VT*	Moderate	5.2 mi	1,000 ft	4 hrs
50	Laraway Lookout *Johnson, VT*	Moderate	3.9 mi	1,400 ft	2.5 hrs
51	Jay Peak *Westfield, VT*	Moderate	3.4 mi	1,638 ft	3 hrs
SECTION 4 // NORTHEASTERN VERMONT					
52	Burke Mountain *Burke, VT*	Strenuous	6.2 mi	2,080 ft	4.5 hrs
53	Barr Hill *Greensboro, VT*	Easy	0.8 mi	120 ft	45 mins
54	Mount Pisgah *Westmore, VT*	Moderate	4.8 mi	1,395 ft	3 hrs

Trip highlights	Trip features
Varied landscapes, tons of spring wildflowers	▨ ▨ ▨ ▨ ▨
Shoreline loop hike with views and swimming	▨ ▨ ▨ ▨ ▨ ▨ ▨ ▨ ▨ ▨ ▨
Four peaks, remote forest ridge	▨ ▨ ▨ ▨ ▨
Fun rock scrambling, unusual summit terraces, views	▨ ▨ ▨ ▨ ▨
Steep ledges, bald summit, views	▨ ▨ ▨ ▨ ▨
Loop hike, fire tower, views, balanced boulder on ridgeline	▨ ▨ ▨ ▨ ▨ ▨ ▨
Loop hike through varied forests	▨ ▨ ▨ ▨ ▨
Accessible boardwalk, views of Smugglers' Notch	▨ ▨ ▨ ▨ ▨ ▨ ▨
Views from bald spot on mountainside	▨ ▨ ▨
Open ridgeline hike, alpine tundra, highest point in Vermont	▨ ▨ ▨ ▨ ▨ ▨ ▨
Loop hike, tundra, views	▨ ▨ ▨ ▨ ▨ ▨ ▨
Steep, scenic notch and high mountain pond	▨ ▨ ▨ ▨ ▨ ▨ ▨ ▨
Views from rock outcrop	▨ ▨ ▨ ▨ ▨ ▨ ▨
Rock scrambling in narrow ravine, pond shore, views from shelter	▨ ▨ ▨ ▨ ▨
Overhanging rocks, views	▨ ▨ ▨ ▨ ▨ ▨
Open ridge and summit, views	▨ ▨ ▨ ▨
Mature, open hardwoods, fire tower, views	▨ ▨ ▨ ▨ ▨ ▨
Multiple viewpoints, loop hike	▨ ▨ ▨ ▨ ▨ ▨
High, rocky perches over scenic lake	▨ ▨ ▨ ▨

Trip number	Trip name and location	Difficulty rating	Round-trip distance	Elevation gain	Estimated time
55	Mount Hor *Sutton, VT*	Easy–Moderate	2.9 mi	601 ft	1.5 hrs
56	Wheeler Mountain *Sutton, VT*	Moderate	4.1 mi	870 ft	3.5 hrs
57	Bald Mountain (Westmore) *Westmore, VT*	Moderate	4 mi	1,450 ft	2.5 hrs
58	Moose Bog *Ferdinand, VT*	Easy	1 mi	34 ft	30 mins
59	Bluff Mountain *Island Pond, VT*	Moderate	3.3 mi	1,110 ft	2.5 hrs
60	Brousseau Mountain *Norton, VT*	Easy–Moderate	1.6 mi	590 ft	1 hr

Trip highlights	Trip features
Ridge walk to varied views, including Lake Willoughby	🚶 🥾 🐕 🔍 ☀️
Clifftop views	🧗 🐕 ☀️
Views from a fire tower, overnight cabin on summit	🥾 🐕 🔍 ⛺ ☀️ 🗼
Wetlands viewing platform, dense spruce forest	🥾 🐕 ♿ 💧 🔍
Loop hike, steep ledges, views	🧗 🐕 🔍 ☀️
Rocky outcrop, views	🧗 🥾 🐕 🔍 ☀️

PREFACE

Welcome to the third edition of *AMC's Best Day Hikes in Vermont*. The first edition was published in 2013, adding Vermont to a popular series of day-hiking guidebooks for hikers of all skill levels. The first and second editions, authored by Jen Lamphere Roberts, aimed to give hikers an overview of Vermont's landscapes by covering a diverse range of trails, from meandering walks through mature forests and easy trips to waterfalls and ponds for swimming, to rugged mountain treks that end with sweeping views among rare alpine plants.

The third edition of the book is coauthored by Tara Schatz and Jen Lamphere Roberts, who worked together to check each trail description for accuracy; identify trees, plants, and birds along each route; record Global Positioning System (GPS) tracks; and take an overabundance of photographs. Input from land managers has ensured that each trail description and corresponding map are up-to-date.

Of course, it's impossible to cover even a small fraction of the network of trails that crisscross Vermont, and with each edition, new hikes are added and others are retired. You may wonder how we decide which hikes to include, with so many amazing choices. The goal is always to choose hikes that cover a range of lengths and difficulties, spread evenly across the geographic landscape. Sometimes hikes are chosen for their unusual or remarkable natural features and sometimes simply because they are iconic and a guidebook wouldn't be complete without them.

For the third edition, we've added a few hikes that are, at least in part, universally accessible and suitable for people of all abilities. Both Raven Ridge (Trip 32) and Barnes Camp Loop (Trip 43) include accessible boardwalks with beautiful wetlands views. Another addition—Moose Bog (Trip 58)—is a 1-mile universally accessible hike on a graded path that leads to a wide boardwalk into Moose Bog. Yes, moose are common in the bog, as are beaver, blueberries, and numerous songbirds.

On the more rugged end, we've added the challenging hike along Bucklin Trail to the top of Killington Peak (Trip 16), Vermont's second-highest mountain at 4,230 feet. While much of Killington is developed as part of Killington Resort, the peak itself provides 360-degree views of the Green Mountains. We've also replaced a few popular trips on the Long Trail with routes that are a bit more remote, including two new hikes in the Taconic Mountains: Gettysburg Quarry and Owl's Head in Dorset (Trip 9) and Mount Zion Major and Minor (Trip 19) in Hubbardton.

We enjoyed discovering new hikes to add to this edition and are encouraged to know that there are many more to uncover for future editions. We hope you will use this book to find new trails and revisit old favorites. Most important, we hope you find as much delight in exploring Vermont's exceptional hiking trails as we have.

—Jen Lamphere Roberts and Tara Schatz

ACKNOWLEDGMENTS

I am so grateful to Tara Schatz for her care and thoroughness as she tackled the big project of third edition updates. Her photography alone improves the book dramatically, and her new hikes and essays are interesting, informative, and fresh. Thanks to AMC Senior Book Editor Tim Mudie for bringing Tara and me together on this project and for deftly shepherding us through the publication wilderness.

—Jen Lamphere Roberts, 2023

We had a tremendous amount of assistance putting this third edition together. Vermont has many smart, dedicated professionals working for the benefit of its natural places. We are fortunate to have benefited from their time and expertise to improve the descriptions in this book. Thanks to the following people for reviewing trips and helping update this third edition: Luke O'Brien, Brian Renfro, Lisa Thornton, Kathryn Wrigley, Ethan Phelps, Emily White, and the rest of the staff of Vermont Department of Forests, Parks, and Recreation; Danna Strout, Holly Knox, and Seth Coffey of the U.S. Forest Service; Lynn McNamara of The Nature Conservancy; Rick LaDue of Equinox Preservation Trust; Elsa Gilbertson of the Vermont Division for Historic Preservation; Maggie Stoudnour of Rivendell Trails Association; Geordie Heller of Putney Mountain Association; Betsy Cieplicki of Shelburne Parks and Recreation; Jeff O'Donnell of Lake Champlain Land Trust; Kay Emery from Marsh-Billings-Rockefeller National Historical Park; Amy Alfieri of the Vermont Fish and Wildlife Department; and Rachel Batz of the Town of Dorset.

For the third edition, I owe gratitude to Eric Schatz for picking up the slack at home and for slowing down on the trail so that I could mark waypoints, identify plants, and take photos. Thanks to Gabriel Schatz and Mackenzie Bourgeois for accompanying me to the Northeast Kingdom, and to Jen Lamphere Roberts for providing contacts, expertise, and advice as I worked through the process of scouting new trails. Finally, thanks to Tim Mudie and Abigail Coyle from AMC Books for giving me such a fun opportunity to explore more of Vermont.

—Tara Schatz, 2022

INTRODUCTION

Vermont is a small state, ranked 49th by population and 43rd by land area. Even Vermont's mountains are modest compared with those of its neighbors to the east and west, and mere hills when compared with the snowcapped peaks in the western half of the United States. But what Vermont lacks in size it makes up for in diverse, widespread, and abundant recreational opportunities.

Vermonters have an ingrained appreciation for the outdoors, evidenced by the vast network of hiking, biking, and ski trails crisscrossing the state, not to mention numerous town, county, and state parks, national forestlands, wildlife management areas, and other preserved tracts of land that make up the rural character of a state that is 78 percent forested. Whether people strap on skis to make fresh tracks in newly fallen snow, cast a line in a mountain stream for the first brookies of spring, or simply put one foot in front of the other en route to a magnificent vista, Vermont's forests, lakes, and mountains are for everyone, and they beg to be explored.

The Green Mountains (*Vert Mont* in French, giving Vermont its name), run north to south, bisecting the entire length of the state with rounded, ancient peaks. They are part of the larger Appalachian Mountain range, which stretches south all the way to Alabama and north to Newfoundland. Most of the hikes in this book are in the Green Mountains, with their rocky summits, expansive views, and numerous lakes, ponds, streams, and waterfalls. Running across the spine of the Green Mountains is the nation's oldest long-distance hiking trail. The 270-mile Long Trail begins at Vermont's southern border and travels north to the town of Jay on the Canadian border. Ten hikes in this guidebook travel on sections of the Long Trail, which has been captivating visitors since 1910.

While many of Vermont's most iconic day hikes require an arduous uphill climb to reap the reward of a spectacular view, just as many trails can be enjoyed without much effort. The easiest trips in this book are as short as a mile in length, without significant elevation gain, and are suitable even for small children to enjoy. Children are eager explorers and will be as enthralled with a fern-covered ledge, a meandering stream, or a patch of ripe berries as with a mountain vista. Hiking with kids is good for you, too—you may be itching to conquer your next peak, but as you meander along with your child, you can rediscover the magic of a woodland walk.

The trails in this book were chosen both for their remarkable features and for their representation of Vermont's different landscapes. They are spread out across the state and visit remote ponds and bogs, rare natural communities, waterfalls, historical sites, and even an island on Lake Champlain that is only reachable by boat. Several trails are universally accessible and suitable for those with limited mobility, and all of them give hikers opportunities to slow down and appreciate the incredible gift that Vermont's natural areas and wild spaces give to us all.

HOW TO USE THIS BOOK

With 60 hikes to choose from, you may wonder how to decide where to go. The locator map at the front of this book will help you narrow down the trips by location, and the at-a-glance trip planner that follows the table of contents will provide more information to guide you toward a decision.

Once you settle on a destination and turn to a trip in this guide, you will find a series of icons that indicate recommended or permitted activities, fees for parking or admittance to a property, potential hazards, and features such as water and scenic vistas.

Information on the basics follows: location, rating, distance, elevation gain, estimated time, and maps. The difficulty ratings are based on the authors' perception and are estimates of what the average hiker will experience. You may find hikes to be easier or more difficult than stated. The distance and estimated hiking time shown are for the entire trip, whether it's an out-and-back hike, a loop, or a one-way hike. The estimated time is also based on the authors' perception. Consider your own pace when planning a trip, especially if hiking with kids.

For hikes with the good-for-kids icon, the authors suggest an age range of children who might enjoy the trip, but of course children's interests and abilities vary tremendously. These suggestions are geared toward children who are not athletic prodigies but whose families hike together regularly. Some of the hikes designated as kid-friendly visit waterfalls or cliff lookouts that are great rewards for the effort to get there but can be hazardous. To determine whether a hike is appropriate for all family members, adults ultimately will have to gauge children's levels of interest, motivation, and ability.

The elevation gain is calculated from measurements and information from U.S. Geological Survey (USGS) topographic maps, landowner maps, and Google Earth. Information is included about the relevant USGS maps, as well as where you can find trail maps.

This section also includes Global Positioning System (GPS) coordinates for parking lots. Whether or not you own a GPS device, it is wise to bring an atlas, such as DeLorme's *New Hampshire and Vermont Atlas & Gazetteer* (2015), which shows small roads and forest roads in detail.

Contact information for the hiking location is also included here.

"Directions" explains how to reach the trailhead by car.

In "Trail Description," you will find detailed instructions on the given hike, including turn-by-turn directions. You will learn about the natural and human history along the route, as well as about flora, fauna, and any landmarks or objects you will encounter.

The trail maps that accompany each trip help guide you, but it is always wise to have an official trail map. Official maps are often—but not always—available online, at the trailhead, or at the visitor center. For each trip, see the list of relevant maps included in the basic information.

"Did You Know?" provides interesting facts about the area.

Each trip ends with a section called "More Information" that provides details about access times and fees, as well as the rules and regulations of the property on which the hike is located. "Nearby" offers suggestions for places to continue the experience once you've finished the hike—including swimming, paddling, or mountain-biking destinations—and where to find the closest shops and restaurants.

TRIP PLANNING AND SAFETY

You will be more likely to have an enjoyable, safe hike if you take proper precautions. Planning is the first step to a successful hike. Some of the trips in this guide ascend to bare, high-elevation summits where winds and low temperatures necessitate extra clothing. Other hikes visit clifftops or waterfalls where you'll need to use extra caution with children and dogs. Learn about the terrain you will travel through so you can pack the right gear and prepare for the experience. Allow extra time for potential delays.

Pack as if you will be out on the trail for hours longer than you hope to be, and you will have the supplies you need to stay comfortable and well fed in case an injury or a lost hiker keeps you on the trail into the evening or even overnight. Before heading out, consider the following:

- Select a hike that everyone in your group is comfortable taking. Match the hike to the abilities of the least capable person in the group. If anyone is uncomfortable with the weather or is tired, turn around and complete the hike another day.

- Plan to be back at the trailhead before dark. Before beginning your hike, determine a turnaround time. Monitor your group's pace and progress and turn around in time to get off the trail by dark, even if you have not reached your intended destination.

- Check the weather and assume it will be cooler and windier on the mountain than at the base. Weather conditions can change quickly, and any changes are likely to be more severe the higher you are on the mountain. In New England, planning for wet weather is always a good idea, regardless of the forecast.

Bring a pack with the following items:

- Water: Two quarts per person is usually adequate, depending on the weather and the length of the trip. You can carry less if you know you will be able to find water along the trail and if you bring a means of sterilizing found water, such as iodine, a filter, or a SteriPEN.

- Food: Even if you are planning just an hour-long hike, bring some high-energy snacks, such as nuts, dried fruit, or protein bars.

- Map and compass: Make sure to pack a map of your route. As backup, you might take a photo of the map with your phone or camera and pack extra batteries for that device. A handheld Global Positioning System device may also be helpful but shouldn't take the place of a paper map. If you pack a compass, make sure you know how to use it.

- Cell phone: Be aware that cell phone service is still unreliable in many parts of Vermont, and mountains may block signals even from nearby towers. Mute your phone while in the woods to avoid disturbing the backcountry experience for other hikers.

- Headlamp or flashlight, with spare batteries
- Extra clothing: rain gear, wool or fleece sweater, hat, and mittens
- Sunscreen
- First-aid kit, including adhesive bandages, gauze, nonprescription painkillers, moleskin, and any necessary prescription medication needed if on the trail longer than expected
- Pocketknife or multitool
- Waterproof matches or a lighter
- Toilet paper and double plastic bag to pack it out; do not leave toilet paper "flowers" strewn in the woods
- Whistle
- Insect repellent
- Sunglasses
- Binoculars (optional)
- Camera (optional)

Wear appropriate footwear and clothing. Waterproof boots or sneakers equal dry feet and more comfortable, happier hiking. Wool or synthetic hiking socks keep your feet drier than cotton and help prevent blisters. Cotton clothing, in general, absorbs sweat and rain, making it effective at helping cool you down but problematic or even dangerous if the weather conditions change. If you choose to wear cotton while hiking, bring a synthetic, wool, or silk layer to change into. Polypropylene, fleece, silk, and wool all wick moisture away from your body and keep you warm in wet or cold conditions. To help avoid insect bites, you may want to wear pants and a long-sleeved shirt.

Vermont's woods are home to biting insects that can be a minor or a significant nuisance, depending on seasonal and daily conditions. West Nile virus and eastern equine encephalitis (EEE) virus can be transmitted to humans by infected mosquitoes and cause rare but serious diseases. Reduce your risk of being bitten by using insect repellent, wearing long sleeves and pants, and avoiding hiking in the early morning and in the evening, when mosquitoes are most active. A variety of options are available for dealing with bugs, ranging from sprays that include the active ingredient DEET, which can potentially cause skin or eye irritation, to more skin-friendly products. After you complete your hike, check yourself for deer ticks, which can transmit numerous illnesses, including Lyme disease.

When you are ahead of the rest of your hiking group, wait at all trail junctions until the others catch up. This avoids confusion and keeps people from getting separated or lost.

If downed wood appears to be purposely covering a trail, it probably means the trail is closed.

When a trail is muddy, walk through the mud or on rocks, never on tree roots or plants. Water-resistant boots will keep your feet comfortable. Staying in the center of the trail will keep it from eroding into a wide hiking highway.

Leave your itinerary and the time you expect to return with someone you trust. If you see a logbook at a trailhead, be sure to sign in when you arrive and sign out when you finish your hike.

Stay alert for poison ivy, particularly at lower elevations near water. To identify the plant, look for clusters of three leaves that shine in the sun but are dull in the shade. If you do come into contact with poison ivy, wash the affected area with soap as soon as possible.

Wear blaze-orange items in hunting season. In Vermont, hunting begins in September; although most seasons end in December, some may extend later into winter. Yearly schedules are available at vtfishandwildlife.com and in flyers and brochures available at town halls, general stores, and other public areas.

Many trails are closed during mud season, and even if they are not, it's a good idea to avoid hiking when trails are especially susceptible to damage. Mud season is loosely defined as most of April and May—essentially, spring in Vermont—but in reality, mud season begins whenever the ground starts to thaw and lasts until the ground has dried out. The same conditions—saturated, partly frozen soils—can also occur in late fall and during winter thaws. Mud season begins and ends earlier in the warmer valleys than on the cool mountain slopes; you may be able to stagger your hikes according to when the trails dry out. If muddy conditions cause you to begin hiking on the sides of the treadway rather than in the middle, turn around.

Winter hiking can be an enjoyable way to experience the Green Mountains in their snowy splendor, but it requires extra gear and planning. Once the snow piles up, many trailheads are not reachable by car, so plan to hike farther than the distance shown in this guidebook. The presence of alpine ski areas may alter your route and your experience, particularly on Pico and Jay peaks. Skis with traction (wax, skins, or a pattern etched in the base) or snowshoes keep you more or less on top of the snow, letting you travel more efficiently without creating "postholes" by sinking into the snowpack. Snowshoeing is an easy activity for beginners to pick up because it is basically walking. Skiing on ungroomed backcountry trails requires considerable skill. Cross-country skiers should be aware that difficulty ratings given for hikes in this book do not apply to skiing, which is generally more challenging. All winter travelers need to bring more food and warm layers than they would in summer and exercise more caution; fewer daylight hours, colder temperatures, and slower travel times magnify any problems that may occur, such as getting lost or twisting an ankle. Prudent winter travelers do not go out alone. Make sure at least one person in the group has a sleeping bag, something to use for emergency shelter (such as a small tarp), and a camp stove. When properly prepared, winter hikers can safely and comfortably experience the deep quiet and spectacular beauty of Vermont's frozen landscape.

GREEN MOUNTAIN CLUB

The Green Mountain Club (GMC) is a nonprofit organization founded in 1910. GMC built and maintains Vermont's Long Trail, and the organization's advocacy and education efforts also safeguard the state's many other hiking trails. At sensitive high-use areas, GMC sponsors caretakers who perform trail and shelter maintenance, provide first aid, and talk with hikers about fragile summit ecosystems, local regulations, and Leave No Trace principles. For more information, visit GMC headquarters in Waterbury Center or see greenmountainclub.org.

GREEN MOUNTAIN NATIONAL FOREST

Green Mountain National Forest encompasses more than 400,000 acres in southwestern and central Vermont, forming the largest contiguous public land area in the state. The forest includes eight federally designated Wilderness Areas and three nationally designated trails (the Appalachian Trail, the Long Trail, and Robert Frost Interpretive Trail—a National Recreation Trail), as well as approximately 900 miles of multiple-use trails. For more information, visit fs.usda.gov/gmfl.

LEAVE NO TRACE

 The Appalachian Mountain Club (AMC) is a national educational partner of Leave No Trace, a nonprofit organization dedicated to promoting and inspiring responsible outdoor recreation through education, research, and partnerships. The Leave No Trace program seeks to develop wildland ethics: ways in which people think and act in the outdoors to minimize their impact on the areas they visit and to protect our natural resources for future enjoyment. Leave No Trace unites four federal land management agencies—U.S. Forest Service, National Park Service, Bureau of Land Management, and U.S. Fish and Wildlife Service—with manufacturers, outdoor retailers, user groups, educators, organizations such as AMC, and individuals.

The Leave No Trace ethic is guided by the following seven principles:

1. **Plan Ahead and Prepare.** Know the terrain and any regulations applicable to the area you're planning to visit, and be prepared for extreme weather or other emergencies. This will enhance your enjoyment and ensure that you've chosen an appropriate destination. Small groups have less impact on resources and on the experiences of other backcountry visitors.

2. **Travel and Camp on Durable Surfaces.** Travel and camp on established trails and campsites, rock, gravel, dry grasses, or snow. Good campsites are found, not made. Camp at least 200 feet from lakes and streams, and focus activities on areas where vegetation is absent. In pristine areas, disperse use to prevent the creation of campsites and trails.

3. **Dispose of Waste Properly.** Pack it in, pack it out. Inspect your camp for trash or food scraps. Deposit solid human waste in cat holes dug 6 to 8 inches deep, at least 200 feet from water, camps, and trails. Pack out toilet paper and hygiene products. To wash yourself or your dishes, carry water 200 feet from streams or lakes and use small amounts of biodegradable soap. Scatter strained dishwater.

4. **Leave What You Find.** Cultural or historical artifacts, as well as natural objects such as plants and rocks, should be left as found.

5. **Minimize Campfire Impacts.** Cook on a stove. Use established fire rings, fire pans, or mound fires. If you build a campfire, keep it small and use dead sticks found on the ground.

6. **Respect Wildlife.** Observe wildlife from a distance. Feeding animals alters their natural behavior. Protect wildlife from your food by storing rations and trash securely.

7. **Be Considerate of Other Visitors.** Be courteous, respect the quality of other visitors' backcountry experience, and let nature's sounds prevail.

AMC is a national provider of the Leave No Trace Master Educator course. AMC offers this five-day course, designed especially for outdoor professionals and land managers, as well as the shorter two-day Leave No Trace Trainer course at locations throughout the Northeast.

For Leave No Trace information and materials, contact the Leave No Trace Center for Outdoor Ethics, P.O. Box 997, Boulder, CO 80306. Phone: 800-332-4100 or 302-442-8222; fax: 303-442-8217; web: lnt.org. For information on the AMC Leave No Trace Master Educator training course schedule, see activities.outdoors.org.

Southern Vermont stretches from the Massachusetts border north to US 4, an area defined by two distinct mountain ranges, a long and narrow valley, high plateaus, low foothills, and the floodplains of the Connecticut River as it widens on its way to Long Island Sound. While just 40 miles wide, southern Vermont's diverse landscape offers day-hiking opportunities that travel past abandoned relics created by European settlers, through working farms and forests, and into natural communities that are rare in Vermont.

Let's start in southwestern Vermont, where the Taconic Mountains straddle the border between New York and Vermont as they make their way north from Massachusetts. These irregularly shaped, tree-covered mountains rise steeply from the Vermont Valley, reaching their highest point—3,839 feet—at Mount Equinox (Trip 8) and becoming smaller as they stretch into central Vermont. Mount Equinox towers above the town of Manchester and the Battenkill Valley, and its eastern slopes are part of one of the most expansive, rich northern hardwood forests in the northeastern United States. These wide tracts of land provide critical habitat for large and small animals, including black bears, bobcats, foxes, white-tailed deer, and numerous songbirds.

The limy bedrock of the Taconic Mountains dissolves readily when exposed to water, and the steady erosion has created a network of caves throughout the hills, as well as a maze of underground streams, seeps, and springs. The calcium-rich soil, combined with the relatively warm climate, supports a vast diversity of plant life, including prolific wildflower displays in spring. Taconic rocks include limestone, marble, and slate, all of which have been mined extensively since the 1700s. The Gettysburg Quarry in Dorset (Trip 9) opened in 1866 and remained in operation until 1897. Most of the marble went to Philadelphia to be used for buildings and monuments. The abandoned quarry, along with many others in the region, is now surrounded by forests.

The southern Green Mountains run south to north through the center of the state, and consist of high, rolling land that is more a plateau than a sharply defined range of mountains. As a whole, the mountains in the southern region of the Green Mountains are smaller than those up north, but Killington Peak (Trip 16), in south-central Vermont is an exception. At 4,230 feet, it's the second-tallest mountain in the state, and while much of Killington is developed as a ski resort, the bald peak offers hikers 360-degree views after a rigorous climb. The Appalachian Trail and the Long Trail run together through the southern Green Mountains, paralleled by Catamount Trail, a long-distance cross-country ski trail open to the public.

The terrain of the southern Green Mountains was historically difficult for humans to settle due to its acidic soil, short growing season, and numerous boggy wetlands. Remnants of previous activity, such as fire towers, ranger cabins, sawmills, and charcoal kilns, remain.

Nearly 60,000 acres of federally designated Wilderness Areas have been protected as part of the larger Green Mountain National Forest. Wilderness Areas, managed to preserve their wild character with minimal roads and signage, are home to large animals, including black bears, moose, and bobcats. These animals need broad tracts of undeveloped forests, such as the deep woods east of Lye Brook Falls (Trip 7). Glastenbury Wilderness, northeast of Bennington, protects 22,330 acres of wild ridgeline and sweeping stands of mature beech trees that support a significant number of black bears, as well as many bird species, including the threatened Bicknell's thrush and numerous warblers. Enter Glastenbury Wilderness on Bald Mountain Trail (Trip 1) to explore the southeast corner of this remote mountain forest.

The foothills to the east of the Green Mountains are dissected by rivers and streams that flow swiftly into the Connecticut River, which travels the length of the state along the Vermont–New Hampshire border. The Southern Vermont Piedmont (the word *piedmont* literally means "foothills") is characterized by fertile farmland, warm temperatures, and small hills, lower than 1,500 feet. A notable exception is 3,099-foot Mount Ascutney (Trip 14), which towers over the Connecticut River valley and has more in common geologically with the White Mountains of New Hampshire. Mount Ascutney is a classic monadnock, an isolated mountain of erosion-resistant rock rising above a predominantly flat plain.

Much of the Southern Vermont Piedmont is forested with sugar maple, ash, beech, and yellow birch, but a few natural communities on the drier hilltops are uncommon in Vermont and associated with more southerly climates. These include a rare black gum swamp in the town of Vernon and a 70-acre rocky woodland community consisting of pitch pine, oak, and heath on the summit of Black Mountain (Trip 4).

1 BALD MOUNTAIN (BENNINGTON/WOODFORD)

Glastenbury Wilderness holds many secrets, including this unusual ridgeline peak with views across southern Vermont.

Features 🚶 🐕 ✍ ☀ 🌲

Location Bennington and Woodford, VT

Rating Moderate

Distance 5.6 miles one-way

Elevation Gain 2,099 feet

Estimated Time 4.5 hours

Maps USGS Bennington; U.S. Forest Service: fs.usda.gov/Internet/FSE _DOCUMENTS/fseprd573938.pdf

GPS Coordinates Bennington trailhead: 42° 53.40′ N, 73° 10.83′ W; Woodford trailhead: 42° 54.38′ N, 73° 07.38′ W

Contact Green Mountain National Forest, Manchester Ranger District, 2538 Depot Street, Manchester Center, VT 05255; 802-362-2307; fs.usda.gov/gmfl

DIRECTIONS

To Bennington trailhead
From the traffic light at US 7/South Street and VT 9/Main Street in downtown Bennington, go east on VT 9/Main Street 0.8 mile and turn left onto Branch Street. Go 0.3 mile and turn right onto North Branch Street. Go 0.5 mile and turn right onto an unmarked dirt road where North Branch Street curves sharply left. The trailhead parking area is immediately on the right (space for about twelve cars).

To Woodford trailhead
From the traffic light at US 7/South Street and VT 9/Main Street in downtown Bennington, go east on VT 9/Main Street, which becomes Molly Stark Trail, for 3.9 miles and then turn left onto Harbour Road. Go 0.8 mile and turn left onto an unmarked dirt road at a water tower. Park on the grass off the left side of the road (space for about eight cars).

TRAIL DESCRIPTION

Bald Mountain (2,857 feet) is the southern sentinel of a ridgeline that marks the western edge of the 22,330-acre Glastenbury Wilderness. Bald Mountain Trail crosses the ridge west to east (or vice versa) and is a fun 5.6-mile one-way hike, if you can leave a car or a bike at the other end. You can also hike each approach separately as an out-and-back trip (see "More Information" on page 6).

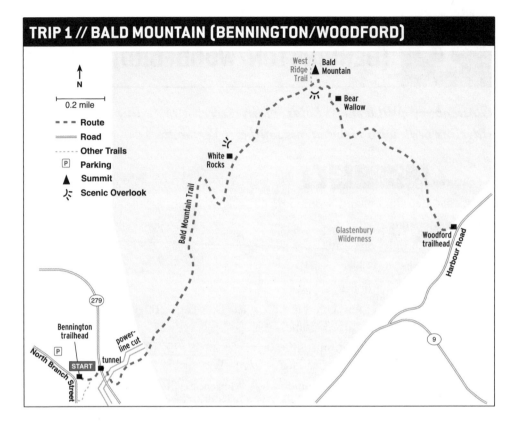

Bennington Trailhead

The western leg of Bald Mountain Trail rises 3.7 rocky miles from Bennington to the ridgeline, passing the popular White Rocks lookout point at 2.9 miles. This route is a bit more difficult than the one up the other side of Bald Mountain from Woodford trailhead. Take this approach if you want a little challenge.

Woodford Trailhead

The eastern leg of Bald Mountain Trail climbs more steeply to reach the ridge in 1.9 miles. For a peaceful round-trip hike, use this quieter, shorter eastern side.

For this one-way trip, either trailhead works; the route below is described west to east. The Bennington Trailhead route is not recommended for children younger than 10, given the distance and elevation gain.

Bennington to Woodford—one way

The Bennington side of Bald Mountain Trail starts with a staircase from the parking area, climbs past a kiosk, and zigzags through the brush of a power-line cut for 0.5 mile. Blue blazes on rocks mark the path in this open area. Before entering the woods, turn around for a view of Bennington Battle Monument soaring over the town. A sign here incorrectly indicates the West Ridge Trail junction on top of Bald Mountain is 4.0 miles away; it is actually 3.2 miles from this point.

Cross a wooded hillside and intersect with an eroded woods road in a gully. Turn right onto the woods road and follow the woods road uphill, through the colorfully painted Free

A hiker enjoys the views from Bald Mountain.

Expression tunnel beneath VT 279, and back across the power-line cut, entering woods on the far side. Blue blazes indicate the route across streams and past several unsigned intersections with old woods roads. At 1.0 mile, turn left off the woods road where it curves sharply to the right, and continue to follow the blue blazes. In another 0.3 mile, enter Glastenbury Wilderness.

The footing becomes challenging as Bald Mountain Trail traverses often-soupy spots and long stretches of loose rock before finally rising onto the drier hillside where fir trees line the path. After a couple of switchbacks, openings appear in the woods where scree spills down the mountainside. At 2.9 miles, a massive pile of rocks appears to block the way, and a side path leads left 100 feet. Follow it to the White Rocks ledges for westward views across the Vermont Valley and Taconic Mountains before returning to the main trail.

The final 0.8 mile of climbing crosses several fields of loose rock (known locally as cobble) and ascends ledges before arriving atop the shrubby ridge amid spruces, blueberries, and surprising white sand from disintegrated quartzite. The highest point of Bald Mountain Trail (2,810 feet) is here at the junction of West Ridge Trail, and the view south is spectacular, even if partially screened. The summit of Bald Mountain is 0.1 mile north on the blue-blazed West Ridge Trail. The whole ledgy, shrubby area, with its various views, is worth exploring before descending.

From the trail junction, continue east on Bald Mountain Trail toward Woodford. The white sand underfoot quickly gives way to conifer needles and duff. At 4.0 miles, an old sign for Bear Wallow marks a faint trail north to a seasonal spring. Continue steadily downward on Bald Mountain Trail, passing through a beautiful softwood forest, which gradually transitions to hardwoods and a wetter, wider treadway. At 5.3 miles, exit Glastenbury Wilderness and bear right onto an old road, following it the final 0.3 mile to the Harbour Road trailhead and your return vehicle.

DID YOU KNOW?

Glastenbury Wilderness has featured prominently in many mysterious happenings and is well known for spooking hikers with unexplained sounds and eerie sensations. Look for books by Vermont writers Joe Citro and Tim Simard to scare yourself silly.

MORE INFORMATION

Although the one-way hike is described here in detail from Bennington to Woodford, you can start at either trailhead for an out-and-back hike with a single car. From the Bennington trailhead, it's a moderate round-trip hike of 7.4 miles, gaining 2,099 feet and taking 5.5 hours. From the Woodford trailhead, it's a moderate round-trip hike of 3.8 miles, gaining 1,509 feet and taking 3.5 hours.

Glastenbury Wilderness is a place where human impact is kept to a minimum: do not leave any personal property or use any wheeled device, such as a mountain bike or a wagon. Bald Mountain Trail and Glastenbury Wilderness are managed by Green Mountain National Forest.

NEARBY

Swim, paddle, and camp at Woodford State Park, Vermont's highest-elevation state park at 2,400 feet. Head to downtown Bennington for restaurants, shops, the Battle Monument, and the fabulous Bennington Museum.

2 HAYSTACK MOUNTAIN (WILMINGTON)

This pleasant hike up a mellow ridge leads to a rocky top with views of nearby Haystack Pond and distant peaks.

Features 👥 🐕 💧 🔍 ✳️

Location Wilmington, VT

Rating Moderate

Distance 4.2 miles round-trip

Elevation Gain 1,025 feet

Estimated Time 3 hours

Maps USGS Mount Snow; U.S. Forest Service: fs.usda.gov/Internet/FSE_MEDIA/stelprdb5315088.pdf

GPS Coordinates 42° 53.99′ N, 72° 54.66′ W

Contact Green Mountain National Forest, Manchester Ranger District, 2538 Depot Street, Manchester Center, VT 05255; 802-362-2307; fs.usda.gov/gmfl

DIRECTIONS

From the western junction of VT 100 and VT 9 in Wilmington, go west on VT 9 for 1.1 miles and turn right onto Haystack Road. (A large sign on the grass reads "Chimney Hill.") Drive 1.2 miles and turn left onto Chimney Hill Road. Proceed 0.2 mile and turn right onto Binney Brook Road, which weaves past many turnoffs and ends after 1.1 miles at Upper Dam Road. Turn right and follow Upper Dam Road 0.3 mile (staying left at a junction, as marked) to park on the right shoulder (space for about six cars), where a gravel road heads uphill into the woods.

TRAIL DESCRIPTION

Haystack Mountain (3,410 feet) is a recognizable, pointed peak on the southern end of a ridge dominated by Mount Snow (3,586 feet), identifiable by the many ski trails along its southeastern slope. The hike to Haystack's small, rocky summit traverses easy-to-moderate grades until the slightly steeper final 0.3 mile, making it a good hike for kids 6 and older.

From the roadside parking area near a trailhead with a kiosk, follow Haystack Mountain Trail on a gravel woods road uphill into the woods and around a metal gate. Occasional blue plastic diamonds mark the woods road, which leads to Wilmington's water supply at Haystack Pond. Hiking among yellow birch and beech trees, you begin to hear Binney Brook as it tumbles through a ravine on your left. At 0.5 mile, where No Trespassing signs indicate the start of the Wilmington Watershed Protection Area and the brook flows

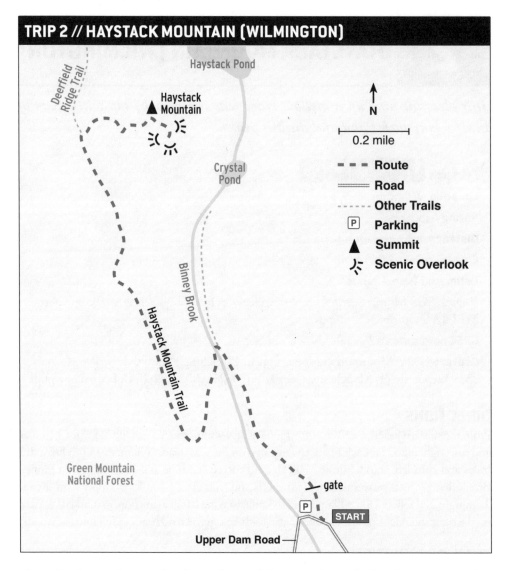

through a large culvert under the road, turn left onto a footpath. For the next 1.3 miles, Haystack Mountain Trail coincides with Deerfield Ridge Trail.

The narrow, rooty treadway heads southwest to circle the end of the long ridgeline leading to Haystack's summit. Wood nettle, with its stinging hairs, spreads along the edges of the path as it rolls gently 0.3 mile from the woods-road junction. The path then bends sharply back northwest and begins a moderate, steady climb across a rocky hillside. The climbing is pleasantly interrupted by level stretches and gradual pitches, and at 1.3 miles, a sharp S-curve brings you to the ridgeline. Lilies and ferns fill in the forest floor alongside rose twisted stalk, with its flowers and berries dangling beneath its arched, leafy stem.

Passing through some wide muddy areas, Haystack Mountain Trail rounds the western side of Haystack's summit cone. At 1.8 miles, a wooden sign directs you to turn right off

Deerfield Ridge Trail, which continues straight. Haystack Mountain Trail immediately moves from a northern hardwood forest on the ridgeline to a shady, thick boreal forest as you climb the summit knob. The path ascends switchbacks to a small, rocky opening at the summit. The view east is dominated by Haystack Pond in the basin below. Beyond that, the north–south valley carrying VT 100 is backed by rows of low, gently sloping hills. In the distant northeast, Mount Ascutney juts above the horizon, and far to the east, the huge hump of Mount Monadnock rises above southwestern New Hampshire. Mount Snow's summit chairlift is just visible over the treetops to the north.

For views to the south and west, climb down through a narrow cleft in the rocks to another outlook, on the south face of the summit. This perch provides a clear view of the 2,200-acre Harriman Reservoir (also called Lake Whitingham), one of the largest bodies of water within Vermont's borders. Built in 1923 to provide hydroelectric power, the lake is a dammed stretch of the Deerfield River. The Deerfield Valley village of Mountain Mills was abandoned to make way for the reservoir, and boaters today can occasionally spot the submerged foundation of the old mill. Another version of electrical production is visible to the west, where wind turbines in Searsburg spin on top of a ridge. On a clear day, visitors can see Massachusetts's highest point, Mount Greylock (3,491 feet), in the distant southwest.

To return to the parking area and end your hike, simply retrace your steps.

DID YOU KNOW?

Haystack Mountain's alpine ski area closed to the public in the early 2000s after 40 years of operation. It has since been transformed into a private recreation and vacation club.

A winter view of the Green Mountains from the top of Haystack Mountain in Wilmington.

MORE INFORMATION

Haystack Mountain is part of the Green Mountain National Forest.

NEARBY

Swim in and paddle on Harriman Reservoir, 3.5 miles south. Camp at Woodford State Park, 6.4 miles west, which also has great swimming and paddling on a high-elevation lake, or at Molly Stark State Park, 6.1 miles east (Trip 3: Mount Olga). Restaurants and shops are in Wilmington, 3.8 miles southeast.

3   MOUNT OLGA

The loop trail to Mount Olga's fire tower is a pleasant ramble through a rich forest.

Features

Location Wilmington, VT

Rating Easy to Moderate

Distance 1.8-mile loop

Elevation Gain 520 feet

Estimated Time 1.5 hours

Maps USGS Wilmington; Vermont Department of Forests, Parks, and Recreation: vtstateparks.com/assets/pdf/molly-stark-trails.pdf

GPS Coordinates 42° 51.29′ N, 72° 48.88′ W

Contact Molly Stark State Park, 705 Route 9 East, Wilmington, VT 05363; 802-464-5460 or 888-409-7579; vtstateparks.com/mollystark.html

DIRECTIONS

From the junction of VT 9 and VT 100 in downtown Wilmington, drive 3.3 miles east on VT 9 to Molly Stark State Park on your right. A parking lot (space for about twenty cars) is near the park office. When the park is closed, park at the base of the entrance road and add 0.4 mile to the hike.

TRAIL DESCRIPTION

Mount Olga (2,418 feet) has all the attractive features of a big mountain—including a variety of hiking terrains and terrific views—in a small package, making it an excellent destination for families or those with limited time. The trail on the north side of the loop is a little shorter (0.7 mile to the summit) and therefore a little steeper—a better choice for the ascent. Descend on the more gradual 1-mile trail that ends at the top of the campground. The southern side of the loop is suitable for cross-country skiing, while the northern leg is better for snowshoeing. Children as young as 5 will enjoy the accomplishment of summiting this small mountain.

Begin across the park road from the office, where Mount Olga Trail descends wooden steps to cross a stream. Follow blue blazes up a moderate climb, through a young forest of yellow birch, spruce, and fir. Where a rock wall ascends from the right, the trail turns sharply left and zigzags up a steep, rooty pitch. Mount Olga Trail continues to climb moderately for the first few tenths of a mile. Then, entering a spruce–fir stand, the trail levels and crosses more rolling terrain. Canada violets blossom in early spring in these damp

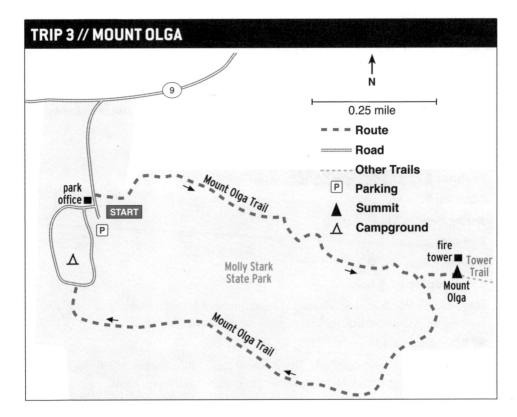

woods, their white petals unfurling to reveal a yellow center; look for striking dark purple veins on the lowest petal.

Climbing moderately again, the trail leaves the coniferous forest and emerges into mixed deciduous woods. Ascend rock steps to a trail junction on the hillside, with ledges rising around you. Go left, climbing the 0.1-mile spur path to a grassy summit area surrounded by tall trees.

From the cab, or lookout room, of Mount Olga's steel fire tower, Mount Greylock looms to the southwest. To the northwest, Haystack Mountain's pointed peak (3,410 feet) juts from the prominent ridgeline leading north over Mount Snow (3,586 feet) and Stratton Mountain (3,940 feet). A small slice of Harriman Reservoir (Lake Whitingham) is visible, tucked into the hills directly west. Searsburg Wind Farm turbines sprout from the ridge just north of the reservoir. Far to the east, Mount Monadnock (3,130 feet) rises 2,000 feet higher than the New Hampshire hills surrounding it.

Go back down the summit spur path (avoiding a trail that heads east to Marlboro). Returning to the junction with Mount Olga Trail, head straight onto the southern leg of the loop, climbing over a little ridge before dropping downhill through a beech stand with remarkably twisted branches. After passing through a corridor between boulders and crossing a low bridge over a stream, Mount Olga Trail curves to the right and begins a gentle downward grade, which it maintains for most of the remainder of the hike. If the leaves are off the trees, you can look back across the stream valley and see Olga's summit.

The deciduous woods here are rich with understory plants. In spring, look for tall, slender stalks of wild oats and trout lilies, as well as early yellow violets. Mats of evergreen partridgeberry and ferns spread across the forest floor. Shelf fungus and large, rectangular holes made by pileated woodpeckers appear on rotting trunks. About 0.8 mile from the summit, Mount Olga Trail meets a rock wall and follows it to the campground. Emerge next to site 10, turn right (east), and follow the campground road back to the trailhead.

DID YOU KNOW?

Did you hear drumming resonating through Mount Olga's forests or see a large, dark bird with a strikingly red head? Pileated woodpeckers drum to mark their territory and to attract a mate. They excavate dead trees in search of carpenter ants and other wood-boring insects and to make nests, leaving cavities that become shelters for other birds and small mammals.

MORE INFORMATION

Molly Stark State Park operates from Memorial Day to Indigenous Peoples' Day; it is open for day use from 10 A.M. to official sunset. A day-use fee applies in summer. Off-season use is allowed.

NEARBY

Swim and boat at Harriman Reservoir, 5 miles west, or at the high-elevation Adams Reservoir in Woodford State Park, 13 miles west. The Southern Vermont Natural History Museum, 1.5 miles east, has year-round exhibits and seasonal events focusing on the environment of this region. Restaurants and shops are along VT 9/VT 100 in Wilmington, 3 miles west.

Mount Olga's slopes burst with wildflowers: wild oats (pictured), trout lilies, and early yellow violets.

STANDING TALL: THE LEGACY OF FIRE TOWERS IN VERMONT

If you're not afraid of heights, you won't find a better way to take in unobstructed 360-degree views than from the top of a spindly Vermont fire tower swaying gently in the wind. Of course, the towers weren't originally intended for the recreational enjoyment of hikers. As the name suggests, fire towers were built to protect valuable forestland after several forest fires created panic within the timber industry in the early twentieth century.

A series of wildfires across Vermont in the early 1900s led to the creation of a fire protection program, and by 1908, the Vermont Forest Service was established to help manage a problem of growing concern. The very first fire tower was a wooden structure built in 1912 on top of Burke Mountain with private funds from landowner Elmer Darling. The tower lasted 20 years before it succumbed to Vermont's harsh winter weather. The second Burke Mountain tower, also made of wood, didn't fare as well; it was destroyed by a storm in 1938 (towers on Elmore Mountain, Mount Olga, and Stratton Mountain were destroyed by the same storm). The steel tower that replaced the previous wooden structures on Burke Mountain was built in 1984 and is still standing today.

As many as 38 fire towers once stood on Vermont summits, with caretakers on duty to watch for rising smoke so that fledgling blazes could be swiftly extinguished. More than half of these lookout stations were built in the northeastern corner of the state (known as the Northeast Kingdom), thanks in part to the Vermont Timberland Owners Association, which partnered with the state of Vermont to construct eighteen towers. The heyday of fire

The current fire tower on top of Bald Mountain in Westmore (Trip 57) was built in 1938–39 after a storm destroyed the original.

lookout stations was short-lived in Vermont, and by the late 1980s, the towers were decommissioned and replaced by airplane surveillance programs.

Fortunately for hikers, the legacy of Vermont fire towers lives on, with credit to forward-thinking land managers and outdoors lovers who saw value in the towers, not for seeking out wildfires, but for enjoying the beautiful surroundings.

Fire tower hikes in Vermont are as varied as the landscapes in which they're found. The shortest one in this guidebook is a pleasant ramble to the top of Mount Olga (Trip 3), with a round-trip distance of just 1.8 miles. The current tower on Mount Olga was used as a fire lookout until 1974, first on nearby Bald Mountain in Townshend and then at its current site. The tower was listed on the National Historic Lookout Register in 1996 and delivers unparalleled views of the southern Green Mountains and peeks into New Hampshire and Massachusetts.

The stone fire tower on top of Owl's Head (Trip 30) in Groton State Forest is one of the many highlights of a hike that is easy enough for most kids. This outing is also perfect for hikers who are queasy about heights, because the stone octagon on Owl's Head requires only a few steps up, and the views are lovely. The tower was built by the Civilian Conservation Corps in 1935.

A 60-foot fire tower on the top of Okemo Mountain (Trip 13) provides courageous climbers with a vista across all of southern Vermont and beyond. This structure was originally built in 1935 and restored in 2010. The Okemo tower was used as a fire lookout until 1970 and was put on the National Historic Lookout Register in 1998.

Want more? Mount Ascutney (Trip 14), Spruce Mountain (Trip 29), Elmore Mountain (Trip 41), Burke Mountain (Trip 52), and Bald Mountain (Westmore) (Trip 57) all have fire towers on their summits.

4 BLACK MOUNTAIN

Hike through a blueberry-filled forest to an unusual rocky woodland habitat on Black Mountain's summit, including a sprawling mountain laurel population.

Features

Location Dummerston, VT

Rating Moderate

Distance 3 miles round-trip

Elevation Gain 875 feet

Estimated Time 2.5 hours

Maps USGS Newfane; The Nature Conservancy: nature.org/content/dam/tnc/nature/en/documents/VTHiking_Topo_BlackMountain.pdf

GPS Coordinates 42° 54.68′ N, 72° 36.38′ W

Contact The Nature Conservancy, 575 Stone Cutters Way, Montpelier, VT 05602; 802-229-4425; nature.org/vermont

DIRECTIONS

From the junction of VT 30, VT 9, and US 5 in Brattleboro, head north on VT 30 (Linden Street, which becomes West River Road) for 4.3 miles. Turn right onto Green Iron Bridge and cross West River. At the end of the bridge, turn right onto Rice Farm Road and drive 1.0 mile to the trailhead parking area (space for about five cars) on the left, marked with a Nature Conservancy sign. A second parking area has been recently added a half-mile east on Rice Farm Road, providing another access to the Black Mountain trails.

TRAIL DESCRIPTION

Black Mountain (1,279 feet) is a steep-sided, horseshoe-shaped peak with a rolling, wooded summit ridgeline studded with granite outcroppings. Its dry crest supports Vermont's only pitch-pine and scrub oak woodland, a natural biosphere more commonly found along New England's coasts. The hike through Black Mountain Natural Area features frequent steep climbs, but the footing is not difficult, and the variety of landscapes is pleasantly distracting. Painted white and blue blazes mark a previous land boundary and should be ignored; follow the yellow-and-green plastic trail markers put in place by The Nature Conservancy (TNC).

From the parking lot, Black Mountain Trail begins climbing northward, crossing the hillside on a grassy woods road speckled with wild strawberries and violets. Just past a metal gate is a three-paneled kiosk with pertinent hiking information. The trail enters the woods, rounds a switchback, and climbs onto a flat, bench-like area. Tall pines shade a path

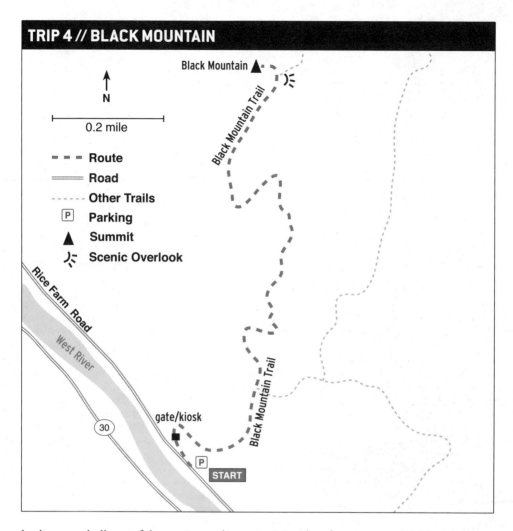

Black Mountain ▲

N

0.2 mile

- - - Route
=== Road
----- Other Trails
P Parking
▲ Summit
)ɛ Scenic Overlook

Black Mountain Trail

Rice Farm Road

West River

30

gate/kiosk

Black Mountain Trail

P

START

leading to a hallway of dense pine saplings. At 0.3 mile, after passing a TNC registration box fixed high on a tree, Black Mountain Trail crosses a series of boardwalks and begins a moderate climb across a rooted slope. Dwarf ginseng blooms in early summer here, with yellowish berries replacing the clusters of white flowers later in the season.

Now the trail begins a series of switchbacks up a hill. Black Mountain's steep sides are a result of its volcanic history. Most Vermont mountains were pushed up by tectonic plate movement, but Black Mountain is a granite pluton, formed when magma inside an ancient volcano that never erupted cooled and hardened. Softer rocks surrounding the hardened magma wore away over time, revealing the granite dome. As you climb, notice the change in the forest that occurs as the soil becomes thinner and more acidic on the upper mountain. Partway up this steep slope, red and black oaks and blueberries mix in with the beeches, pines, and hemlocks. As you go higher, you'll see more blueberries and oaks and fewer beeches, pines, and hemlocks.

Climb several rock staircases onto a dry, ledgy plateau. Look for pileated woodpecker holes in the pines. Spotted wintergreen, with a pale stripe on its dark, pointy leaves, grows

Black Mountain treats hikers to a variety of forests, including dense pines, broadly spaced hemlocks, and beeches at middle elevations, with short, skinny scrub oaks and pitch pines across the summit.

low among the blueberries on the forest floor. Mounting this more moderate slope, zigzag through large beech trees and moss-and lichen-covered ledges to the base of another steep pitch, where switchbacks begin again.

Ascend into a dry pine-oak-heath forest dominated by red pine with patches of scrub oak (endangered in Vermont) and pitch pine. The low canopy allows a fair amount of sunlight, and blueberry bushes and granite ledges cover the ground between the small trunks. At about 1.1 miles, Black Mountain Trail begins its undulating course over the summit ridge. Continue northward, passing several stands of mountain laurel. In June, white-and-pink flowers blanket these evergreen shrubs in a stunning display.

Descending briefly, the trail arrives at a series of southeastern-facing ledges. Obstructed views through the branches reveal the tall point of New Hampshire's Mount Monadnock in the background and rock slabs on the eastern half of Black Mountain in the foreground. The south-facing bowl within the horseshoe of Black Mountain captures solar heat, supporting plants that typically thrive 200 miles to the south. At a junction, follow the trail left, uphill to the highest ledge, surrounded by blueberries and wintergreen. When returning to the junction, turn right to go back downhill the way you came up.

DID YOU KNOW?
Pitch pines are adapted to wildfires. Their bark is heat resistant, and some of their pine-cones do not open to disseminate seeds until they've been exposed to the heat of a fire.

MORE INFORMATION
Black Mountain Natural Area is limited to passive recreational activities, such as hiking, snowshoeing, bird-watching, photography, and nature study. Bicycles and motorized vehicles are not permitted. Dogs are not allowed except for service dogs. Do not remove plants, animals, artifacts, or rocks, and do not build fires.

NEARBY
For excellent biking, ride West River Rail Trail, which starts across from the easternmost parking lot for Black Mountain and travels 3.5 miles south to Brattleboro. West River has great paddling opportunities and several swimming holes, including one under the 267-foot-long West Dummerston Covered Bridge, the longest covered bridge open to traffic in Vermont, 2 miles north of the trailhead for Black Mountain Trail. (*Caution*: Before swimming, double-check the safety of swimming holes, as flooding may have altered the landscape.) Head to downtown Brattleboro, 6 miles south, for food and shopping. Camp at Fort Dummer State Park, 6.4 miles south, or Townshend State Park, 12.5 miles northwest.

5 PUTNEY MOUNTAIN

Walk through a variety of lovely forests on this loop hike to a grassy summit with views across southern Vermont and New Hampshire.

Features

Location Putney, VT

Rating Easy

Distance 1.2-mile loop

Elevation Gain 140 feet

Estimated Time 1 hour

Maps USGS Putney, USGS Westminster West; Putney Mountain Association: putneymountain.org/web/trails

GPS Coordinates 42° 59.78′ N, 72° 35.93′ W

Contact Putney Mountain Association, P.O. Box 953, Putney, VT 05346; putneymountain.org

DIRECTIONS

From I-91, Exit 4, drive north 0.7 mile on VT 5 and turn left onto Westminster Road/ Kimball Hill. After 1.1 miles, turn left onto West Hill Road and go 2.3 miles to Putney Mountain Road, on the right. Drive 2.2 miles to the trailhead parking area on the right (space for about fifteen cars). The gravel road is often adversely affected by mud season; check the Putney Mountain Association website (putneymountain.org) for road and trail conditions.

TRAIL DESCRIPTION

Putney Mountain's open, field-like summit (1,667 feet) with panoramic views is the reward at the end of a pleasant ridgeline ramble. Kids 5 and older will have fun exploring interesting natural features described on interpretive signs along the trail.

A kiosk marks the trailhead and sits at the junction of the two legs of the summit loop. At the kiosk, go left onto West Cliff Trail and follow the yellow markers onto a shady hillside of mature hemlocks that effectively block the sun, leaving the understory sparse. Rock cairns—piles of stones used to mark backcountry routes—have been artfully and frequently arranged along this stretch of trail. (*Note*: These are placed by hikers and thus are not reliable trail markers; trust the yellow blazes on the trees instead.) Step across small streams and the remnants of an old stone wall—evidence that this steep slope was previously cleared pasture. At 0.7 mile, leave West Cliff Trail as it turns left, and follow blue markers straight onto Summit Trail.

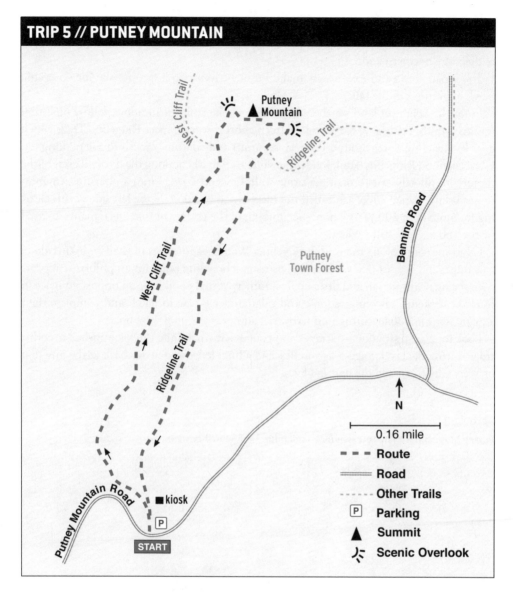

As soon as you start uphill on Summit Trail, the deep red-gold hues of the conifer forest recede, replaced by the light, airy white and green of a birch stand. Follow this gentle slope to the open summit of Putney Mountain. Small footpaths wander the grassy, shrubby area, looping and dead-ending through a variety of plants, such as raspberry thickets, that colonize cleared forests at this latitude and elevation. In the summer months, you may encounter sheep within fenced areas brought in to help control invasive glossy buckthorn. Nubs and stripes of durable white quartzite jut out of the softer bedrock of gray phyllite. A few glacial erratics, large boulders dropped by receding ice, reveal the area's glaciated past.

Walk up to the height-of-land to see the rocky summit of New Hampshire's Mount Monadnock, visible in the distance to the southeast. Turn around to admire the long ridgeline of the Green Mountains to the west. The pointed peak of Haystack Mountain anchors the southern end of this chain, and the ski trails on Stratton Mountain can be seen at the more northern end.

The broad views and easy access make Putney Mountain a favorite site for observing hawk migrations in the fall.

From the height-of-land on the eastern side of the summit meadow, follow blue trail markers south, reentering the woods. After a short distance, meet Ridgeline Trail, which goes left (leading north around Putney's summit) and continues south to the parking lot. Go straight on Ridgeline Trail, following white trail markers along the forested crest of the mountain. Shortly after crossing a stone wall, descend a ledge into a clearing. An enormous, oddly shaped white ash called the Elephant Tree stood on the left side of this clearing for more than 200 years before succumbing to the ravages of time; its remains, scarred by fire and age, are still evident.

Continue south along the rolling ridgeline. Water accumulates in shallow basins along this ridge, and at least one vernal pool, a seasonal breeding pond for amphibians, appears each spring near the trail and dries up in summer. Vernal pools have an important place in forest ecosystems, allowing tadpole and salamander larvae to hatch and complete their aquatic stage before maturing into terrestrial adults as the pool dries up.

Look for glacial striations—scrapes and gouges left when mile-thick ice pushed over this ridge during the last ice age—as you descend a final ledge and arrive back at the junction of West Cliff Trail and the parking lot.

Putney Mountain is a fantastic spot for winter hiking and snowshoeing.

DID YOU KNOW?

The Putney Mountain Association, a membership-supported group that owns Putney's summit and maintains the trails, sponsors the annual Fall Putney Mountain Hawk Watch to gather data about raptor migration patterns.

MORE INFORMATION

Camping and fires are not permitted on Putney Mountain. Motorized vehicles are not permitted, except as needed to make the trails accessible to people with disabilities. Snow-mobiles are permitted on this trail in winter.

NEARBY

West Dummerston's historical covered bridge spanning West River on VT 30 is a popular spot to picnic and swim. A few restaurants and a food co-op are in Putney, near the junction of Westminster Road and VT 5, with more dining options 10 miles south in Brattleboro.

6 GROUT POND AND SOMERSET RESERVOIR

Pack your tent, canoe, and hammock. Once you find your way to the prettiest pond in Vermont, you'll want to set up camp and stay awhile.

Features

Location Stratton, VT

Rating Easy

Distance 4.6-mile loop

Elevation Gain 250 feet

Estimated Time 2.5 hours

Maps USGS Stratton Mountain; U.S. Forest Service (Grout Pond Recreation Area): fs.usda.gov/Internet/FSE_DOCUMENTS/stelprdb5434687.pdf

GPS Coordinates 43° 02.83' N, 72° 57.10' W

Contact Green Mountain National Forest, Manchester Ranger District, 2538 Depot Street, Manchester Center, VT 05255; 802-362-2307; fs.usda.gov/gmfl

DIRECTIONS

From VT 100 in West Wardsboro, take Stratton-Arlington Road 6.2 miles west to Grout Pond Road on the left. (From East Arlington, follow Old Mill Road east, which becomes Kansas Road. After crossing a bridge over US 7, go 0.4 mile farther and turn right onto Kelley Stand Road. Drive 11.2 miles east to Grout Pond Road on the right.) Follow Grout Pond Road 1.2 miles through a campground and past a boat launch to the trailhead parking lot (space for about twenty cars). In winter, Grout Pond Road is plowed for approximately 1 mile from Kelley Stand Road; a winter lot is at the top of the road.

TRAIL DESCRIPTION

Grout Pond and Somerset Reservoir are nestled between low hills in a remote section of the high, rolling plateau that characterizes the southern Green Mountains. Their clear waters offer refreshing swimming and provide for long views over the otherwise thickly forested region. A trailhead at the north end of Grout Pond provides access to a network of rambling trails, including the long-distance Catamount Trail (best used for skiing), numerous loops through the forest, and a pedestrian route to the pond's appealing shoreline campsites. Kids of all ages will enjoy the flat first leg of this hike along Grout Pond's shore, but after that, the rolling terrain is best suited to kids 4 and older. The route described below follows close along the water on the east side of Grout Pond and then descends to the edge

TRIP 6 // GROUT POND AND SOMERSET RESERVOIR

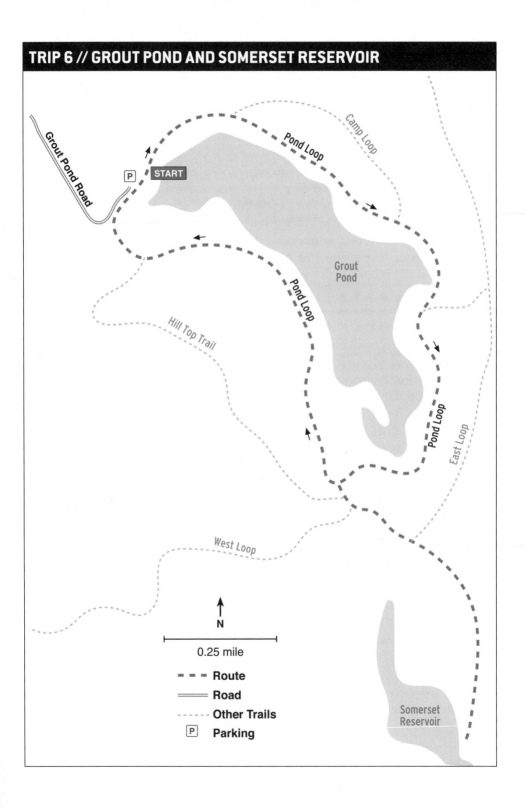

of Somerset Reservoir before returning to finish the loop on the hillside above Grout Pond's western shore. It is one of many hiking options in the immediate vicinity, and if you are fortunate enough to be able to stay a few days, you can explore them all. Bring footwear appropriate for encountering the inevitable muddy areas in this often-soggy landscape.

From the trailhead kiosk on the edge of the parking lot, descend a short distance to a T junction and go left on Pond Loop. Follow blue diamond blazes along the wide gravel trail as it curves around the top of the pond, which is not quite visible through the foliage. The Catamount Trail enters from the left via a spur path to East Loop, and shortly after that, at 0.2 mile, narrow Camp Loop Trail departs to the left. Stay on Pond Loop and round a curve to a long, flat straightaway with the first views of the pond. Campsites on the right provide access to the shoreline at regular intervals as you head southeast. Ski trails on the north slope of Mount Snow are visible over the treetops at the end of the pond. The trail narrows and rises away from the pond near campsite 10, traversing bog bridges, step stones, and turnpikes—gravel-filled wooden boxes—in this wet area. Pass the southern end of Camp Loop on your left and at 0.9 mile arrive at a trail junction. East Loop bears left, away from the pond; go right, continuing through thick woods on Pond Loop and the Catamount Trail, marked with blue diamond markers. Raspberries, ferns, and hobblebushes crowd the trail edges, and moss grows thickly beneath bog bridges as you round the muddy southern end of Grout Pond. Cross a wide bridge over the dark, tumbling outlet stream and weave through attractive wetlands on bog bridges before arriving at a four-way trail junction at 1.7 miles.

Straight ahead, Hill Top Trail climbs to the ridge. Pond Loop, your eventual return route, turns right here and extends 0.9 mile back to the campground. Before taking Pond Loop back, turn left and follow the Catamount Trail southbound, marked by blue diamond markers, on a wide swath through the woods. In 500 feet, West Loop departs to the right; bear left to continue on the woods road, part of the big East Loop, following blue diamond blazes and descending through the forest. A bridge leads you back across a lower stretch of Grout Pond's outlet stream. Then, at 2.1 miles, East Loop goes left. Stay straight on the Catamount Trail 0.4 mile more, through rolling terrain to a descent that brings you alongside an arm of Somerset Reservoir. At a point where the Catamount Trail turns sharply left and climbs away from the water, an informal path goes straight to the shoreline at a pleasant spot for a picnic with a view south. This is a good turnaround site, although you can continue to follow the Catamount Trail south along the water as far as you like before turning around (you'll reach the south end of the lake in about 6 more miles). The 1,568-acre Somerset Reservoir is fed by the remote headwater streams of the Deerfield River, and access is difficult, with only one long dirt road to the dam on the southern tip. Swim and enjoy the peaceful surroundings, but don't fish for your dinner here. Mercury and acidity have impaired the health of aquatic wildlife.

Hike back the way you came, returning to the four-way junction of Pond Loop and Hill Top Trail. Go straight on the western leg of Pond Loop and climb a gentle grade through pretty, open hardwoods. Nettle fills the gaps between widely spaced yellow birch, maple, and beech trunks, and the pond waters are distantly visible through the tree branches. The trail gradually ascends and descends numerous times as it traverses the hillside, finally rising to exit the woods next to a campsite where Hill Top Trail also ends. Go straight on a

The trail around Grout Pond leads to beautiful fall-foliage views in early October, and it's also a great spot for paddling.

dirt road between two more campsites and arrive at Grout Pond Road. Turn right to return to the trailhead.

DID YOU KNOW?

Grout Pond's outlet stream is stained deep brown by tannins, substances that leach from plants into soil and water. Tannins are recognizable in the dry, astringent feeling you get when biting into a tart apple or sipping black tea or red wine.

MORE INFORMATION

Grout Pond's primitive campsites are available by online reservation through recreation.gov and are currently $16 per night. Camping is allowed only at designated sites. The campground is open year-round, but access is challenging in snowy conditions. Dogs must be leashed in Grout Pond Recreation Area.

NEARBY

West River, renowned for paddling, also offers swimming holes and camping at Jamaica State Park, 14 miles northeast. Food and lodging are in Dover, 11 miles southeast, and in Arlington, 15 miles west. Mount Snow in Dover has mountain-bike trails and activities for all abilities, from guided cross-country tours to a lift-served, downhill bike park.

WALKING THE DISTANCE

"No person should attempt to tramp The Trail without a light axe, and a good compass." So advised the 1921 edition of the *Long Trail Guide*. Hiking was not new in America at that time, but the idea of a long-distance hiking trail was. The Green Mountain Club (GMC), formed in 1910 to create better access to the mountains, began cutting the Long Trail (LT) that same year. By 1920, the trail extended almost 200 miles, from Johnson, Vermont, to the Massachusetts border. Long-distance hiking in America had begun.

The LT now extends the length of Vermont, 272 miles, and likely was an inspiration for the 2,190-mile Appalachian Trail (AT), which was born as a proposal in an architectural journal in 1921. Today, the AT and LT share their corridors for 105 miles in southern Vermont, and hiking either one end-to-end has become a badge of fortitude.

The two long-distance trails have developed similar subcultures of ambitious hikers striving to walk great distances over rugged terrain, and there are as many ways to hike as there are adventurous spirits to try it. Thru-hikers complete a trail in one long walk, while section-hikers cover the distance in smaller chunks over a longer time. Some hikers adopt ultralight practices, forgoing luxuries to shave weight: going without a sleeping bag in warmer months, for instance, or cutting the handle off a toothbrush if they're really counting ounces. Others travel old-school style, wearing wool and leather. Some people hike barefoot, and one man who is blind completed the AT with a Seeing Eye dog. Slack-packers carry just water and snacks, heading to town at day's end for dinner, a shower, and a bed. Some thru-hikers are purists, resisting the urge to blue-blaze—that is, to skip a section of the AT proper by hiking a blue-blazed side trail and then rejoin it later on, perhaps after a pizza and a beer and a pint of ice cream. Others view the hike as a series of experiences linked by the general route of the trail but not bound to it. (Bill Bryson's book *A Walk in the Woods* [Broadway Books, 1999] is a humorous example of this philosophy.) However it's tackled, the challenge of a thru-hike requires as much emotional stamina as it does physical, and for most who complete it, the journey is transformational.

7 | LYE BROOK FALLS

A magnificent 125-foot waterfall hides deep in a narrow wilderness valley just outside one of Vermont's most-visited towns.

Features 🚶 🐕 〰️ 📍 ⛷️ 🌲

Location Manchester, VT

Rating Moderate

Distance 4.4 miles round-trip

Elevation Gain 740 feet

Estimated Time 3 hours

Maps USGS Manchester; U.S. Forest Service: usfs-public.app.box.com/s/7u3hl6880cqp4uyo2rcaqa08biptul34

GPS Coordinates 43° 09.55′ N, 73° 02.50′ W

Contact Green Mountain National Forest, Manchester Ranger District, 2538 Depot Street, Manchester Center, VT 05255; 802-362-2307; fs.usda.gov/gmfl

DIRECTIONS

From the junction of US 7 and VT 11/VT 30 in Manchester, head east on VT 11/VT 30 for 0.5 mile. Turn right onto East Manchester Road and drive 1.2 miles. Turn left onto Glen Road, which quickly forks. Turn right onto Lye Brook Access Road and drive 0.4 mile to the road's end, at the Lye Brook Wilderness parking area (space for about twenty cars).

TRAIL DESCRIPTION

From the bustling village of Manchester, Lye Brook Valley appears as an intriguing, narrow slice in the steep wall of eastern mountains. The valley provides access to 18,122-acre Lye Brook Wilderness, a high, forested plateau laced with streams, ponds, and bogs. On the way to these upland wilds, Lye Brook Falls, one of the highest waterfalls in Vermont, plummets down the wall of the valley. Lye Brook Trail alternates between climbs and level stretches; it is most likely to be enjoyed by kids 8 and older. The terrain also provides a fun cross-country ski adventure.

Lye Brook's trailhead kiosk, with details about the Wilderness Area, is a few steps into a dim hardwood and hemlock forest. Beyond the kiosk, go left at the junction of several trails—mostly informal exploratory paths around the river and parking area—and ascend blue-blazed Lye Brook Trail along the edge of Lye Brook's ravine. The wide treadway and the woods surrounding it are bursting with rocks, although you soon arrive on smoother ground. Lye Brook Trail continues this pattern of alternating between very rocky and very smooth terrain the whole way to the Falls Trail junction.

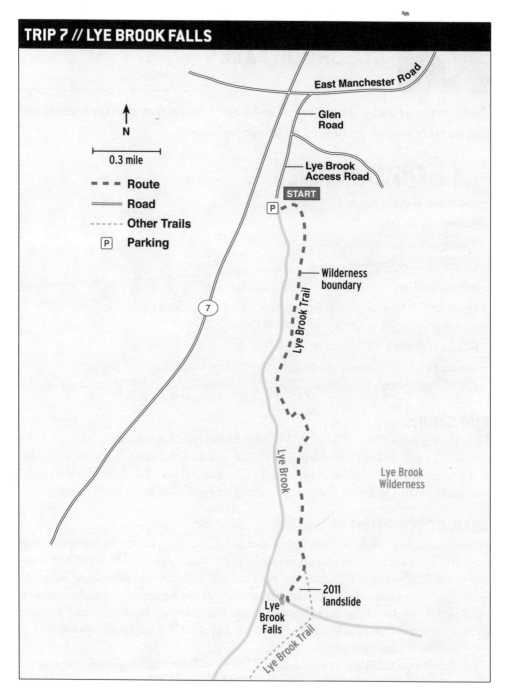

N

0.3 mile

- - - Route
——— Road
- - - - Other Trails
P Parking

East Manchester Road

Glen Road

Lye Brook Access Road

START

P

Wilderness boundary

Lye Brook Trail

Lye Brook

7

Lye Brook Wilderness

2011 landslide

Lye Brook Falls

Lye Brook Trail

Leveling out, the trail passes a hiker register box (please use it!) and briefly follows the straight corridor of a former railroad bed before arriving at the Wilderness Area boundary. Continuing in a southwesterly direction across a gentle slope, Lye Brook Trail crosses a wide tannic stream on rocks. Climbing gradually, it passes a small stand of brilliantly white, smooth gray birches on the left.

Lye Brook Falls is one of the tallest waterfalls in Vermont.

Step easily across several small streams before entering a steeper, narrower section of Lye Brook Valley at 1.0 mile. Curving left, Lye Brook Trail begins to climb a moderate pitch, entering a hemlock stand. Lye Brook drops away to the right, deep in its ravine. Curving north and then back to the south again, the trail climbs steadily for 0.6 mile over alternately rocky and then smooth ground before leveling across the steep hillside high above Lye Brook.

At 1.8 miles, a spur path to Lye Brook Falls diverges to the right, while Lye Brook Trail continues uphill to the left. Head right, following the narrow spur to the falls as it traverses a rocky sidehill, gradually descending past dripping ledges and more rock-filled stream gullies. At 2.1 miles, cross a 2011 landslide path, now revegetating. This dramatic slide, 60 feet across and about 500 feet long, was the result of heavy rains during Tropical Storm Irene, whose floods rearranged the landscape of many valleys in southern Vermont.

The approach to Lye Brook Falls, 0.1 mile past the landslide, is a little unclear due to multiple unblazed trails that spiderweb off the main route. Stay high and go left for the best view of the cascade. The steep edges of the stream's ravine are unprotected. Lye Brook Falls spills down a narrow rock chute for at least 125 feet; some estimates put it at 160 feet, before twisting and turning through boulders in the streambed below. The winter landscape here is a marvel of frozen sheets of ice draped over the rocks and hanging from the sides of the ravine.

Retrace your steps to return to the trailhead.

DID YOU KNOW?

Can you identify different types of waterfalls within Lye Brook Falls? A plunge exists where water drops over an edge and loses contact with rock. A horsetail happens where the waterfall contacts the rock for part of the drop and then plunges off it. A fan occurs when water spreads horizontally across rock as it descends.

MORE INFORMATION

Lye Brook Wilderness is within the Green Mountain National Forest.

NEARBY

Benson Hole is an informal swimming spot with a great view of Mount Equinox (Trip 8), just downstream from Glen Road's bridge over Bromley Brook, 0.4 mile from the trailhead. Swim, paddle, and camp at Emerald Lake State Park, 8 miles north, off US 7. Restaurants and shops are in Manchester, 2.5 miles west.

8 MOUNT EQUINOX

A long, boreal ridgeline with incredible views is a well-deserved reward at the top of this challenging hike up the highest peak in the Taconic Mountains.

Features

Location Manchester, VT

Rating Strenuous

Distance 6 miles round-trip

Elevation Gain 2,805 feet

Estimated Time 4.5 hours

Maps USGS Manchester; Equinox Preservation Trust: equinoxpreservationtrust
.org/wp-content/uploads/2021/02/ept-trail-map-guide.pdf

GPS Coordinates 43° 09.73′ N, 73° 04.93′ W

Contact Equinox Preservation Trust, P.O. Box 986, Manchester, VT 05254;
802-362-7794; equinoxpreservationtrust.org. Mount Equinox Skyline Drive,
1A Saint Bruno Drive, Arlington, VT 05250; 802-362-1114; equinoxmountain.com

DIRECTIONS

From the junction of VT 7A and VT 11/VT 30 in downtown Manchester, head south on VT 7A for 1.2 miles. Turn right onto Seminary Avenue and follow it 0.2 mile to its end, where it bends left and becomes Prospect Street. Take the second right onto West Union Street and go 0.2 mile to the end of the public road. The parking lot is on the right (space for about ten cars).

The parking area fills quickly during peak season, and cars parked along West Union Street will be ticketed; find additional parking behind the Equinox Hotel on VT 7A or behind Burr and Burton Academy where Seminary Avenue becomes Prospect Street.

TRAIL DESCRIPTION

Mount Equinox (3,839 feet) steals the show in the Battenkill Valley, towering impressively over the village of Manchester. Its very steep sides support diverse natural communities, including rich northern hardwood forests and fen on the lower mountain, an old-growth red spruce–yellow birch stand on the middle of the mountain, and boreal forest and calcareous outcroppings on the upper mountain. The range of habitats led to conservation of much of the eastern slope in the 1990s, with the Equinox Preservation Trust (EPT) organized to manage it. Blue Summit Trail, formerly called Burr and Burton Trail, is the only

TRIP 8 // MOUNT EQUINOX

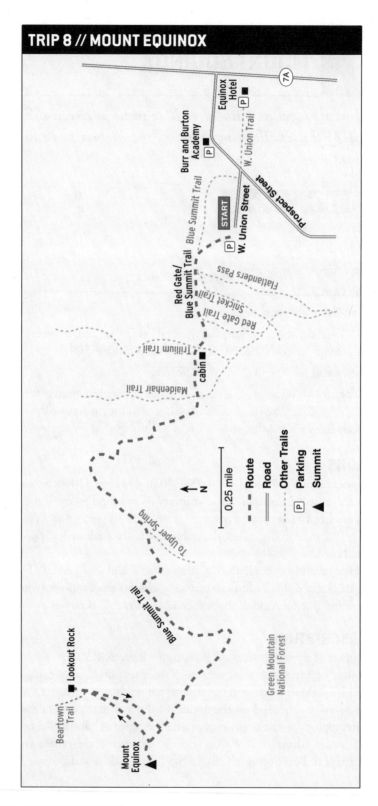

7A

Equinox Hotel

Burr and Burton Academy

W. Union Trail

START

W. Union Street

Prospect Street

Blue Summit Trail

Red Gate/
Blue Summit Trail

Red Gate Trail

Snicket Trail

Flatlanders Pass

Trillium Trail

cabin

Maidenhair Trail

0.25 mile

N

- - - Route
═══ Road
········ Other Trails
P Parking
▲ Summit

To Upper Spring

Blue Summit Trail

Lookout Rock

Beartown Trail

Mount Equinox

▲

Green Mountain National Forest

route on the mountain that EPT designates double black diamond (most difficult), due to its relentlessly steep climb to the ridgeline at 2.1 miles, at which point the pitch lessens for the final 0.5 mile to the summit. Another 0.5 mile of gently sloped trail leads along the crest to Lookout Rock. Given the steep climbs and the fact that ice can often linger until late spring, traction devices, such as microspikes, would be a smart addition to your gear between November and May.

Pass through the parking area gate and begin your hike on Red Gate Trail. After a kiosk, Blue Summit Trail (still called Burr and Burton Trail on the signpost) joins from the right. Together, the two trails follow a gravel woods road past Flatlanders Pass and Snicket Trail. Following a moderate climb, the two trails separate at a fork at 0.3 mile. Go right on Blue Summit Trail, marked with blue blazes, and pass through private land where Trillium Trail crosses next to a small cabin.

Blue Summit Trail reenters EPT land at 0.7 mile, at the crossing of Maidenhair Trail, and the grade increases. For the next 0.8 mile, the woods road jogs back and forth on the mountainside, maintaining a steep rise on every leg. The steady climb passes through beech, red oak, and bitternut hickory, with pale jewelweed, hobblebush, and a variety of ferns and wildflowers spreading across the angled slopes. In spring, look for bloodroot, hepatica, lady's slipper, and trillium; in summer, you may see Herb-Robert and whorled aster.

At about 1.5 miles, cross a very steep rock band where thin yellow birch saplings line the trail like sentries, and small spruces crowd along the narrow shelf. At a junction, the woods road continues to Upper Spring; go right to remain on Blue Summit Trail, leaving the road for a rugged footpath, and continue up steeply for another 0.6 mile.

A view of Manchester Village from the top of Mount Equinox.

The grade eases, and the forest becomes more boreal at 2.1 miles, where an enormous yellow birch growing next to a large fir marks your arrival on the ridge. Climb directly up a moderate slope, passing the junction with a yellow-blazed trail at 2.4 miles. To continue to the top, stay straight, following the blue blazes, pass a cell tower station, and go left (west) where a wide path leads to the summit in another 0.1 mile. The Saint Bruno Scenic Viewing Center is open from 9 A.M. to 4:15 P.M. daily between Memorial Day and November 1; no shelter is available on the summit in the coldest months of the year. Carthusian monks own 7,000 acres of the western side of Mount Equinox, including the road and summit, and manage the trails along the ridgeline. Hikers should be aware that trail markings are limited or nonexistent on the summit. Views from the top are expansive—across four states on a clear day.

To go to Lookout Rock, follow Blue Summit Trail the way you ascended and stay left at the cell tower junction, following a wide, rocky path. Beartown Trail drops off the ridgeline to the left just before you arrive at Lookout Rock's bench with its bird's-eye view of Manchester. (Lookout Rock and the bench are about 75 yards to the right off the trail. Pay attention because it is not currently marked and to miss it means a long hike down the ridgeline with poor cell phone coverage.)

To descend, return to the cell tower and follow Blue Summit Trail back to the trailhead.

DID YOU KNOW?

The Taconic Mountains are so steep because the lower slopes are composed of soft rock that erodes more readily than the rock forming the upper slopes, thus washing away what once were more gradual hillsides.

MORE INFORMATION

Dogs are welcome but must always be leashed and under control. Most of the trails and the eastern side of the mountain are managed by the Equinox Preservation Trust. Summit trails are managed by Mount Equinox Skyline Drive.

NEARBY

Benson Hole is an informal swimming spot on Bromley Brook near Glen Road Bridge, 2.8 miles east of the Mount Equinox trailhead. Camp, swim, and paddle at Emerald Lake State Park, 10 miles north. Battenkill River has many scenic paddling stretches. Restaurants and shops are abundant in Manchester.

9 GETTYSBURG QUARRY AND OWL'S HEAD

This trail starts as an easy walk through a young hardwood forest to an abandoned marble quarry and becomes a steep climb to the top of Owl's Head, with southwesterly views of the Taconic Mountains.

Features 🚶🐕💧🍃✳️

Location Dorset, VT

Rating Moderate

Distance 5.1-mile loop

Elevation Gain 1,545 feet

Estimated Time 3.5 hours

Maps USGS Manchester; Town of Dorset: dorsetvt.org/hike.html

GPS Coordinates 43° 14.36′ N, 73° 4.54′ W

Contact Owl's Head Town Forest, Town of Dorset, 112 Mad Tom Road, P.O. Box 715, East Dorset, VT 05253; 802-362-4571; dorsetvt.org/hike.html

DIRECTIONS

From the junction of VT 7A and VT 11/VT 30 in downtown Manchester Center, head north on VT 30 for 4.4 miles. Turn right onto Raptor Lane and follow it for 0.7 mile to a small dirt road on the left, marked by a trail sign. Follow this road to the end and park just beyond the trailhead. The parking lot is on the right (space for about six cars). Raptor Lane and the parking area are not maintained in winter. Winter parking is available at J.K. Adams, a local kitchen store, and adds 1.0 mile to the hike.

TRAIL DESCRIPTION

Owl's Head (2,474 feet) is a wooded peak of the Taconic Mountains, which begin in the Berkshires of Massachusetts and run north along Vermont's border with New York for 80 miles. This unassuming peak and the surrounding forest hide a rich geological and human history that includes old marble quarries, stone cellar holes, and abandoned industrial equipment. The area also includes plants found in calcium-rich outcroppings, which in this case are part of a temperate calcareous natural community. The first half of the hike is easy enough for kids, who will enjoy trekking up to Gettysburg Quarry. After the quarry, however, the trail becomes more difficult, hugging the side of the mountain on a narrow, rocky path requiring careful steps. If you want to hike with kids, consider skipping Owl's Head; walk the yellow-blazed trail up to Gettysburg Quarry and loop back to your car on the blue-blazed trail (2.5 miles).

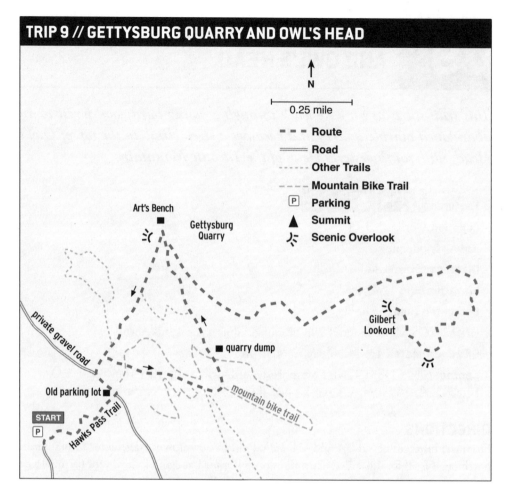

From the parking area, walk back along the gravel road you just drove in on and enter the woods on a small footbridge near the trail kiosk. Hawks Pass Trail is marked with diamond-shaped yellow blazes. This gradual climb through a mixed hardwood forest showcases many of the diverse understory plants that are indicative of a rich northern hardwood forest: maidenhair ferns, wild columbine, dutchman's breeches (in spring), and wild leeks.

At 0.3 mile, pass over the remnants of an old stone wall and turn left at the trail junction before a gravel road. This short section of trail brings you to a parking area that is no longer in use. From here, the trail is blazed in both blue and yellow, heading uphill. Follow the yellow blazes, veering right off the blue-blazed trail in approximately 300 feet. The yellow-blazed trail continues a gradual ascent up a wide, well-traveled path lined with wildflowers in spring and shaded by young maple, white ash, cherry, and beech trees. Pass several junctions with marked mountain-bike trails as you make your way up the hill.

Continue to follow the yellow blazes, turning left at a grassy trail junction at 0.7 mile. From here the path narrows, passing a marble quarry dump on the right; these giant slabs of marble appear as if they've been tossed down the mountain, which isn't far from the

Abandoned Gettysburg Quarry is being slowly reclaimed by the forest.

truth. Much of the marble found in these hills wasn't good enough for the retail market, so it was piled up and left behind. Eventually the quarry dump gives way to a sheer rock precipice on your right, followed by a blue-blazed trail junction leading up to Owl's Head. Bypass this trail for now and continue straight for another 250 feet to visit Gettysburg Quarry. The yellow-blazed trail ends at 1.0 mile, and then blue blazes begin.

The Gettysburg Quarry is one of the many old marble quarries in Dorset that are slowly being reclaimed by the forest. Wild columbine grows from crevices in the marble, and water drips eerily into the turquoise pools framed by massive walls of cut stone. It's hard to imagine a bustling quarry in such a quiet and peaceful spot.

From Gettysburg Quarry, a little detour is in order. At the sign for Art's Bench, follow an unblazed spur path 200 feet southwest to a quarry dump turned viewpoint. Art's Bench, dedicated in 2016, honors Dorset resident Arthur W. Gilbert, who worked for 30 years in Owl's Head Town Forest. The marble bench was built by members of the Vermont Youth Conservation Corps and provides excellent views of Mount Equinox (Trip 8), Mother Myrick Mountain, and Mount Antone (Trip 10).

From Art's Bench, retrace your steps past Gettysburg Quarry and follow the signs toward Owl's Head and Gilbert's Lookout. The trail is marked by both yellow and blue blazes. Turn left onto the blue-blazed trail, climbing a few marble steps as you begin the hike toward Owl's Head. The trail switchbacks for a short distance. In early summer, numerous red efts appear on the trail—watch your step to avoid crushing them. These are small salamanders, in the second stage of growth in the life cycle of the eastern newt.

You are entering a temperate calcareous outcropping natural community; this is an uncommon natural community in Vermont that supports a diverse array of calcium-loving plants, including yellow lady's slipper, Hooker's orchid, spreading juniper, and four-leaved milkweed. The trail levels out, passing a view of the Taconics to the west. (*Caution*: Poison ivy lines the route in some spots here.) It curves gently clockwise around Owl's Head, dropping into a dark forest glade carpeted with violets, ferns, and foamflowers. Tall birch trees mingle with maples, beeches, and oaks, while hermit thrushes provide the soundtrack.

After this mellow section, the trail curves to the right and starts climbing steeply toward the summit. At 1.6 miles, pass a junction with the trail that formerly led to Gilbert's Lookout. It is now closed due to erosion and dangerous conditions. Continue straight on the main trail, now blazed with red. Stone steps provide tight switchbacks before giving way to a narrow, rocky path along the steep side of the mountain. Footing is tricky here; every step requires careful placement. As the trail curves around the eastern slope of Owl's Head, it enters a dark hemlock forest and continues to switchback up the mountain. Owl's Head summit is forested, but the woods open up a bit at the top, allowing for a breeze and long views through the understory.

After a quick pass over the summit, switchback downhill on a short, steep descent. The narrow, slippery trail leads to a small rock outcropping, which is a lovely spot for one or two people to rest, recharge, and take in the views to the south. Pick your way another 0.1 mile to Gilbert's Lookout, a larger rock outcropping that provides an expansive vista of Dorset and the Taconic Mountains beyond.

To end the hike, retrace your steps back to Gettysburg Quarry. From there, follow blue-blazed Gettysburg Quarry Trail, which descends steeply on an old logging road for 0.5 mile, where it meets the old trail junction and intersects with the yellow-blazed trail. From this point, retrace your steps past the gravel road onto the yellow-blazed trail for another 0.5 mile back to the parking area.

DID YOU KNOW?

The diverse, wooded landscape you see here today did not exist 100 years ago. Gettysburg Quarry, one of many marble quarries in the area, opened in 1866 and remained in operation until 1897. Most of the marble quarried here went to Philadelphia to be used for buildings and monuments. Instead of forest, there were farmed fields on the hillside, and numerous roads led to the quarries.

MORE INFORMATION

Trails are part of the Owl's Head Town Forest and managed by the Town of Dorset.

NEARBY

Swim in nearby Dorset Quarry, the oldest marble quarry in the United States, 0.2 mile north on VT 30. Camp, swim, and paddle at Emerald Lake State Park, 10 miles north. Find restaurants and shops in Dorset, 1.7 miles north, with more options in Manchester, 7 miles south.

10 MOUNT ANTONE

Wander through a working farm and beautiful hardwood forests on your way to Mount Antone and a magnificent vista.

Features 🚶 🐕 📍 🎿 ⛷️ 🔆 🏠 🐎

Location Rupert, VT

Rating Moderate

Distance 5.8-mile loop

Elevation Gain 800 feet

Estimated Time 4 hours

Maps USGS Pawlet; Merck Forest & Farmland Center: merckforest.org/wp-content/uploads/2020/09/MFFC_Trail_Map_2020-_geocache-_data_for_avenza.pdf

GPS Coordinates 43° 16.46′ N, 73° 10.45′ W

Contact Merck Forest & Farmland Center, 3270 Vermont Route 315, P.O. Box 86, Rupert, VT 05768; 802-394-7836; merckforest.org

DIRECTIONS

From the junction of VT 30 and VT 315 in East Rupert, follow VT 315 west 2.6 miles to the height-of-land. Turn left and follow the 0.5-mile driveway to Merck Forest & Farmland Center's parking area (space for about 100 cars).

TRAIL DESCRIPTION

Climbing Mount Antone (2,600 feet) at Merck Forest & Farmland Center is a pleasantly different kind of hiking experience. The nonprofit center uses its 3,160 acres of farm and forest to demonstrate sustainable agriculture, and the public is invited to observe, participate, or simply explore the landscape on 30 miles of trails. No fee is charged, but donations for upkeep of the trails are appreciated. Mount Antone is steep but not terribly high, with an amazing picnic spot on its wide, grassy shoulder. Kids 8 and older will enjoy the hike, if you can get them past the farm animals. Dogs must be leashed near the visitor center and the farm.

The visitor center next to the parking area has maps and restrooms, among other offerings. Go around a gate and walk 0.3 mile on a dirt road to the field that is the hub of farm activities. Animals graze along the road, and a large sugarhouse and barn invite further exploration. Continue straight through a four-way junction of dirt roads, descending between open fields on Old Town Road. Climbing from the low spot, Wildlife Trail heads to the right, through a pasture, and a little farther on, Gallop Road heads left. At 0.6 mile into your hike, turn right onto McCormick Trail.

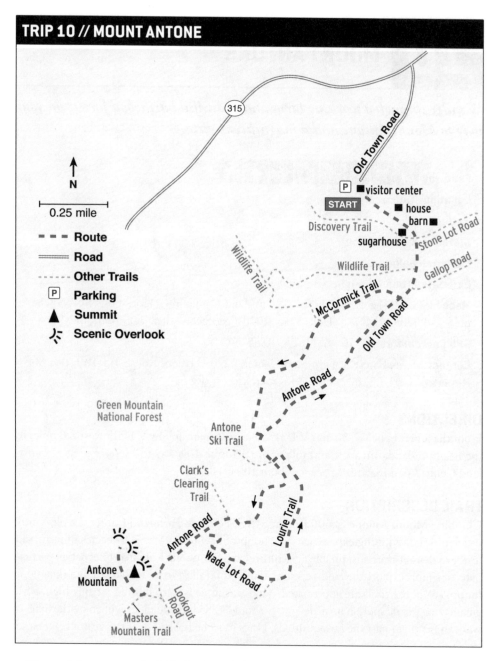

The trail drops across the hillside through birches and maples before leveling out through widely spaced hardwoods, where ferns and jewelweed create a meadow across the forest floor. At the lowest point, Wildlife Trail joins from the right, and McCormick Trail begins a moderate climb that becomes steep as it curves left and follows the edge of a ravine. At the top of a ridge, McCormick Trail descends for a short distance to meet Antone Road in a clearing at 1.5 miles. Bear right across this small field and follow signs leading south on Antone Road.

Antone Ski Trail diverges to the right near a little cabin, and Lourie Trail heads left, next to sap lines strung in sugar maples. Stay straight on Antone Road for a steep 0.3-mile climb to the mountain ridge. The grassy woods road switchbacks a few times, but some pitches are simply straight up. Antone Road rolls along the high land, passing the top of Antone Ski Trail on the right and then Wade Lot Road, your return route, on the left at 2.2 miles. Pass Lookout Road and climb a rocky, rooty pitch to a four-way junction at 2.5 miles. Turn right to continue on Antone Road and ascend the last 0.2 mile to the summit.

A small clearing provides a window northeast, back toward where you started. For a really spectacular view, go 350 feet down the far side of the summit to a grassy field with a bench under an oak tree. A northern panorama stretches across the horizon, from the Champlain Valley in the northwest over the diminishing Taconics and tall Green Mountains to the big, 160-year-old barn anchoring Merck's farm fields.

Return 0.6 mile along Antone Road and turn right down Wade Lot Road. This curving, grassy woods road drops steeply through one of the most beautiful forests on the property, with ferns and grass spread beneath widely spaced hardwoods. Ned's Place, a camping cabin, is visible downhill to the right.

At 3.6 miles, turn left and follow the sign onto Lourie Trail. Continue through the same lovely forest, and as you curve north around the mountain, the woods fill with shrubby saplings. Blackberries, raspberries, and purple-flowering raspberries (also called thimbleberries) line the path as it crosses the steep mountainside before arriving at Clark's Clearing Trail at 4.3 miles. Turn right onto Antone Road and retrace your steps to the meadow at the top of McCormick Trail. From there, follow Antone Road's gradual descent for 0.4

Capturing the view of the Taconic Mountains from Mount Antone.

mile to Old Town Road. Go left on Old Town Road and return downhill 0.6 mile to the barn and sugarhouse. Retrace your steps to the parking lot.

DID YOU KNOW?

In 1850, most of the forest on this property was pasture cleared for sheep, with only the mountaintops remaining forested. See historical photos of the changing landscape at the visitor center.

MORE INFORMATION

The grounds are open dawn to dusk, seven days a week, year-round. Camping is permitted, and cabins and three lean-to shelters are available (reservations required).

NEARBY

Emerald Lake State Park is 14.5 miles east and offers camping, swimming, and paddling. Battenkill River, 20 miles southeast, has scenic paddling. Restaurants are available in Dorset, 5 miles east, with more options in Manchester, 11 miles southeast.

11 HAYSTACK MOUNTAIN (NORTH PAWLET)

Popular with day-hikers, Haystack has hillsides rich in biodiversity, as well as panoramic views from its cliffy summit.

Features

Location Pawlet, VT

Rating Moderate

Distance 4 miles round-trip

Elevation Gain 770 feet

Estimated Time 3 hours

Maps USGS Wells; The Nature Conservancy: nature.org/content/dam/tnc/nature/en/documents/VTHiking_Topo_NorthPawletHills.pdf

GPS Coordinates 43° 22.65′ N, 73° 09.89′ W

Contact The Nature Conservancy, 575 Stone Cutters Way, Montpelier, VT 05602; 802-229-4425; nature.org/vermont

DIRECTIONS

From the junction of VT 30 and VT 133 in Pawlet, head north on VT 30 for 1.7 miles and turn right onto Waite Road. Go uphill (with the obligatory stop on the way to photograph Haystack's cleft south face) for 1.2 miles and park in the dirt pull-off on the left at the bottom of Tunket Road (space for about eight cars). Do not drive up or block private Tunket Road or the entrance to the adjacent agricultural field. If the natural area is busy and does not have available parking, please consider returning during off-peak hours. Do not block the road, driveways, or any gates.

TRAIL DESCRIPTION

Haystack Mountain (1,730 feet) is the southernmost of the striking Three Sisters in the North Pawlet Hills, jutting abruptly from the rolling farmland and beckoning hikers with its low, attainable summit and a rocky top that promises breezes and fabulous views. As with many of its Taconic Mountains siblings, Haystack is short but wickedly steep, and this trail goes almost straight up. You'll work for this summit, but it will be worth the effort. This is a good hike for kids 7 and older. Other than service animals, dogs are not allowed in North Pawlet Hills Natural Area, and it's best to check with Vermont Audubon for closures related to peregrine falcon nesting season before heading up Haystack.

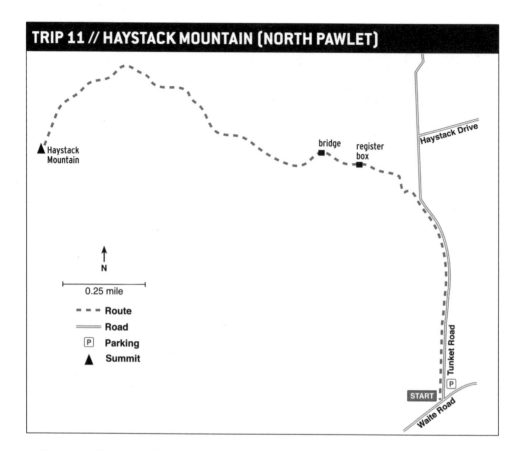

Start by walking uphill between cow pastures on jewelweed-lined Tunket Road (do not drive on this privately owned road). Stay straight uphill when a wide driveway departs to the left; the road becomes rougher and enters the woods. Shagbark hickories, with their scruffy, peeling trunks, are easy to recognize here. At the top of the hill, an open meadow permits a view north to Bald Hill, the tallest of the Three Sisters at a little more than 2,100 feet.

At 0.6 mile, at the end of the meadow, turn left off the road and follow green-and-white The Nature Conservancy (TNC) trail markers across the grass and into a conifer stand. Descend to a register box and then continue downhill to cross a stream, at 1.0 mile, on a bridge built by the Vermont Youth Conservation Corps in 2017. Ascend a rooty slope from the stream and begin a steady climb through hardwoods. The open understory is due to the relatively warm climate (for Vermont) and shallow soil, which combine to provide drought-like conditions. The trail rises persistently until a relocation of the route at 1.7 miles provides welcome switchbacks through the woods. The respite is short, however, and soon you're climbing steeply again.

As you gain the ridgeline, the trees are noticeably smaller and widely spaced, and blueberries fill in the understory. This dry oak woodland is rare in Vermont, although fairly common here in the Taconics. The trail crosses many ledges and passes through a slight depression before ascending the final pitch to Haystack's grassy, rocky, open summit at 2.0

miles. Mettowee Valley farmland stretches from the base of the North Pawlet Hills. The darkly forested Taconic Mountains march south, while the ridge of the Green Mountains fills the eastern horizon. Far to the northeast, the prominent point of Killington Peak (4,230 feet) is visible in the Coolidge Range. Foothills of the Adirondacks rise to the northwest. Look north for Haystack's two "sisters," Middle Mountain and Bald Hill.

The top of Haystack Mountain was privately owned until 2012, when a local group formed an organization called the Friends of Haystack. The group bought the summit to keep it open to hikers and to conserve and protect its natural communities. The Friends of Haystack and TNC work together to maintain the trail. Much of the surrounding landscape is owned and managed by TNC as 1,437-acre North Pawlet Hills Natural Area.

Keep an eye out for peregrine falcons while you're taking in the scenery. The cliffs you're sitting on make good hunting territory for these predators, and the birds sometimes nest here as well. Other animals that call the North Pawlet Hills home are bobcats, turkeys, deer, and grouse.

Return downhill the way you hiked up.

DID YOU KNOW?

Haystack is within the Slate Valley, a 24-mile-long, 6-mile-wide region along the Vermont–New York border that produces most of the colorful roofing slate sold in the United States. A quarry in nearby Granville, New York, is distinctly visible from the summit.

Views all around from Haystack's summit make this a perfect option for families with children.

MORE INFORMATION

North Pawlet Hills Natural Area is limited to passive recreational activities, such as hiking, snowshoeing, bird-watching, photography, and nature study. Bicycles and motorized vehicles are not permitted. Service dogs are welcome; otherwise, dogs are not allowed. Be aware that hunters may be in the area from October 1 to December 31 and in May; find hunting season information at eregulations.com/vermont/hunting. Remove no plants, animals, artifacts, or rocks; do not build fires. Camping is not allowed.

NEARBY

Some restaurants are in Pawlet, with more options in the college-campus town of Poultney, 12 miles north. Slate Valley Trails, also in Poultney, is a volunteer community group that provides a network of single-track and gravel road mountain-bike trails, as well as more walking routes in this region. Swim, paddle, and camp at Lake Saint Catherine State Park, 9 miles north. The Slate Valley Museum (wheelchair accessible) in Granville, New York, has exhibits featuring the massive machinery of quarrying and artistic works inspired by the rock and the industry. The Pember Library and Museum, also in Granville, houses a community free library on the first floor and a natural history museum with more than 5,000 displayed specimens on the second floor. Both are open Tuesday through Saturday year-round.

12 WHITE ROCKS ICE BEDS

Hike to the foot of a giant rock slide, where pockets of ice remain through summer, releasing a cold stream and cool breezes on even the hottest days.

Features 👪 🐕 📍 🎆 🪧

Location Wallingford, VT

Rating Easy

Distance 1.8 miles round-trip

Elevation Gain 336 feet

Estimated Time 1.5 hours

Maps USGS Wallingford; U.S. Forest Service: fs.usda.gov/Internet/ FSE_MEDIA/stelprdb5315073.pdf

GPS Coordinates 43° 27.05′ N, 72° 56.61′ W

Contact Green Mountain National Forest, Manchester Ranger District, 2538 Depot Street, Manchester Center, VT 05255; 802-362-2307; fs.usda.gov/gmfl

DIRECTIONS

From the junction of US 7 and VT 140 (School Street) in Wallingford, follow VT 140 east for 2.1 miles. Bear right onto Sugar Hill Road and take the next right onto Forest Road 52 (White Rocks Picnic Road). Follow it 0.5 mile to its end at the trailhead parking lot (space for about 25 cars). Winter hikers: Park alongside the road at the gate and add 0.4 mile to the hike.

TRAIL DESCRIPTION

The steep northwestern side of White Rocks Mountain (2,682 feet) is eroding in a series of dramatic rock slides easily seen from a nearby ridge. After a short climb to the lookout, descend to the foot of one of the slides to experience the microclimate created by sheltered ice beds slowly melting deep within the rocks. This hike ascends and descends in both directions and is fun for kids 5 and older. The rocky outcroppings atop the lookout ridge are particularly amusing places for kids to explore—with supervision, as there are some cliffs—and are far more appealing picnic spots than the tables next to the parking lot. Dogs are permitted but must be leashed.

From the parking area, Keewaydin Trail departs east, and Ice Beds Trail goes southwest onto a low ridge. Follow blue-blazed Ice Beds Trail into a hemlock forest. A rocky ridge descends toward you through the trees, with many unofficial trails created by explorers looking for views. Ice Beds Trail crosses the base of the rocks to rise gradually along the right slope. A series of switchbacks then climbs the steep pitch to arrive at a T junction on

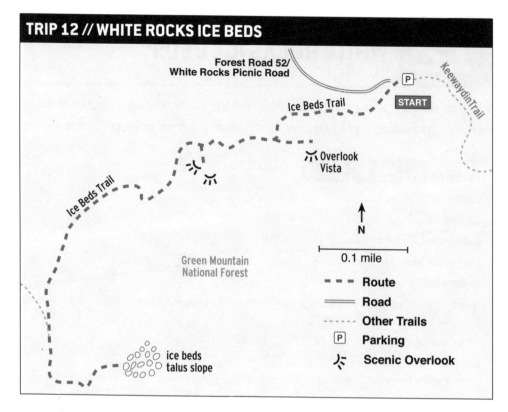

top of the rocky crest at 0.2 mile. Go left on an unmarked spur path to Overlook Vista, where a low rock wall and blueberry bushes line the edge of a cliff. A narrow valley separates the overlook from steep talus slopes on White Rocks Mountain. A sharp escarpment descends from its pointy peak to the valley, and conifers rim the rock slides.

Follow the path back to the junction and go straight to continue along Ice Beds Trail, immediately scrambling up a ridge bristling with rock. At 0.1 mile from the junction, the trail encounters a wall of ledge and turns sharply right to descend off the ridge. Before going down, climb onto the wide, smooth ledge and take in the sights south and west. The western slope of White Rocks Mountain is now visible, dominated by an enormous rock slide that tumbles about 1,000 feet from the summit cliffs to the trees in the valley below. The Vermont Valley stretches south, with Otter Creek—the longest river entirely within Vermont, at 112 miles—snaking northward along the bottom. A limestone quarry lies along the valley floor, and the Taconic Mountains stack up along the southern and western horizons.

Return to the trail and descend into the wooded valley. The route can be challenging to follow through the hemlocks because almost no undergrowth defines the path; keep an eye out for blue blazes. As you drop over the left side of the ridge, the footpath arrives at a dirt road. Go left on the road to continue along Ice Beds Trail, heading downhill into a thicker, more diverse forest, including hobblebushes that tower more than 10 feet over the understory. Cross the wide stream and the flat valley floor, trending left as a rocky hillside rises steeply on the right. Bog bridges extend over damp ground before the trail begins to gradually rise. The open, white slope of talus becomes visible through the trees, and the air

The white rocks spilling down their namesake mountain were once sand on an ocean floor. Squeezed and heated to become quartzite, they can be found all along the western edge of the Green Mountains.

turns noticeably cooler. Touch the stream running out of the base of the slide; the ice beds hidden in the rocks produce an achingly cold rivulet of 35 to 40 degrees Fahrenheit. Ice Beds Trail ends at the bottom of the slide, but steep, eroded bootleg trails ascend the right side, and the jumble of boulders calls to be climbed. (*Caution*: When scrambling here, don't assume the rocks are stable.)

After you've finished exploring, return to the trailhead the way you hiked in.

DID YOU KNOW?

In a rock slide, the sizes of the rocks differ from the top to the bottom. The momentum of large rocks carries them farther, and they end up lower on the slope, while smaller rocks are more easily stopped by obstacles and remain higher on the slide.

MORE INFORMATION

Robert T. Stafford White Rocks National Recreation Area is within the Green Mountain National Forest.

NEARBY

Swim, paddle, and camp at Emerald Lake State Park, 16 miles south. Mill River's Clarendon Gorge is a popular swimming hole 6 miles northwest. Restaurants and shops are in Wallingford, 2.5 miles west.

13 OKEMO MOUNTAIN

A historical fire tower on this tall peak offers a 360-degree vista across all of southern Vermont.

Features 🐕 🌼 🌿 ❄ 🗼

Location Mount Holly, VT

Rating Moderate to Strenuous

Distance 6 miles round-trip

Elevation Gain 1,950 feet

Estimated Time 4 hours

Maps USGS Mount Holly; Vermont Department of Forests, Parks, and Recreation: vtstateparks.com/assets/pdf/okemo_sf_trails.pdf

GPS Coordinates 43° 25.95′ N, 72° 45.70′ W

Contact Okemo State Forest, Vermont Department of Forests, Parks, and Recreation, 100 Mineral Street, Suite 304, Springfield, VT 05156; 802-289-0613; fpr.vermont.gov/okemo-state-forest

DIRECTIONS

From the junction of VT 100 and VT 103, go west on VT 103 for 2.8 miles and turn left onto Station Road. Go 0.7 mile and cross active railroad tracks. Turn left and proceed about 500 feet to the end of the road at the Healdville Trail parking area (space for about six cars). The parking area is plowed in winter for use by snowmobiles on the nearby Vermont Association of Snow Travelers (VAST) network.

TRAIL DESCRIPTION

Okemo Mountain (3,343 feet) is the name often used for Ludlow Mountain due to the ski area called Okemo on the mountain's eastern side and 7,323-acre Okemo State Forest encompassing most of the peak. The hiking trail on its western side, built by youth crews in the early 1990s, is a steady climb for the first half and a cross-mountain trek for most of the second.

Leaving the parking area, walk parallel to the active train tracks for a short distance and then curve right, following blue-blazed Healdville Trail uphill. The Catamount Trail shares the path for a little way and then breaks off at a wide wooden bridge. Healdville Trail starts out wide and mostly smooth as it climbs alongside a stream but becomes narrower and rockier. Pretty cascades tumble down on your right; rose twisted stalk, blue and white cohosh, trillium, and cucumber root line the sides of the trail.

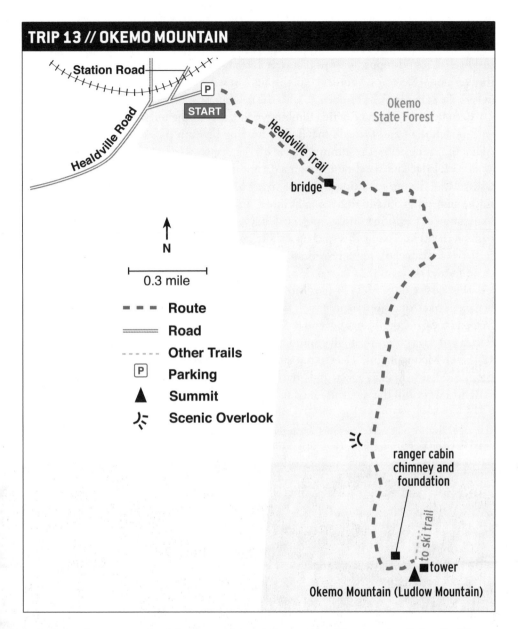

At 0.8 mile, cross a plank bridge and continue up the valley another 0.2 mile. Then a hard-left bend begins a series of switchbacks that lead you up through a northern hardwood forest and among glacial erratics for almost 0.5 mile. A final push straight up the moderate pitch brings you to the cross-mountain section of Healdville Trail at 1.6 miles.

Walk south over undulating ground high on the mountainside, and cross muddy areas on wide, flat step stones. At 2.4 miles, a small outlook opens to the north and west. The Coolidge Range, including Killington Peak (4,230 feet), Vermont's second highest, extends north. To the west, a gap allows VT 103 and the railroad to pass out of the Green

Mountains and into the Vermont Valley, beyond which the Taconic Mountains rise. The Taconics were pushed up millions of years before the Greens and have weathered into steep-sided, round-topped humps that stretch from the Champlain Lowlands south along the Vermont–New York border and through western Massachusetts and Connecticut (where they are generally lumped in with the neighboring Berkshires).

Continue across the mountain, climbing moderately as the forest becomes more boreal, with bunchberry and Canada mayflower growing beneath paper birch, spruce, and fir. About 0.25 mile below the summit, Healdville Trail curves left and climbs steeply, skirting a tall rock ledge and winding through a damp boreal forest. Look for ghost pipe with its waxy, white fingers sprouting from the shady forest floor here. Arriving on the summit ridge, descend gradually to a stone chimney in a clearing, backed by the moss-covered foundation of the former forest ranger cabin. Continue 25 feet farther to the summit spur path on the right. Follow this spur up a short, rocky pitch to the fire tower.

The roofed cab of the tower provides a panoramic view over southern Vermont. Beyond the chairlifts and slopes of the Okemo ski area, the village of Ludlow extends east along the valley. The massive ridge of 3,144-foot Mount Ascutney (Trip 14) dominates the northeastern horizon. Lake Ninevah rests in a high basin to the north, with Salt Ash Mountain (3,286 feet) and the Coolidge Range beyond it. Due west, Robert T. Stafford White Rocks National Recreation Area covers the high ground, with its scenic hike to White Rocks Ice Beds (Trip 12). South Mountain (3,179 feet) is the appropriately named bump close by to the south, with Bromley Mountain (3,275 feet) and Stratton Mountain (3,940 feet) in the southwest.

Return downhill the way you hiked up.

That cute, blaze-orange critter creeping across the forest floor is a red eft, the juvenile stage of the eastern newt. Its color is a warning to predators that toxins make it an unsavory snack.

DID YOU KNOW?

The 4.5-mile auto road up Okemo Mountain, the fire tower, and the ranger cabin were built in the 1930s by Civilian Conservation Corps crews. The auto road can be biked or driven in summer, but it's the mountain's longest ski trail in winter.

MORE INFORMATION

Healdville Trail is open to foot travel only. It is closed during mud season, from snowmelt to about the third week in May.

NEARBY

Swim, picnic, hike, and rent a cabin at Camp Plymouth on Echo Lake, 8 miles north, where group camping is available. Individual campsites are available at Gifford Woods State Park, 25 miles north; Ascutney State Park, 27 miles east; or Emerald Lake State Park, 27 miles southwest. Restaurants and shops are in Ludlow, 5 miles east.

14   MOUNT ASCUTNEY

Cascades and lookout ledges provide scenic rest spots along this challenging hike to the top of southeastern Vermont's most recognizable landmark.

Features 🥾 🐕 〰 🔍 📐 ✳ 🗼

Location Windsor, VT

Rating Strenuous

Distance 5.2 miles round-trip

Elevation Gain 2,450 feet

Estimated Time 4 hours

Maps USGS Windsor, VT–NH

GPS Coordinates 43° 27.42′ N, 72° 25.33′ W

Contact Ascutney Trails Association, P.O. Box 246, Brownsville, VT 05037; ascutneytrails.com

DIRECTIONS

From the junction of US 5 and VT 44 in Windsor, follow VT 44 west for 3.3 miles. Make a left hairpin turn onto VT 44A (Back Mountain Road) and travel 0.2 mile to an Ascutney State Park parking lot on the right (space for about ten cars), marked by a small sign ("Windsor Trail Parking") on the opposite side of the road.

TRAIL DESCRIPTION

Mount Ascutney (3,144 feet) towers over the hills of the Connecticut River valley, its granite and syenite dome—once the magma inside a volcano—more durable than the landscape around it and therefore slower to wear down. The steep sides of the mountain have long drawn adventurers; the peak is home to an auto road, a community ski run, and the foundation of a former stone hut. Five hiking trails ascend from points around the dome and converge along the summit ridgeline. Windsor Trail ascends the northeast side, climbing steadily and often steeply past numerous points of interest on its way to an observation tower with spectacular vistas over the treetops.

From the parking area, follow a mowed path uphill through a field and enter the woods on white-blazed Windsor Trail. Just after entering the forest, cross multiuse blue-blazed Norcross Trail. Pass through hardwoods and sumac to enter a dim hemlock stand, where the trail comes alongside a steep ravine. Windsor Trail follows the right side of this stream valley for about a mile, climbing steadily. Hemlocks give way to hardwoods as you ascend,

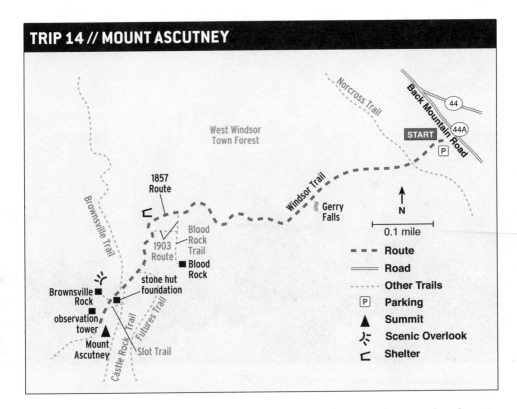

West Windsor
Town Forest

Norcross Trail

Back Mountain Road

44

44A

START

P

1857
Route

Brownsville Trail

Windsor Trail

Gerry
Falls

N

0.1 mile

1903
Route

Blood
Rock
Trail

Blood
Rock

stone hut
foundation

Brownsville
Rock

observation
tower

Mount
Ascutney

Castle Rock Trail

Futures Trail

Slot Trail

- - - Route
═══ Road
······ Other Trails
P Parking
▲ Summit
⅄ Scenic Overlook
⊏ Shelter

and views of Mountain Brook become more common as the ravine becomes less deep. At 0.8 mile, Gerry Falls will be to your left. While it's tempting to climb out to the falls, please stay on the main trail here to reduce erosion and protect water quality.

After a short, steep ascent above the falls, cross the stream with the help of ropes strung between trees at hand height and continue ascending over slippery slabs. Windsor Trail zigzags across Mountain Brook several more times and then heads right to cross a hillside littered with large chunks of rock. A steep, rugged climb leads to the junction of two segments of Windsor Trail at 1.6 miles: the 1857 route leads right, and the 1903 route goes left. (The two legs rejoin in 0.2 mile.) Go right onto the 1857 route. After 0.1 mile, the open front of a log shelter appears, jutting from the steep hillside. The trail veers left, coming close to the impressive stone chimney as it ascends the slope above. A couple of switchbacks bring you to the upper junction with the 1903 route. Stay right.

Climb over roots and mossy rocks for 0.2 mile to reach the junction of Futures Trail on your left. Continue right on Windsor Trail for another 0.2 mile, ascending switchbacks to a boreal forest ridge and a little rock-walled bowl in the mountainside. Castle Rock Trail departs left; stay on Windsor Trail and climb a short pitch to the right, meeting Brownsville Trail at the top. Stay left and climb another 0.1 mile to arrive at the foundation of the old stone hut, 2.3 miles into the hike. From the right side of the clearing, walk 200 feet down a spur path to find wide western views from Brownsville Rock.

The summit trails on Mount Ascutney provide plenty of opportunities for quiet reflection.

Continuing along the ridge on Windsor Trail, pass Slot Trail on the left, and climb a small slope to the observation tower at 2.5 miles. From its open platform, you can see across New Hampshire and Vermont, north into Quebec, and south into Massachusetts. The Connecticut River slips in and out of sight between the hills, and if you're lucky, you may see a hang glider launching from the southwest side of the mountain. The southern view is dominated by a cell tower rising from the trees around Ascutney's true summit, 0.1 mile farther along the trail.

Return downhill the way you ascended. For variety, go right onto the 1903 route, which has the same mileage as the 1857 route. Blood Rock Trail extends south 0.3 mile from the 1903 route to a pleasant view east and north from an uncomfortably angled slope above a cliff. (The origin of the name of the outlook is less dramatic than you might guess: according to the Dartmouth Outing Club, a climber cut his hand trying to carve his initials in the rock.) If you check out the view from Blood Rock, add 0.6 mile to your total trip distance.

DID YOU KNOW?

According to Frank H. Clark's book *Glimpses of Ascutney* (1905), the mountain's original road and the stone hut were built in 1825 in anticipation of a visit by the French general Lafayette. Due to a change in his travel itinerary, Lafayette never ascended the mountain.

MORE INFORMATION

Windsor Trail is maintained by Ascutney Trails Association. For up-to-date maps and seasonal closures, visit Trailfinder; trailfinder.info/trails/trail/mt-ascutney-state-park.

NEARBY

Camp at Mount Ascutney State Park, 2.5 miles south, where less ambitious hikers can drive the auto road to within an easy mile of the summit. Rent kayaks or canoes at Wilgus State Park on the Connecticut River, 5 miles south. For restaurants and shopping, head to Brownsville, 3 miles west, or drive to Windsor, 4 miles northeast.

15

MOUNT TOM'S SOUTH PEAK AND THE POGUE

A gentle climb through a diverse forest leads hikers around a picturesque pond and up to Mount Tom's South Peak with views of the town of Woodstock and the Green Mountains.

Features 🚶 🐕 💧 📍 🎿 ☀ ⛺ 🐎

Location Woodstock, VT

Rating Easy to Moderate

Distance 5.5-mile loop

Elevation Gain 700 feet

Estimated Time 2.5 hours

Maps USGS Woodstock North, VT; National Park Service: nps.gov/mabi/planyourvisit/upload/Walk_Woodstock_Map_Final-Georeferenced-Aug-2019-508.pdf

GPS Coordinates 43° 37.95′ N, 72° 30.99′ W

Contact National Park Service; 54 Elm Street, Woodstock, VT 05091; nps.gov/mabi/index.htm. Trails in Billings Park are maintained by the Town of Woodstock; 31 The Green, Woodstock, VT 05091; townofwoodstock.org

DIRECTIONS

From the junction of VT 4 and VT 12 in Woodstock, follow VT 12 (Elm Street) for 0.5 mile. Turn slightly right onto Old River Road. Park in the Billings Farm & Museum parking lot (space for 50 cars). An overflow parking lot is directly across the street from the museum.

TRAIL DESCRIPTION

Marsh-Billings-Rockefeller National Historical Park is the only national park in Vermont, and according to the National Park Service, it's also "the only national park to tell the story of conservation history and the evolving nature of land stewardship in America." This beautiful forest has been actively managed for wood products, recreation, aesthetics, education, and conservation for more than a century. As you hike along the wide gravel carriage roads, you will pass through several stands of managed forest containing both native and introduced species. The largest specimens of Norway spruce trees in Vermont are found on the property, as well as magnificent stands of sugar maple, eastern hemlock, European larch, white pine, red pine, and red oak. A gentle climb brings you deep into the forest as you make your way to the top of Mount Tom's South Peak (1,250 feet). Leashed

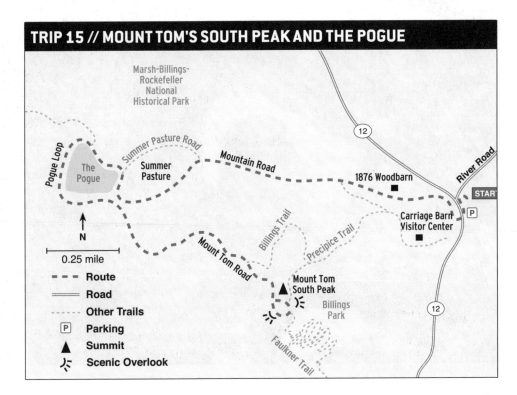

Marsh-Billings-Rockefeller National Historical Park

Pogue Loop

The Pogue

Summer Pasture Road

Summer Pasture

Mountain Road

1876 Woodbarn

River Road

12

STAR

P

Carriage Barn Visitor Center

N

0.25 mile

Billings Trail

Precipice Trail

Mount Tom Road

Mount Tom South Peak

Billings Park

12

Faulkner Trail

- - - Route
=== Road
----- Other Trails
P Parking
▲ Summit
)⟨ Scenic Overlook

dogs are welcome, and because this loop travels on graded carriage roads, it's suitable for jogging strollers. Children as young as 4 will enjoy circuiting the pond and perhaps climbing their very first peak. In winter, the carriage roads and trails are groomed for cross-country skiing by Woodstock Inn & Resort.

From the parking area, carefully walk across Elm Street (VT 12) and enter Marsh-Billings-Rockefeller National Historical Park. The Carriage Barn Visitor Center with information, trail maps, and restrooms is located straight ahead. Take an immediate right onto Mountain Road, following signs to the Forest Center and trails. Mountain Road begins on a wide carriage road leading into a stand of tall Norway spruce trees that were planted in 1888. At 0.2 mile, pass the Forest Center on the right and arrive at the Woodbarn, built between 1875 and 1876. An exhibit inside the upper level of the barn details the history of forest stewardship on Mount Tom. The site also offers information about landscape features of the park and displays a collection of antique carriages.

Follow Mountain Road for 1.3 miles, passing numerous side paths on either side of the carriage road. As you walk, notice the range of tree species and forest stands that have been developed over a century of managed regeneration of agricultural fields. Just past the summer pasture, a trail junction marks the path to the artificial pond known as the Pogue. Follow the trail counterclockwise around the 14-acre pond. On summer days, the water's surface is dotted with yellow waterlilies and lined with cattails and blue irises. In fall, the water reflects the bright colors of the tree leaves. You may spot great blue herons fishing

A barred owl perched in a white pine tree near the trail up Mount Tom.

near the shore or hear the call of barred owls echoing through the forest. Swimming and wading are prohibited, as is ice skating in winter.

After circling the Pogue, backtrack on Mountain Road for a short distance and turn right onto Mount Tom Road. From this point, the trail begins to ascend, passing through several beautiful meadows, a stand of European larch (planted in 1887), and a stand of white pine (planted in 1911), before leaving the national park boundary and entering Billings Park, which is owned and managed by the Town of Woodstock. Notice the variety of ferns along the shaded trail—lady ferns, Christmas ferns, maidenhair ferns, and interrupted ferns grow in this fertile forest.

Pass steep Billings Trail on the left, which leads to Mount Tom's North Peak. At 1,359 feet, North Peak is about 100 feet higher than South Peak, and while the forest views on North Peak provide serenity, there are no dramatic overlooks. Continue along Mount Tom Road, and you will be rewarded at the summit of South Peak with western views of the Green Mountains and southern views of Woodstock. A few strategically placed benches beckon you to relax for a spell and take in the scenery. You'll also see the iconic Woodstock Town Star, which has been illuminated during winter nights for more than 70 years.

Follow the short loop around South Peak to Mount Tom Road. At the intersection with Mountain Road, turn right and walk 1.4 miles back to the parking area.

DID YOU KNOW?

Both Mountain Road and Mount Tom Road are part of the elaborate historical carriage road system constructed by Frederick Billings in the 1870s. The carriage roads were part of an estate plan designed by scientific farmer and landscape planner Robert Morris Copeland in 1869.

MORE INFORMATION

The trails in Marsh-Billings-Rockefeller National Historical Park are managed by the National Park Service. Trails in Billings Park are maintained by the Town of Woodstock. Winter trails are groomed by Woodstock Inn & Resort, and winter walkers can use the carriage roads mentioned in this description free of charge, but the other ski and snowshoe trails in the park require a trail pass, which you can purchase at Woodstock Nordic Center; woodstockinn.com/do/things-to-do/woodstock-nordic-center.

NEARBY

After hiking to South Peak, consider touring the historical mansion at Marsh-Billings-Rockefeller National Historical Park for a small fee. Billings Farm & Museum is adjacent to the national park and provides visitors with a rare window into rural Vermont farm life with indoor and outdoor displays. Camp at Quechee State Park, 8 miles east. Restaurants, shopping, and lodging are all available in Woodstock.

16 KILLINGTON PEAK

Expansive views from Vermont's second-highest peak make this strenuous hike well worth the effort.

Features 🏃‍♂️🧗‍♂️〰️💧🐾⛷️📐☀️

Location Mendon, VT

Rating Strenuous

Distance 7.4 miles round-trip

Elevation Gain 2,335 feet

Estimated Time 4.5 hours

Maps USGS Killington Peak, VT; Vermont Department of Forests, Parks, and Recreation: vtstateparks.com/assets/pdf/coolidge_hiking.pdf

GPS Coordinates 43° 37.19′ N, 72° 52.60′ W

Contact Vermont Department of Forests, Parks, and Recreation, Rutland Office, 271 North Main Street, Suite 215, Rutland, VT 05701; 802-786-0060; fpr.vermont.gov. Bucklin Trail is maintained by the Green Mountain Club, 4711 Waterbury–Stowe Road, Waterbury Center, VT 05677; 802-244-7037; greenmountainclub.org.

DIRECTIONS

From the junction of US 7 and US 4 in Rutland, follow US 4 east for 5.0 miles. Turn right onto Wheelerville Road. Follow Wheelerville Road for 4.0 miles until you reach the Bucklin Trail parking area on the left (space for twenty cars). The parking area is plowed for winter access to the Catamount Trail.

TRAIL DESCRIPTION

Bucklin Trail in Calvin Coolidge State Forest climbs the west face of Killington Peak (4,230 feet), the second-highest mountain in Vermont. While much of Killington is developed as part of Killington Resort, the peak itself provides a 360-degree vista of the Green Mountains, as well as the Adirondack Mountains in New York and the White Mountains in New Hampshire. You may be disconcerted to see tourists in flip-flops enjoying the scenery at the end of your climb, but the beautifully forested and serene route to get there more than makes up for it.

Bucklin Trail begins at the far end of the parking area near a trail kiosk. Follow blue blazes into a mixed forest of Norway spruce and hardwoods, including maple, beech, and cherry trees. Walking is easy on this wide, flat treadway lined with hobblebushes and ferns. For a brief time, Bucklin Trail coincides with the Catamount Trail, Vermont's 300-mile

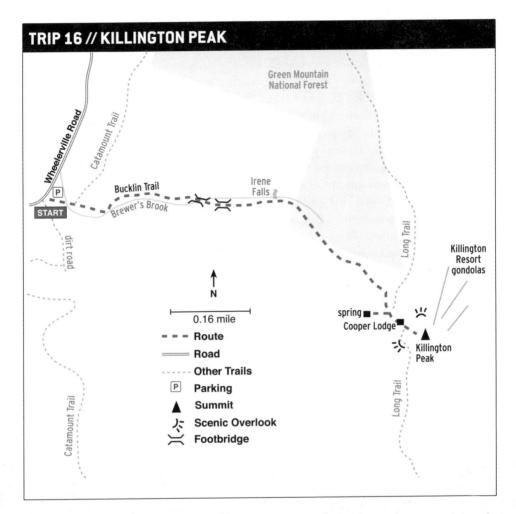

cross-country ski trail. At 0.1 mile, cross the first of three footbridges over Brewer's Brook; the fast-moving water provides a natural soundtrack to your woodland walk for the next 2.0 miles.

The Catamount Trail departs to the left at 0.2 mile. Continue on Bucklin Trail, and at 0.5 mile, reach a junction with two unmarked trails; one is a spur path leading down to Brewer's Brook; the other is a winter trail, which is quite overgrown in summer and fall. Continue to follow the blue blazes as Bucklin Trail turns sharply left. It climbs gradually, passing over numerous bog bridges, up and down wooden steps, and through a few muddy patches before leveling off again.

At 2.0 miles, a spur path on the left leads down a steep embankment to Irene Falls. Three small tributaries join forces here to create a moss-laden, watery sanctuary. Return to Bucklin Trail after enjoying the falls.

At 2.5 miles, the trail curves to the right and begins a steeper ascent. If you are cross-country skiing, this is a good turnaround point. Yellow birch trees become more prominent as you climb, and before long, as the woods thin out, you can see red spruce, balsam fir, mountain maple, and mountain ash. Feel that breeze? The open woods make for better airflow, which is welcome on a summer day.

At 3.4 miles, Bucklin Trail meets up with the Appalachian Trail/Long Trail, and blazes switch from blue to white for a short period to reflect this. A spur path to the right leads to a water source as you reach Cooper Lodge. Built in 1939, Cooper Lodge is the highest shelter on the Long Trail, and while it has fallen into a state of disrepair, it is obviously still used by hikers and locals. Just past the lodge, the AT/LT splits on the right, heading south.

Follow the blue blazes again as you begin the final steep climb. This last 0.2 mile is a bit of a scramble and requires careful footing as you clamber onto the summit. The stunted trees on Killington Peak are part of a subalpine krummholz natural community. *Krummholz* means "crooked wood" in German, and indeed these balsam fir and black spruce trees face such extreme temperatures, high winds, and snowfall that they never reach their full size and are often misshapen.

A 360-degree vista is obscured by a radio tower and an old fire tower that is no longer in use, but you can easily circumvent the peak and the towers for more unobstructed sight lines. On a clear day, the views from Killington Peak are the best in the southern Green Mountains. To the west are the Adirondacks in the distance, including New York's highest peak, Mount Marcy (5,343 feet); to the north, the Coolidge Range gives way to the northern Green Mountains, including both Camel's Hump (4,083 feet) and Mount Mansfield (4,393 feet). Walk around to the south side of the towers to see the southern Green Mountains, including Peru Peak (3,428 feet), Bromley Mountain (3,274 feet), Stratton Mountain (3,940 feet), and Mount Snow (3,596 feet). The solitary peak to the east is 3,144-foot

Irene Falls off Bucklin Trail.

Mount Ascutney (Trip 14), with glimpses of New Hampshire's Mount Monadnock (3,087 feet) to the southeast and Mount Washington (6,288 feet) to the northeast.

A short trail east from the summit leads downhill to the top of the gondola at Killington Resort, as well as a full-service restaurant with restrooms. After enjoying the scenery, follow the blue blazes back to Bucklin Trail and descend the mountain the way you hiked up.

DID YOU KNOW?

Killington Peak was donated to the state of Vermont in 1938. The land around Killington Peak, comprising approximately 6,000 acres, was acquired by the state of Vermont seven years later and is included in Coolidge State Forest. Killington Resort opened as a ski area in 1958.

MORE INFORMATION

Numerous recreational opportunities exist in Coolidge State Forest. The forest is managed by the Vermont Department of Forests, Parks, and Recreation. Bucklin Trail is maintained by the Green Mountain Club.

NEARBY

Camping is available at Gifford Woods State Park, 10 miles northeast. Paddle on Kent Pond, right across Route 100 from Gifford Woods. President Calvin Coolidge State Historic Site, 22 miles southwest, is the birthplace and boyhood home of the 30th president of the United States. Lots of restaurants and lodging options are available in Rutland, 9 miles east.

From Lake Champlain east to the Connecticut River, the broad swath of land that makes up central Vermont is about 60 miles wide and 55 miles from north to south. As with the rest of the state, the Green Mountains are the dominant feature of central Vermont, with multiple smaller, parallel ranges descending on either side toward the Champlain Valley in the west and the foothills and Connecticut River valley in the east.

The southern reaches of Lake Champlain straddle the border of Vermont near Whitehall, New York, and stretch for 109 miles all the way to Quebec. South of the bridge to Crown Point, New York, the lake is narrow and marshy, with warm temperatures and fertile farmland that has been settled as far back as the departure of the last glacier, nearly 11,000 years ago. Otter Creek, the state's longest river, zigzags north through southern and central Vermont, beginning in Emerald Lake in East Dorset and draining into Lake Champlain near Ferrisburgh. This is part of the Atlantic Flyway, an important migratory route for birds, which use the lake as a stopover, as well as a spot to breed, nest, and rear their young. Helen W. Buckner Memorial Preserve at Bald Mountain (Trip 18) is a 4,010-acre ecologically diverse gem along southern Lake Champlain, home to many rare and uncommon plant and animal species, as well as the largest population of golden-winged warblers in New England.

The Taconic Mountains, so prominent in southern Vermont, are more diminutive as they march northward but still provide excellent opportunities for recreation. The combination of pastoral and mountain views is unsurpassed at Taconic Mountains Ramble State Park in Hubbardton, where you can climb the outcroppings of Mount Zion Major and Minor (Trip 19) or picnic in the Japanese gardens at the base of towering rock formations. Farther north, in Addison, the cliffy prominence of 1,287-foot Snake Mountain (Trip 23) rises steeply from the lowlands and provides panoramic vistas of Lake Champlain and the Adirondacks.

East of the Champlain Lowlands, the northern Green Mountains rise steeply, making a dramatic departure from the relatively flat valley floor. From there, mostly parallel ranges stack up to the east, covering the middle of the state with a broad swath of high land. The northern half of Green Mountain National Forest encompasses a large chunk of this landscape, accompanied by numerous state forests. The Breadloaf Wilderness, the Bristol Cliffs Wilderness, and the Joseph Battell Wilderness protect more than 41,000 acres of forest and crag, including the rare plants of Mount Horrid's Great Cliff (Trip 21).

The Appalachian Trail and the Long Trail part ways just below Deer Leap (Trip 17), as the latter continues north parallel to the ski-specific Catamount Trail. In the northern part of central Vermont, two peaks, Mount Abraham (Trip 25) and the iconic Camel's Hump (Trip 27), are high enough to support small above-treeline areas where rare arctic plants grow.

The smaller Braintree and Northfield Mountain ranges—both part of the larger Green Mountains—run parallel east of the big peaks, giving way to the unorganized hills of the Piedmont in east-central Vermont. This hilly region is dissected by rivers and small streams, with a patchwork of villages and farms. Although the Piedmont summits are lower and less popular with hikers than the main range of the Green Mountains, they feature some lovely peaks. A historical fire tower on Spruce Mountain (Trip 29) provides intimate views of the Granite Hills, and nearby Owl's Head (Trip 30) is a convenient alternative with long views to the west and south.

The big, placid Connecticut River forms the eastern border of Vermont. The water mostly snakes through floodplain fields in central Vermont and then slowly backs up behind Wilder Dam in White River Junction. Hikers on Bald Top Mountain (Trip 28) get a good overview of the region known as the Upper Valley, a place defined by the geography of the river more than by the state line dividing it.

17 DEER LEAP

This short hike to a rocky promontory towering over Sherburne Pass leads to panoramic vistas of Pico Peak and the Coolidge Range.

Features

Location Killington, VT

Rating Easy to Moderate

Distance 2 miles round-trip

Elevation Gain 430 feet

Estimated Time 1.5 hours

Maps USGS Pico Peak; U.S. Forest Service: https://www.fs.usda.gov/Internet/FSE_MEDIA/stelprdb5315846.pdf

GPS Coordinates 43° 39.84' N, 72° 49.94' W

Contact Green Mountain National Forest, P.O. Box 220, Rutland, VT 05702; 802-747-6700; fs.usda.gov/gmfl

DIRECTIONS

From the junction of VT 100 and US 4 in Killington, follow US 4 west 1.5 miles to a parking area on the left (space for 30 cars), across from the Inn at Long Trail, which provides parking for inn and tavern guests.

TRAIL DESCRIPTION

Where US 4 crosses the height-of-land at Sherburne Pass, Deer Leap's cliffs seem to rise straight out of the Inn at Long Trail. Getting to the cliffs involves circling behind the outcropping and approaching from the more gradual northern side. Although earlier generations of hikers scaled the steeps more directly, that route is no longer available due to erosion and dangerous conditions, as well as to its more recent preservation as Abenaki sacred space. The Sherburne Pass and Deer Leap Mountain trails to the outlook have rocky, uneven footing, but the short distance and gradual rise make the hike suitable for children 5 and older who can reliably understand the safety precautions needed at the top. The 100-foot drop from the edge of the cliff appears suddenly; watch children carefully and make sure your dog is on a leash.

From the parking area, Sherburne Pass Trail extends on both sides of US 4; it is the renamed former route of the combined Appalachian Trail (AT) and Long Trail (LT). Cross US 4 to the northern trailhead on the far right side of the Inn at Long Trail. At first, blue-blazed Sherburne Pass Trail parallels the road below, gaining elevation gradually as it crosses jumbles of rocks along the hillside. At 0.3 mile, a gentle left curve steers the route

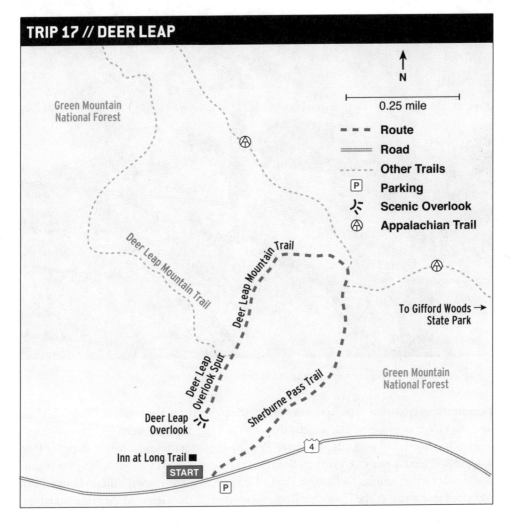

deeper into the woods. Climbing easily through an open hardwood forest, Sherburne Pass Trail arrives at a junction at 0.5 mile. The AT north to Maine heads right; stay straight, following the white-blazed southbound AT for 200 feet, and then turn left onto Deer Leap Mountain Trail, once again following blue blazes.

The route now curves south toward the cliffs, climbing a hardwood hillside. As the trail levels out on top of this knoll, it enters an enchanting forest of widely spaced spruce and paper birch. Weaving between the trees, cross the flat top of the hill and descend over rooty, rocky ground. Look for birch roots arching out of the dirt; their bark is surprisingly black, with striking red stripes. Paper birch is distinguishable from its yellow and gray relatives by its sheets of peeling bark. Paper birch is often called white birch—a name also used sometimes for gray birch—or canoe birch, as its bark is used to construct traditional Abenaki boats.

The woods become thick with spruce and fir as you descend from the knoll to a trail junction. Deer Leap Mountain Trail curves sharply downhill on your right. Stay straight to follow blue-blazed Deer Leap Overlook Spur, continuing over rocky terrain. A

The rocky outcrops of Deer Leap make for an excellent photo opportunity.

boardwalk and wooden steps facilitate the last, steep descent to the overlook. Keep children and dogs close as you leave the woods; the edges of Deer Leap are steep.

Dominating the view across Sherburne Pass are the ski trails and wooded slopes of Pico Peak (3,930 feet). Over Pico's eastern shoulder, the top of the ski trails at Killington Resort are visible farther south. Killington Peak (4,230 feet) is the second-tallest mountain in Vermont and anchors the Coolidge Range, a section of the Green Mountains stretching south from US 4, connecting the southern and northern tracts of Green Mountain National Forest. The Catamount Trail, a long-distance trail that is used by cross-country skiers in winter, parallels the combined AT and LT through the Coolidge Range, although it stays at lower elevations.

Nearby to the west, Blue Ridge Mountain (3,259 feet) rises in a solitary hump. US 4 curves between Blue Ridge Mountain and East Mountain (2,350 feet) as the road descends toward Rutland in the Vermont Valley, a long, narrow lowland running north–south between the Green and Taconic mountains.

Return downhill the way you hiked up.

DID YOU KNOW?

"One could do worse than be a swinger of birches." In his poem "Birches," Robert Frost described the remarkable flexibility of birch trunks and a couple of reasons—factual and fanciful—why you may see them arched, their branches sweeping the forest floor.

MORE INFORMATION

Deer Leap is within Green Mountain National Forest.

NEARBY

Camp in an old-growth forest at Gifford Woods State Park on VT 100, 2 miles northeast (or hike there on the AT from Sherburne Pass Trail). Kent Pond has paddling and swimming with spectacular mountain backdrops 2 miles east. Killington Welcome Center provides public restrooms and tourist information, 1.5 miles east. In addition to the Irish pub at the Inn at Long Trail, there are restaurants, grocery stores, and shops along Killington Road, 1.5 miles east, and on US 4 and in downtown Rutland, 9 miles west.

HELEN W. BUCKNER MEMORIAL PRESERVE AT BALD MOUNTAIN

This loop hike follows cliffs through a parklike forest that is home to rare species and overlooks the southern reach of Lake Champlain.

Features

Location West Haven, VT

Rating Moderate

Distance 2.6-mile loop

Elevation Gain 240 feet

Estimated Time 2.5 hours

Maps USGS Whitehall, NY

GPS Coordinates 43° 34.41′ N, 73° 24.26′ W

Contact The Nature Conservancy, 575 Stone Cutters Way, Montpelier, VT 05602; 802-229-4425; nature.org/vermont

DIRECTIONS

Although the trailhead is in Vermont, visitors must drive through New York to reach it. Traveling west on US 4, 5.1 miles after entering New York from Vermont, cross railroad tracks. Take the second right after the tracks (0.2 mile west of them) onto NY 9A, which is not well marked. Go 0.9 mile, to the end of the road, and turn left onto NY 9. Drive 0.2 mile and take the first right onto NY 10/Doig Street. After 0.5 mile, where NY 10 curves right, bear left onto an unmarked dirt road and follow it 0.1 mile over the Poultney River, reentering Vermont. After crossing the bridge, turn left onto Galick Road and follow it 0.7 mile to a small pull-off at Tim's Trail on the right (space for about three cars).

TRAIL DESCRIPTION

Helen W. Buckner Memorial Preserve at Bald Mountain sits on an ecologically rich peninsula of Vermont that dips into New York, defined by the Poultney River and a long, narrow arm of Lake Champlain. The 3,776-acre preserve provides a habitat for a wide array of rare and uncommon species: eleven animals, eighteen plants, and fifteen natural community types. Some species are notable for their general rarity, such as peregrine falcons and bald eagles; others are rare or unusual elsewhere in Vermont. This landscape represents the very northern extent of the habitat of chestnut and bur oaks, timber rattlesnakes, and five-lined skinks—Vermont's only lizard.

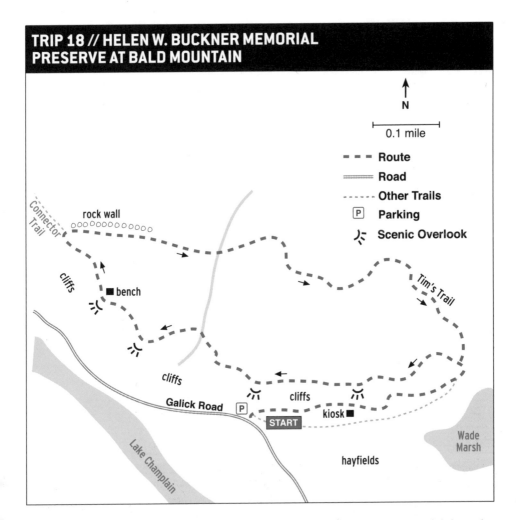

On the southern tip of the peninsula, a band of low cliffs supports a beautiful dry oak–hickory–hop hornbeam forest that is unusual in Vermont. Tim's Trail explores the talus slope beneath the cliffs before climbing through a variety of forest types on top. Talus refers to the accumulation of coarse rock at the base of a mountain or cliff. Southern-facing outcroppings are the preferred basking spots for reptiles that need to absorb solar heat; watch for snakes as you walk. Rattlesnakes are reserved unless they are stepped on or intentionally harassed and will not strike unless they feel threatened. The land's owner, The Nature Conservancy (TNC), recommends the following precautions: wear long pants and ankle-high boots; inspect the ground before you sit; and if you encounter a rattlesnake, back away slowly and give the snake a 20-foot berth. Other than service animals, dogs are not allowed on Buckner Preserve. The interesting terrain and likelihood of spotting a variety of animals makes this hike appealing for kids 6 and older.

Begin the hike following green-and-yellow TNC markers along talus slopes at the base of the cliffs. A kiosk with brochure maps is 0.2 mile down the trail. At 0.4 mile, the trail curves right and appears to go both directions on a woods road. To the right, the mowed path returns to the parking lot along the edge of the field. Go left over bog bridges to the intersection of the two ends of Tim's Trail loop, also blazed with TNC markers. Turn left onto the southern leg and climb for a short distance to arrive on top of the cliffs, where grasslike sedges spread beneath widely spaced, shaggy trunks of hickory, hop hornbeam, cedar, and oak. Climbing along the edge of the cliffs, pass viewpoints overlooking Wade Marsh in the field below, as well as the Champlain Canal and Whitehall, New York, in the distance. Use caution moving around the edge of the cliff.

After passing directly above the trailhead at 0.8 mile into the hike, Tim's Trail turns sharply right, crosses an open area, and descends into a dim hemlock forest. Cross a small stream and resume climbing through a wide hickory meadow, entering an area where tree trunks are scorched from a 2012 fire. A bench at 1.2 miles looks out over steep mountain-sides that drop dramatically to Lake Champlain's South Bay.

From here, the trail rises 0.1 mile to the junction with Connector Trail on the left. Turn right to stay on Tim's Trail, and follow an impressive stone wall downhill, passing eventually into a thicker mixed forest with beech and hemlock. For 0.9 mile from the Connector Trail junction, Tim's Trail descends through a varied forest and crosses two small streams. Joining a woods road, it curves around the edge of a deep ravine and drops back to the loop junction.

Return across bog bridges and follow either the trail along the base of the cliffs or the path that parallels the field edge to the trailhead.

Northern leopard frogs may leap out of your path atop the cliffs of Tim's Trail.

DID YOU KNOW?

Leopard frogs may jump out of your way as you hike here. Many of these spotted amphibi-ans recently have been noted for their missing or deformed legs. Biologists have been study-ing them, which is why you may notice short aluminum fences along the field wetlands.

MORE INFORMATION

The preserve is owned by The Nature Conservancy.

NEARBY

Paddle on the Poultney River, 0.7 mile east. Camp, swim, and paddle at Bomoseen State Park, 15 miles northeast. A limited number of restaurants are available in Whitehall, New York, 2.5 miles south. More dining options are along VT 4A in Castleton, 14 miles east.

19 MOUNT ZION MAJOR AND MINOR

Explore varied terrain that includes a Japanese garden, massive boulders, dark forests, and far-reaching views of the Taconic Mountains.

Features 🏃🚶🐕🏇🔍💥⛺

Location Hubbardton, VT

Rating Moderate

Distance 1.8-mile loop

Elevation Gain 326 feet

Estimated Time 1 hour

Maps USGS Bomoseen; Vermont Department of Forests, Parks, and Recreation: vtstateparks.com/assets/pdf/taconic-trails-western.pdf

GPS Coordinates 43° 41.13' N, 73° 8.56' W

Contact Taconic Mountains Ramble State Park, 321 St. John Road, Hubbardton, VT 05743; 802-273-2997; vtstateparks.com/taconic.html

DIRECTIONS

From US 7 in Rutland, go west on US 4 to Exit 5. Turn north onto East Hubbardton Road, which becomes Monument Hill Road. In 6.4 miles turn left onto St. John Road and follow it for 0.3 mile. Parking is on the left (space for twenty cars).

TRAIL DESCRIPTION

Taconic Mountains Ramble State Park encompasses a diverse network of hiking trails meandering over 204 acres of fields, forests, gorges, cliffs, and gardens. Numerous viewpoints offer big payoffs for very little effort. Start your journey in a Japanese garden before climbing gently to rock outcroppings known as Moot Point and Mount Zion Minor, with views of the Taconics from north to southeast. After a bit of backtracking, switchbacks lead to the 1,207-foot peak of Mount Zion Major, where a solitary picnic table offers views to the north and east. The rocky terrain and steep dropoffs make this trip suitable for kids older than 7 with some hiking experience.

From the parking area, follow the gravel path toward a low-slung blue house, the private residence of the property caretaker. Pass a sign for the Japanese garden, followed by several Adirondack chairs looking south and east over the meadows toward the Taconic Mountains. The property was designed with such views in mind, and this rambling hike offers many opportunities to pause and admire them.

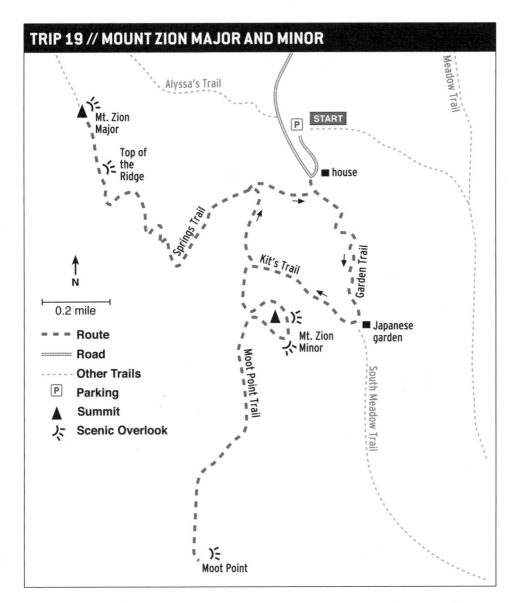

The route switchbacks down the hill, alternating between stone steps and a well-main-tained gravel path. Several tall white pines make a striking backdrop, framing the moun-tains you pass. Cross a small footbridge, which brings you to the Japanese garden at 0.2 mile, nestled against a wall of massive boulders. This property was purchased by Carson and Margaret (Kit and Mickie) Davidson in 1966, and they created a trail network that they opened to the public. Kit's Japanese garden was developed to provide a setting for reflection and tranquility. He incorporated elements found in traditional Japanese gardens, including small ponds, winding paths, waterfalls, seating areas, and bridges. Kit bequeathed the property to the state of Vermont just before his death in 2016.

After enjoying a moment of reflection in the garden, follow the white blazes marking Kit's Trail into the woods. Climb a set of wooden steps, cross a small footbridge, and follow the trail to the right as it hugs an overhanging boulder. This section is a bit of a scramble over numerous rocks and roots. A couple of unmarked trails head to the left. Bypass these and continue on Kit's Trail through a shaded collection of rocks and boulders. After climbing a second set of wooden steps, pass a yellow-blazed trail ascending to the left and continue straight to the intersection of Kit's Trail and Moot Point Trail at 0.3 mile toward Mount Zion Minor.

Turn left onto Moot Point Trail, continuing to follow the white blazes. Mature oak, beech, cherry, and maple trees provide plenty of shade, and ferns carpet the understory. In spring, red and white trilliums, trout lilies, and wild columbine line the path. This is the back of the rock escarpment called Mount Zion Minor. The trail, a reroute of the much steeper yellow-blazed trail that you passed earlier, switchbacks gently up the side of the rocky hill. Ignore any unmarked trails that lead away from the hill.

At the signed trail junction (0.37 mile), continue to follow white-blazed Moot Point Trail. This is a quiet route, often a stark contrast to the busy parking area and Japanese garden, at least on summer weekends. The path travels over a few bog bridges on muddy ground before climbing a gentle ridge that leads to Moot Point at 0.6 mile. Views of the Taconics to the east are framed by mature oaks.

From Moot Point, retrace your steps to the signed trail junction marking Moot Point Trail and Mount Zion Minor. Turn right to explore the overlooks on Mount Zion Minor Loop Trail, blazed with yellow. This very short trail loops counterclockwise to connect a series of outcroppings with more views to the east, including some views of the Japanese garden directly below the rocks. Continue around the loop, climb down a set of stone steps, and turn left to retrace your steps on the switchbacks on Moot Point Trail.

When you reach the intersection with Kit's Trail, turn left, cross a short footbridge and walk approximately 400 feet on a level path until it intersects with Springs Trail. Turn left on Springs Trail to begin the 0.3-mile climb to the top of Mount Zion Major. Easy switchbacks on a path lined with boulders climb out of the woods and onto a rocky outcropping carpeted with wild blueberry bushes. This first outcropping is Top of the Ridge, with views of the Taconic Mountains Ramble State Park meadows and the Taconic Mountains.

Continue along the ridge and go back into the woods for a moment before reaching the rocky summit. Mount Zion Major (1,207 feet) provides a variation on the Taconic Mountain views you've already experienced, but you also get a glimpse of Hubbardton Battlefield, site of the only American Revolution battle fought in Vermont, and distant views of the Adirondacks to the north. A lone table at perhaps one of the loveliest picnic spots in all of Vermont may entice you to stay awhile.

After enjoying the scenery, and possibly lunch or a snack, descend the way you came up. When you reach the junction with Kit's Trail, continue straight on Springs Trail, which takes you out of the woods. Follow the gravel path to the left back to the parking area.

Long views of the Taconic Mountains from the path leading to the Japanese garden.

DID YOU KNOW?

One of the most successful rearguard actions in American history, the Battle of Hubbardton was the only American Revolution battle fought entirely in Vermont. From the top of Mount Zion Major, you can see the site where well-trained, seasoned British soldiers met the resistance of the Americans. Although it was a tactical victory for the British, it's considered an American strategic victory in the northern campaign of 1777.

MORE INFORMATION

Taconic Mountains Ramble State Park is an undeveloped state park with no amenities other than a single portable toilet near the parking area. It is open year-round from 10 A.M. to sunset. Smoking and fires are not permitted.

NEARBY

Half Moon State Park, 8 miles west, and Bomoseen State Park, 10 miles southwest, offer camping, paddling, and swimming. Hubbardton Battlefield State Historic Site includes an interpretive trail that tells the story of the Battle of Hubbardton. Restaurants are in Castleton, 7 miles south, with more options in Rutland, 20 miles east.

20 MOUNT INDEPENDENCE

Interpretive panels help you imagine the fort that once stood on this hill as you wander through regrown forest and fields toward views across Lake Champlain.

Features 🚶🐕♿💧🗺️⛷️✳️⬆️💲

Location Orwell, VT

Rating Easy to Moderate

Distance 3-mile loop

Elevation Gain 200 feet

Estimated Time 2 hours

Maps USGS Ticonderoga NY–VT; handout maps at museum

GPS Coordinates 43° 49.07′ N, 73° 23.08′ W

Contact Mount Independence State Historic Site Administrator, 8149 Vermont Route 17W, Addison, VT 05491; 802-948-2000 in season or 802-759-2412; historicsites.vermont.gov/directory/mount-independence

DIRECTIONS

Go west on VT 73 from its junction with VT 22A in Orwell. After 0.3 mile, when VT 73 curves right, stay straight on Mount Independence Road. After 4.7 miles, stay on Mount Independence Road around a sharp left turn uphill, toward the Mount Independence State Historic Site parking area (space for 100 cars).

TRAIL DESCRIPTION

In 1776, Mount Independence (302 feet) was cleared of trees, topped with a star-shaped fort, and covered with numerous defenses to support Colonial soldiers during the American Revolution. Today, the only building on the reforested hill next to Lake Champlain is the boat-shaped Visitors Center Museum, built in 1996, with a swooping roofline and curved walls. The terrain is mild, with gentle elevation changes, appropriate for hikers of varying ages and abilities, including kids as young as 3.

To start, swing by the museum to purchase an entry ticket ($6 per adult; no fee for children 14 and younger) and pick up an interpretive map. Checklists of the mountain's birds and wildflowers are also available. Find the trailhead for Baldwin Trail to the left of the building. The trail was named for the chief engineer of the Mount Independence defenses, whose diary provided important clues about the American fortification. This part of the

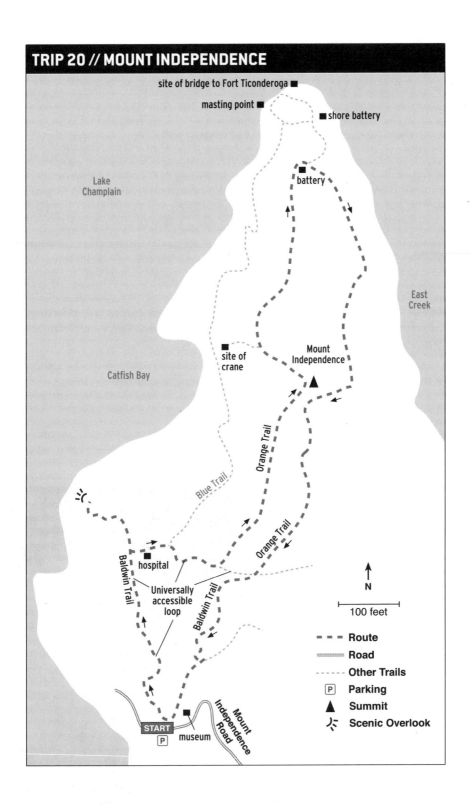

site of bridge to Fort Ticonderoga ■

masting point ■

■ shore battery

Lake
Champlain

■ battery

East
Creek

■ site of
crane

Mount
Independence

▲

Catfish Bay

Orange Trail

Blue Trail

Orange Trail

Baldwin Trail

■ hospital

Universally
accessible
loop

Baldwin Trail

N

100 feet

Route
Road
Other Trails
P Parking
▲ Summit
⅄ Scenic Overlook

Mount
Independence
Road

START
P ■ museum

path is universally accessible crushed aggregate and suitable for outdoor wheelchairs. Ascend gradually through open grass and enter the forest, where loose strips of bark on hop hornbeam and shagbark hickory make it seem like the trees are shedding.

Baldwin Trail flattens as it heads north along the ridge and, after a short distance, comes to a fork. Go left to a viewing area on a promontory. Look for bald eagles soaring over the lake here. While still endangered in Vermont, bald eagles are slowly returning to nest.

The reconstructed walls of Fort Ticonderoga are visible across the narrow stretch of Lake Champlain. When the British came to attack in fall 1776, the sight of the combined fortresses caused them to retreat. They returned the next summer and occupied Mount Independence, but when they learned of the British general John Burgoyne's surrender in Saratoga that fall, they burned all the buildings to the ground and abandoned the fort.

Return to the Baldwin Trail fork and go left, heading east to the middle of the peninsula. Pass Blue Trail on the left; a short distance farther, turn left onto the wide, grassy Orange Trail, marked with orange blazes. This tree-lined swath leads along the height-of-land to a grassy clearing at the summit of Mount Independence, the center of the former fort. The path continues northwest into a deciduous forest dotted with historical sites and to a clearing at the tip of the peninsula. Cannons were aimed at the lake from this high point. Return to the head of the clearing, where Orange Trail continues left, back into the forest. You immediately arrive at a fork. Go right to return south toward the museum, gradually climbing the side of Mount Independence, surrounded by red oak, white pine, and eastern red cedar.

Just across Lake Champlain (and the Vermont–New York state line) is Fort Ticonderoga: a large, eighteenth-century, star-shaped fort built by the French during the Seven Years' War.

Orange Trail ends at a T junction with Baldwin Trail. Turn right and then immediately left, downhill on the return leg of Baldwin Trail. Descending through the woods, pass the former locations of a storehouse and a blockhouse. A spur path leads left; stay straight to return to the grassy field next to the museum.

DID YOU KNOW?

More than 300 shipwrecks are scattered along the bottom of Lake Champlain, including at least two near the bridge that once connected Mount Independence and Fort Ticonderoga. The Lake Champlain Underwater Historic Preserve provides public access for divers who want to explore the wrecks, and it protects the artifacts from anchor damage and looting.

MORE INFORMATION

Camping and overnight parking are not allowed. Pets must be leashed. Digging, collecting any materials (including plants), and using metal detectors are all forbidden. The grounds of Mount Independence State Historic Site are open year-round; in winter the parking lot is not plowed, and parking on the edge of Mount Independence Road is prohibited. The museum is currently open from Memorial Day through mid-October, Tuesday through Sunday, 9:30 A.M. to 5 P.M.; trail fees are charged during operating hours.

NEARBY

Half Moon State Park, 23 miles southeast in Hubbardton, offers paddling and swimming. Some restaurants can be found in Orwell, 7 miles east, or in Benson, 12 miles south, with more options in Brandon, 19 miles east. The Lake Champlain Maritime Museum in Vergennes, 37 miles north, has full-size replicas of Colonial-era vessels on the lake, as well as a shipwreck tour.

21 MOUNT HORRID'S GREAT CLIFF

Rare plants and wide vistas await hikers on this rugged clifftop in the Joseph Battell Wilderness.

Features

Location Goshen, VT

Rating Moderate

Distance 1.6 miles round-trip

Elevation Gain 620 feet

Estimated Time 1.5 hours

Maps USGS Mount Carmel

GPS Coordinates 43° 50.382' N, 72° 58.114' W

Contact Wilderness Area: Green Mountain National Forest, Rochester Ranger District, 99 Ranger Road, Rochester, VT 05767; 802-767-4261; fs.usda.gov/gmfl. The Long Trail: Green Mountain Club, 4711 Waterbury–Stowe Road, Waterbury Center, VT 05677; 802-244-7037; greenmountainclub.org

DIRECTIONS

US 7 and VT 73 coincide through the village of Brandon. From the southern junction of these two roads, head east on VT 73 for 7.7 miles to the U.S. Forest Service Brandon Gap parking area on the right (space for twenty cars).

TRAIL DESCRIPTION

Mount Horrid's Great Cliff (2,860 feet) supports a remarkable diversity of life, including rare and uncommon plants, as well as peregrine falcon nesting sites. Some years, depending on where the falcons nest, the cliffs may be closed between March 15 and August 1 to protect the chicks. Check with Audubon Vermont (vt.audubon.org) or Green Mountain National Forest (fs.usda.gov/gmfl) for details. The hike is relatively short but steep and rocky. Use caution on the cliff; the edge is sudden and unprotected.

From the parking area, cross VT 73 and follow a dirt path through chokecherries to a signed intersection and a kiosk. Beyond the signs, enter the Joseph Battell Wilderness, an L-shaped tract bounded by Brandon Gap to the south and Middlebury Gap to the north. While the north–south leg of the L surrounds the Long Trail, the east–west leg encompasses Monastery Mountain (3,224 feet) and Philadelphia Peak (3,203 feet), which together make up the longest roadless and trailless ridgeline in Green Mountain National Forest. (*Note*: Wilderness Areas are designated by the U.S. Congress to provide retreats

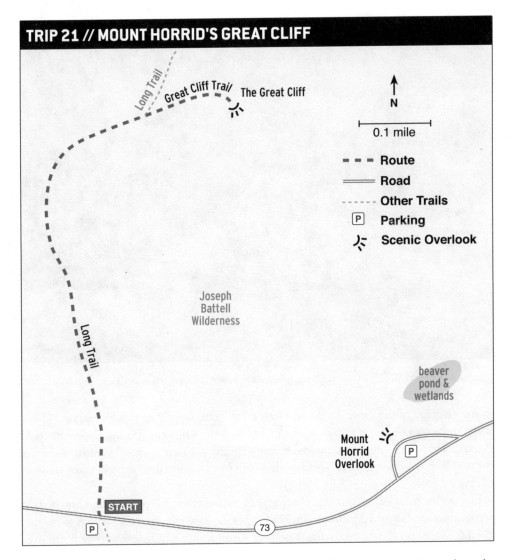

from civilization, where humans are visitors and nature takes precedence. Natural conditions dominate the character of the landscape, so travel may be slower due to downed trees, few signs, or a lack of bridges across streams. This section of trail to Great Cliff, however, has clear signage at its single junction and no large streams to cross.)

Blazed in white, this route is part of the Long Trail (see "Walking the Distance," page 28). The hike starts steeply on a rock-choked path through boulders and skinny striped maples (also called goosefoot maples because their large leaves resemble webbed feet). The trail switches back and forth across the steep slope as it ascends from the road up the west side of the hill.

The climb moderates as the trail crosses to the east side of the hill and follows a smooth bedrock path through a grassy birch forest. After a short distance, Great Cliff rises on your right, and the climbing gets steep again. Multiple rock staircases pass the ledge and ascend

Overlooking nearby Round Mountain, Mount Horrid's Great Cliff supports rare plants.

to the junction of the Long Trail and Great Cliff Trail. Go right onto blue-blazed Great Cliff Trail, which climbs a short distance before flattening out. Exiting the forest, pass through a band of ferns and goldenrod before stepping onto a narrow ledge with an uneven surface. Between the rocks, in pockets where soil has accumulated, mats of three-toothed cinquefoil grow.

Directly in front of you, a ridge running east to west rises steeply, cresting into several summit points. Goshen Mountain (3,292 feet) is the easternmost peak. In the southeast, Round Mountain (3,342 feet) lifts its pointed summit skyward before sloping north over Corporation Mountain (3,142 feet). If you're lucky, you might spot a beaver or a moose in the wetlands directly below your perch.

Seventeen rare, threatened, or endangered plants have been reported on Mount Horrid over the years, many of them on and around Great Cliff. At the lookout, you are amid a variety of interesting species. Northern single-spike sedge (sometimes called Scirpus-like sedge in Vermont) is rare in the state but widespread on Great Cliff. Among the common American mountain ash growing around Great Cliff is some uncommon showy mountain ash, with more-rounded leaf tips and larger fruit. The best treat to stumble across may be blueberry bushes. Black bears, finding a good habitat in the remote Joseph Battell Wilderness, would agree.

Return the way you hiked up.

DID YOU KNOW?

The black bear is the smallest of the three North American bear species (brown and polar being the other two) and the only kind living in Vermont. While you are unlikely to see one of these elusive creatures, if you do, alert it to your presence by clapping, waving your arms, and talking, and then back away slowly.

MORE INFORMATION

No personal property may be left in the Joseph Battell Wilderness, and no motorized or wheeled devices of any kind are allowed. The Wilderness Area is part of Green Mountain National Forest. The Long Trail is maintained by the Green Mountain Club. Audubon Vermont (vt.audubon.org) and the Vermont Fish and Wildlife Department (vtfishandwildlife .com) provide information related to peregrine falcon closures.

NEARBY

Branbury State Park on Lake Dunmore, 10.8 miles northwest, offers swimming and paddling. Both Brandon, 7.5 miles west, and Rochester, 9.9 miles east, have restaurants and shops.

22 ROBERT FROST INTERPRETIVE TRAIL

This winding path through woods, wetlands, and berry fields is adorned with posted poems inspired by these landscapes.

Features 🚶 🐕 ♿ 🔍 ⛷ ⛱

Location Ripton, VT

Rating Easy

Distance 1-mile loop

Elevation Gain 17 feet

Estimated Time 45 minutes

Maps USGS East Middlebury; U.S. Forest Service: fs.usda.gov/Internet/FSE_MEDIA/stelprdb5315866.pdf

GPS Coordinates 43° 57.48′ N, 73° 00.67′ W

Contact Green Mountain National Forest, P.O. Box 220, Rutland, VT 05702; 802-747-6700; fs.usda.gov/gmfl

DIRECTIONS

From the junction of US 7 and VT 125 south of Middlebury, head east on VT 125 for 6.2 miles. The trailhead parking area is on the right (space for about ten cars).

TRAIL DESCRIPTION

Two connected trail loops, totaling approximately 1 mile, wander through varied landscapes that inspired the poet Robert Frost and that, in turn, are augmented by his poems, mounted on posts throughout. Designed for universal accessibility, the trails offer a wetlands lookout, boardwalk segments, and occasional benches, which provide the opportunity to linger along this short hike. This easy walk is friendly to hikers of all ages and abilities. The Robert Frost Interpretive Trail is also a great place to explore on skis, with rolling terrain and a connector trail leading to Water Tower Trails, a series of cross-country ski loops. Dogs are welcome but must be leashed.

From the trailhead, which contains a kiosk and a vault toilet, go right into the trees along a wide gravel path. After a short distance, the path becomes an elevated boardwalk traversing wetlands thick with alders. "A winter garden in an alder swamp," begins the poem posted here. Robert Frost (1874–1963), the winner of four Pulitzer Prizes, spent time in Ripton almost every year from 1921 to 1963, and many of his poems include references to the local landscapes. Curving left, the trail comes to an intersection; go right to cross a bridge spanning the South Branch of the Middlebury River and to walk the second loop. Turning left returns you to the trailhead and parking lot.

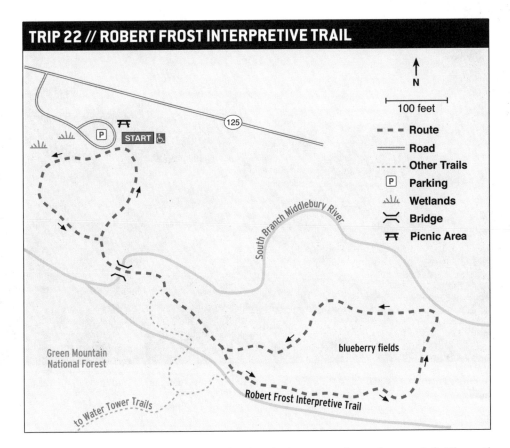

At the end of the footbridge, enter a dim hemlock grove as the trail curves left. The trail rises gently and passes a bench and a small clearing, where one of Frost's most famous works, "The Road Not Taken," is posted. Bypass a spur path to the right, which crosses a small footbridge into the woods, and continue straight on the gravel path lined with young birch trees. Of the birch, Robert Frost observed: "The only native tree that dares to lean, / Relying on its beauty, to the air. / (Less brave perhaps than trusting are the fair.)"

Trout lilies and ferns cover the forest floor between the trees, and hobblebushes spread their large leaves alongside the path. The young woods start to thin out, and several tall white pines mark the edge of the forest and the beginning of the meadow. You are now at the eastern edge of the field and the beginning of the second loop.

Follow the path to the right, skirting the meadow. Blueberries and huckleberries attract many animals, including humans, to this open area, which the U.S. Forest Service maintains through prescribed burns. A bench and a rumination from the poem "The Black Cottage" are situated with a view north across fields and the river to the steep slope of Breadloaf Mountain (3,835 feet). With almost 25,000 wooded and formerly logged acres, the Breadloaf Wilderness, surrounding its namesake peak, supports considerable numbers of black bears and moose.

Head downhill through the fields and curve left along the bank of the Middlebury River. An interpretive sign and the poem "The Last Mowing" address the succession of

The U.S. Forest Service maintains the meadows along Robert Frost Interpretive Trail through prescribed burns.

fields and forests before you arrive back at the beginning of this loop. Go right, retracing your steps to the shorter hiking loop on the other side of the river. Bypass this loop and follow the signs to the parking area.

DID YOU KNOW?

Robert Frost taught at the Bread Loaf School of English on the nearby campus of Middlebury College for 42 years, and the college maintains his Ripton farm as a National Historic Landmark.

MORE INFORMATION

The trail is in Green Mountain National Forest.

NEARBY

Swim, hike, mountain bike, and camp at Branbury State Park, 10 miles southwest. Restaurants and shops are in Middlebury, 10 miles northwest.

23 SNAKE MOUNTAIN

Hike through a mature forest—rare in the Champlain Lowlands—and be rewarded with panoramic vistas of Lake Champlain and the Adirondacks from summit cliffs.

Features

Location Addison, VT

Rating Moderate

Distance 3.6 miles round-trip

Elevation Gain 900 feet

Estimated Time 2 hours

Maps USGS Snake Mountain

GPS Coordinates 44° 02.57′ N, 73° 17.31′ W

Contact The Nature Conservancy, Vermont Chapter, 575 Stone Cutters Way, Montpelier, VT 05602; 802-229-4425; nature.org/vermont. Snake Mountain Wildlife Management Area: Vermont Fish and Wildlife Department, 1 National Life Drive, Davis 2, Montpelier, VT 05620; 802-828-1000; vtfishandwildlife.com

DIRECTIONS
Follow VT 22A south 2.9 miles from its junction with VT 17 and turn left onto Wilmarth Road. Go 0.5 mile to a T intersection at Mountain Road. Turn left, toward a parking lot on the left (space for ten cars). Parking is limited and this is a very popular destination. If the natural area is busy and does not have available parking, please consider returning during off-peak hours or choose another hike.

TRAIL DESCRIPTION
Snake Mountain's serpentine ridge slithers north to south through farmland along Lake Champlain. The 1,287-foot mountain's sudden rise from the surrounding lowlands creates an island of mature hardwood forest amid open fields and gives hikers an extraordinary view of the broad Champlain Valley. The Nature Conservancy (TNC) owns 81-acre Wilmarth Woods, which protects the forest on the mountain's west side; the Vermont Fish and Wildlife Department's 1,215-acre Snake Mountain Wildlife Management Area conserves wildlife habitats along its crest. In 2020, this trail was named Arthur Gibb Trail to honor the state representative from Weybridge who championed conservation around the state and donated land to Snake Mountain Wildlife Management Area. A parallel trail that runs along the cliff is closed during peregrine falcon nesting season; signs at the start of this

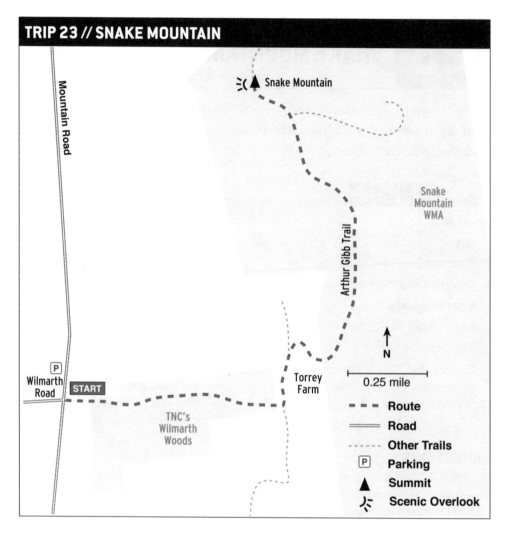

trail indicate its closure period. Hunting is allowed in the wildlife management area, so wear orange during open seasons; find hunting season dates at vtfishandwildlife.com/hunt/seasons. This short hike is fun for kids 8 and older.

A metal gate across from the end of Wilmarth Road marks the Arthur Gibb trailhead; cross a clearing beyond it and enter TNC's Wilmarth Woods on a wide unblazed trail heading east. From the late 1700s until 1992, this land was part of the 200-acre Wilmarth family farm. This particular area was a woodlot and a shady cow pasture; today, it is one of the largest stands of mature mesic red oak/northern hardwood forest in the Champlain Lowlands. Arthur Gibb Trail passes through stands of large beech and maple trees, some of which are 150 years old and host breeding cerulean warblers. Look for the bright sky-blue back of the male and the more muted turquoise back of the female as they flit through the upper canopy, foraging for insects from spring through midsummer.

Arthur Gibb Trail rises gradually on an old road that used to be a carriage road to the hotel that stood on the summit in the late 1800s. Look for interpretive signs along the route that describe the ecology, natural history, and cultural history of the mountain. At 0.7 mile, the trail turns abruptly left at a T junction (no signs or blazes). You will encounter few directional signs on Snake Mountain, and logging activities may change the appearance of trail junctions; when in doubt, search for the most-worn footpaths and for piles of brush or rows of rocks across one trail, providing a vague suggestion to choose the other path.

Heading north, Arthur Gibb Trail climbs more steeply. After a very short distance, stay right at an unmarked fork. The trail now heads eastward, entering Snake Mountain Wildlife Management Area. Because the mountain is a small, rocky refuge of upland forest in an otherwise heavily farmed part of Vermont, it provides important wildlife habitats, including a white-tailed deer wintering area and wetlands near the summit known as Cranberry Bog. Signs indicate closed or sensitive sections to avoid. The trail turns north again and follows Snake Mountain's central ridgeline to the summit.

The hike becomes rolling and pleasant, passing several unmarked trail junctions. At a final junction at 1.1 mile, stay left, heading toward open sky along the western edge of the ridge. Arthur Gibb Trail exits the woods and arrives on a concrete pad that was the beginning of a residence that was never completed at 1.8 mile.

The vistas south, west, and north are jaw-dropping. Immediately beneath you, a patchwork of farmland spreads in all directions, cut by the muddy, tree-lined bends of Dead Creek as it makes its way north to join Otter Creek before emptying into Lake Champlain. Across the lake, the foothills of the Adirondacks seem to rise from the water, while the high

Snake Mountain, like so many Taconic peaks, seems to pop straight up from Champlain Valley farmland, giving a big, dramatic view in exchange for a relatively small hiking effort.

peaks cut a jagged line across the sky. If you visit in fall, Snake Mountain's quartzite cliffs provide an excellent seat from which to watch hawk migrations.

Return to the trailhead the way you climbed up.

DID YOU KNOW?

About 10,000 years ago, Snake Mountain was an island in the Champlain Sea, a temporary arm of the Atlantic Ocean. Marine life, such as seals and beluga whales, swam here, leaving behind skeletons that gave nineteenth-century settlers their first clues to the valley's oceanic past.

MORE INFORMATION

The first 0.5 mile of Arthur Gibb Trail (called Snake Mountain Trail on some maps) is managed by The Nature Conservancy's Vermont Chapter. Bicycles, motorized vehicles, camping, and fires are not allowed in Wilmarth Woods. Per ordinance by the Town of Addison, dogs must be under direct control of their owners on Snake Mountain. The Snake Mountain Wildlife Management Area is owned and managed by the Vermont Fish and Wildlife Department and is open to regulated hunting, trapping, hiking, and wildlife viewing. Motorized and wheeled vehicles, including mountain bikes, are prohibited. Groups larger than ten individuals or associated with a commercial operation need a special-use permit from the Fish and Wildlife Department.

NEARBY

The Vermont Fish and Wildlife Department's Dead Creek Visitor Center is 4.6 miles away on VT Route 17 West in Addison and has variable weekend hours during summer, with expanded hours in fall. Stop by the center or visit vtfishandwildlife.com for up-to-date hours of operation. Branbury State Park, 25 miles southeast in Salisbury, offers lake swimming and camping. Middlebury, 11.4 miles southeast, has restaurants, grocery stores, and a variety of shops.

24 SUNSET LEDGE

This rolling ridge hike on the Long Trail leads to western-facing ledges with magnificent vistas of Lake Champlain and the Adirondacks.

Features 🦌🐕📍🌸🌲

Location Lincoln, VT

Rating Easy

Distance 2.2 miles round-trip

Elevation Gain 387 feet

Estimated Time 1.5 hours

Maps USGS Lincoln

GPS Coordinates 44° 05.70′ N, 72° 55.70′ W

Contact Breadloaf Wilderness: U.S. Forest Service, Rochester Ranger District, 99 Ranger Road, Rochester, VT 05767; 802-767-4261; fs.usda.gov/gmfl. The Long Trail: Green Mountain Club, 4711 Waterbury–Stowe Road, Waterbury Center, VT 05677; 802-244-7037; greenmountainclub.org

DIRECTIONS

From the intersection of VT 100 and Main Street in Warren, travel 0.7 mile south on VT 100. Turn right onto Lincoln Gap Road (labeled Lincoln Mountain Road in places) and follow it 4.0 miles to the Long Trail crossing at Lincoln Gap, where parking is allowed along either side of the road. The height-of-land accommodates about twenty vehicles; a lower parking area holds an additional fifteen. (Lincoln Gap Road is not maintained in winter; snowshoers should park at the gate and add 1.2 miles to the hike.)

TRAIL DESCRIPTION

Sunset Ledge (2,811 feet) juts from the side of a gradually sloping ridge between Mount Grant (3,623 feet) and Lincoln Gap (2,424 feet). This section of the Long Trail undulates over rock slabs and through small hollows, making the walk almost as scenic and interesting as the broad views at the destination. Children of most ages will enjoy scrambling along the ridgeline after an initial steep pitch.

From Lincoln Gap, follow the white-blazed Long Trail south into the Breadloaf Wilderness. The largest of Vermont's eight designated Wilderness Areas, Breadloaf encompasses almost 25,000 acres of the main ridge of the Green Mountains between Lincoln Gap Road and VT 125. As in other designated Wilderness Areas, trail work and signage are not always evident. Once heavily logged, the mountains of the Breadloaf Wilderness are mostly reforested and now well populated by moose. A fair number of black bears roam here as well.

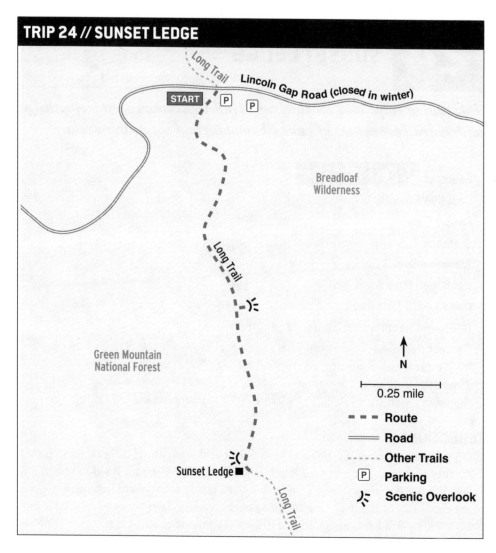

The Long Trail climbs steadily for a few tenths of a mile after entering the Wilderness Area. After a switchback at the top of a sidehill climb, the trail eases to a gradual pitch through beeches and sugar maples, with hobblebushes and ferns filling in the understory. A right turn leads to a ledgy, rooty scramble up an S-curve. Halfway up, an informal path goes left to a rock with a view north and east over the spruce trees to the Northfield Range, paralleling the high ridge of the Green Mountains on the opposite side of the Mad River valley.

Continuing uphill around another couple of curves, the Long Trail tops the ridge. Sky appears through the branches on both sides of the treadway as it rolls along over low ledges. In spring, look for deep maroon blooms of purple trillium and showy white-and-pink petals of painted trillium in these low spots. In late summer, a bright red berry replaces the trillium flower, perched at the top of the stalk and surrounded by three broad leaves.

At 1.1 miles, the forest opens on the right to reveal Sunset Ledge and wide vistas to the west. Keep children close and keep dogs leashed in this cliffy area. The mountainside falls away beneath the ledge, swooping down into a forested and pastoral valley, where the town of Lincoln lies, and up into the Bristol Cliffs Wilderness. A sharp notch in the ridgeline allows views of Lake Champlain spreading across broad lowlands. The Adirondacks rise above everything, the tallest of these distant peaks reaching elevations of more than 5,000 feet. If you're on Sunset Ledge in colder months, look for the Adirondacks' snow-covered landslide scars.

The cliffs continue raggedly northward, with dark green conifer spires on top and smooth, deciduous canopy below. High above, the pointy peak of Mount Abraham (Trip 25) pokes into the sky at a little more than 4,000 feet. Below it, the rounded tops of the Hogback Mountains march north. To the south, Robert Frost Mountain (2,411 feet) rises between the towns of Middlebury and Ripton.

Retrace your steps to return to the trailhead.

DID YOU KNOW?

Lincoln Gap and the town of Lincoln were not named for our country's 16th president, as nearby Mount Abraham was. Instead, these sites honor Major General Benjamin Lincoln, a farmer from Massachusetts whose militia repelled the British in the Battle of Bennington during the American Revolution.

This hike offers views east to the Northfield Range (shown) and west across the Champlain Valley.

MORE INFORMATION

The Breadloaf Wilderness is a place where human impact is kept to a minimum: do not leave any personal property or use any wheeled device, such as a mountain bike or a wagon. The Breadloaf Wilderness is managed by the U.S. Forest Service. The Long Trail is maintained by the Green Mountain Club.

NEARBY

Swim in the Mad River at various holes in Warren, 4 miles east, and along VT 100 north through Waitsfield, 10 miles northeast. The multiuse Mad River Path parallels the river, and whitewater paddling is popular downstream of Warren. Sugarbush, 8.2 miles northeast, offers alpine skiing, mountain biking, disc golf, and other outdoor activities. Restaurants and grocery stores are on VT 100 in Waitsfield and along VT 17 in Bristol, 9.5 miles west.

25 MOUNT ABRAHAM

Hike a section of the celebrated Monroe Skyline to find rare arctic plants and 360-degree vistas on this rocky summit.

Features ❀ 🐕 👓 ◿ ✳

Location Lincoln, VT

Rating Strenuous

Distance 5.2 miles round-trip

Elevation Gain 1,589 feet

Estimated Time 3.5 hours

Maps USGS Lincoln

GPS Coordinates 44° 05.70′ N, 72° 55.70′ W

Contact Mount Abraham: Green Mountain National Forest, Rochester Ranger District, 99 Ranger Road, Rochester, VT 05767; 802-767-4261; fs.usda.gov/gmfl. The Long Trail and Battell Shelter: Green Mountain Club, 4711 Waterbury–Stowe Road, Waterbury Center, VT 05677; 802-244-7037; greenmountainclub.org

DIRECTIONS

From the intersection of VT 100 and Main Street in Warren, travel 0.7 mile south on VT 100. Turn right onto Lincoln Gap Road (labeled Lincoln Mountain Road in places) and follow it 4.0 miles to the Long Trail crossing at Lincoln Gap, where parking is allowed along both sides of the road (space for twenty cars). A lower parking lot holds an additional fifteen vehicles. (Lincoln Gap Road is not maintained in winter; snowshoers should park at the gate and add 1.2 miles to the hike.)

TRAIL DESCRIPTION

Mount Abraham (4,006 feet) is Vermont's fifth-highest peak, just over the 4,000-foot line that marks the approximate edge of alpine tundra in the Green Mountains , though it does not actually feature that habitat (see "The Sparse Tundra of Vermont," page 197). The hike from Lincoln Gap is relatively short, but difficult footing in places makes it more challenging than the distance alone would imply.

The 272-mile Long Trail (see "Walking the Distance," page 28) crosses the highest point of Lincoln Gap Road. From the parking area, head north on the Long Trail, following white blazes up a steep pitch into the woods. The path traverses the hill above the road for a short distance and then turns away and climbs moderately through beech, maple, and fir. The rocky, narrow trail is lined with club moss, trillium, and blue-bead lily.

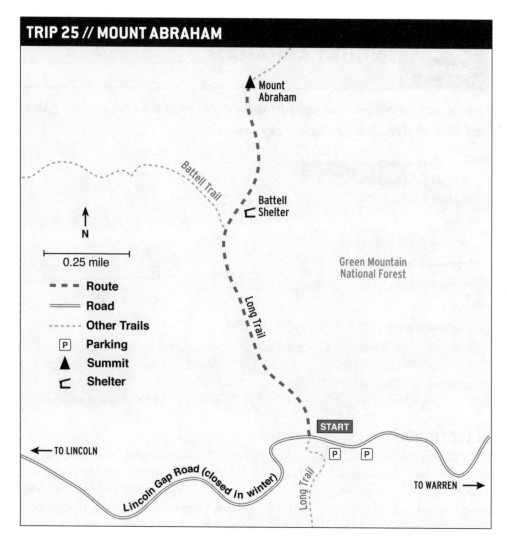

Mount
Abraham

Battell Trail

Battell
Shelter

N

0.25 mile

- - - Route
=== Road
----- Other Trails
P Parking
▲ Summit
⊏ Shelter

Green Mountain
National Forest

Long Trail

START

← TO LINCOLN

P   P

Lincoln Gap Road (closed in winter)

Long Trail

TO WARREN →

After a short descent and a left curve over a sloping ledge, you can see the ridgeline ahead through the trees. Mount Abraham marks the southern end of the spectacular ridge walk known as the Monroe Skyline. Extending north to the Winooski River valley, the 30-mile route follows high ridges with numerous vistas and bald summits.

The shift to high-elevation forest comes early on the hike up Mount Abraham (known locally as Mount Abe). This transition occurs around 2,700 feet, and your nose may alert you before your eyes do: balsam firs are exceptionally fragrant. When you enter the spruce–fir forest, the climb steepens, but as you round the mountain, the pitches are interrupted by brief level respites. Where the path is not on sloping ledges, it's across uneven slopes of half-buried rocks crisscrossed with tannic streams.

At 1.7 miles, blue-blazed Battell Trail joins from the left. One-tenth of a mile farther, Battell Shelter provides a resting place in advance of the final 0.8-mile push to the summit. (A Green Mountain Club caretaker collects a $5 fee from hikers who want to spend the

Mount Abraham's summit patch of tundra vegetation allows hikers a close-up view of these special, hardy plants as well as a break in the forest for long views in every direction.

night in the shelter.) From the shelter, the Long Trail climbs up ledges and over bog bridges. The trees grow shorter until, a little more than 0.5 mile above the shelter, you climb out of the branches as you pass the treeline. The sights along the final ascent to the summit are magnificent. An enormous egg of quartz rests beside the trail, providing a perfect perch for admiring the ridge that stretches south into the Breadloaf Wilderness. You can follow the route of the Long Trail with your eyes, scanning the high ground on the side-by-side peaks of Grant (3,610 feet) and Cleveland (3,470 feet) and beyond, to the prow of Breadloaf Mountain (3,835 feet), which seems to plow westward.

At the summit, the ridgeline path of the Long Trail is evident as it continues northeast, first to Lincoln Peak (3,950 feet), 0.8 mile away, where a viewing platform perches over the ski trails of Sugarbush, and then on to the high crest of Mount Ellen (4,083 feet). To the west, 125-mile-long Lake Champlain sprawls beneath the Adirondack Plateau and its high peaks.

Mount Abraham's 1-acre summit is a patchwork of Bigelow's sedge; schist studded with quartz and covered with map lichen; and stunted, gnarled spruce and fir trees called krummholz ("crooked wood"). Hikers should leash their dogs here and walk only on rocks to avoid trampling the summit vegetation. Areas of particular concern may be designated by low rock walls or string perimeters.

Descend the way you came up.

DID YOU KNOW?

As you hike uphill, the temperature typically drops between 3.5 and 5.5 degrees Fahrenheit for every 1,000 feet you climb—and that's before accounting for windchill. Humidity traps heat, so on dry days the temperature drop is greater than if it's raining or snowing.

MORE INFORMATION

Mount Abraham is in Green Mountain National Forest. The Long Trail and Battell Shelter are maintained by the Green Mountain Club.

NEARBY

Swim in the Mad River at various holes in Warren, 4 miles east, and along VT 100 north through Waitsfield, 10 miles northeast. The multiuse Mad River Path parallels the river, and whitewater paddling is popular downstream of Warren. Sugarbush, 8.2 miles northeast, offers alpine skiing, mountain biking, disc golf, and other outdoor activities. Restaurants and grocery stores are on VT 100 in Waitsfield and along VT 17 in Bristol, 9.5 miles west.

26 BURNT ROCK MOUNTAIN

This bare summit provides a fun rock scramble along one of the most scenic sections of the Long Trail.

Features 🐕 ♿ 〰️ 💧 🔍

Location Fayston, VT

Rating Strenuous

Distance 5.2 miles round-trip

Elevation Gain 2,090 feet

Estimated Time 3.5 hours

Maps USGS Waterbury, USGS Huntington

GPS Coordinates 44° 14.98′ N, 72° 52.43′ W

Contact Green Mountain Club, 4711 Waterbury–Stowe Road, Waterbury Center, VT 05677; 802-244-7037; greenmountainclub.org

DIRECTIONS

From the village of Waitsfield, follow VT 100 north 3.0 miles and turn left onto North Fayston Road. After 4.0 miles, at the forked junction with Center Fayston Road and unmarked Sharpshooter Road, go right onto Sharpshooter Road. Turn immediately left onto Big Basin Road and follow it 0.9 mile to the parking lot for Hedgehog Brook Trail. Parking is on either side of the gravel road (space for eight cars).

TRAIL DESCRIPTION

This hike up Hedgehog Brook Trail and along a section of the Long Trail starts gently and gradually gets steeper and more challenging—and more fun! The payoff matches your efforts: the ridgeline leads you through a beautiful stretch of boreal forest and interesting rock formations before culminating in panoramic views on the bare crest of Burnt Rock Mountain (3,159 feet).

Hedgehog Brook Trail starts by descending to a rock hop across its namesake brook. Ascending rock steps on the far side, the narrow, blue-blazed route leads you into a deciduous forest, paralleling the brook on a gradual uphill climb. Hedgehog Brook Trail undulates over hummocks and across small streams and then descends to cross the wide brook. A short distance after this crossing, the trail turns sharply left and becomes wider and sandier—the remnant of an old road. Look for the teeth marks and dangling strips of bark that indicate moose have visited the striped maple saplings along this section of trail. As you walk up the right side of the brook, an enormous mossy boulder with birch and spruce

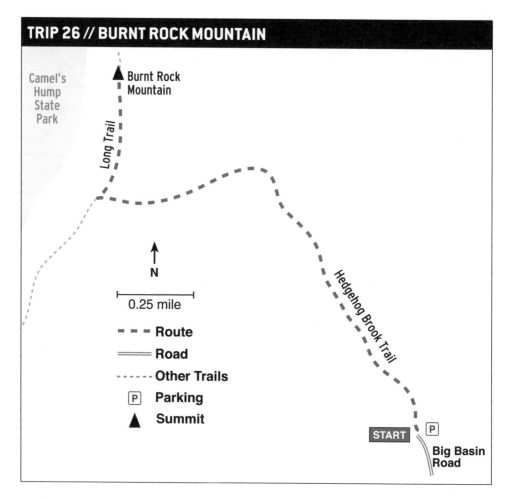

Camel's
Hump
State
Park

Long Trail

▲ Burnt Rock
   Mountain

↑
N

|———— 0.25 mile ————|

- - - **Route**
═══ **Road**
...... **Other Trails**
P **Parking**
▲ **Summit**

Hedgehog Brook Trail

START P

Big Basin
Road

trunks sprouting from its scalp pushes the trail briefly off the straight track, which is lined with purple-flowering raspberry. Hedgehog Brook Trail gradually becomes narrower again and a little rockier and begins to zigzag steeply uphill, leaving the brook far below. A double blaze marks a left turn, and the trail traverses the slope, rising moderately and occasionally following smooth rock spines.

After a rocky stream crossing, the trail again heads steeply uphill. When you enter the Long Trail easement lands, the trees are noticeably shorter. A steep scramble over rocks and up three log ladders brings you into a spruce–fir forest with an occasional mountain ash. Hedgehog Brook Trail jogs back and forth, climbing several ledges before arriving on the ridgeline, where it ends.

Turn right onto the white-blazed Long Trail and head north through a dim, mossy conifer forest. After scrambling through a narrow, rocky canyon and up a steep pitch, break out of the trees and onto the open face of Burnt Rock Mountain. The white blazes are now painted on the rocks, although if you hike early in the season, some may have been scoured off by winter's ice. Making your way through patches of short trees as you climb this rocky crest,

Hikers are treated to dramatic views—such as these trailside cliffs—along the hike up Burnt Rock Mountain, as well as spectacular vistas from its magnificent ridgeline.

you are walking on the spine of the highest range in Vermont. Along most of the Green Mountains' main range, the spine is fully forested, but in some unusual spots such as this one, the bedrock is bare beneath the sky, and visitors get the benefit of a view over the treetops.

To the east, ridgelines stack up one behind the other into the distance. To the south, the dramatic bulk and crests of the high Green Mountains rise, with the ski trails of Sugarbush and Mad River Glen tracing lighter paths through the dark green forests from late spring through summer and fall.

This section of the Long Trail—from Mount Abraham (Trip 25) at the southern end through where you stand on Burnt Rock Mountain and north over Camel's Hump (Trip 27)—is called the Monroe Skyline. Its long stretches of high elevation and magnificent views make it one of the most scenic and interesting parts of the 272-mile Long Trail (see "Walking the Distance," page 28). To the north, Mount Ira Allen (3,450 feet) and Mount Ethan Allen (3,670 feet) lead to the striking summit of Camel's Hump. To the west, the rounded foothills descend to the blue expanse of Lake Champlain; beyond the lake, New York's Adirondack Mountains rise steeply.

Follow the white blazes and then the blue blazes back down to the trailhead.

DID YOU KNOW?

From the summit of Burnt Rock Mountain, the nation's last surviving single-seat chairlift is visible on General Stark Mountain. Its continued use is one of many ways the Mad River Glen ski area resists modern alpine ski culture. At Mad River Glen, snowmaking is minimal, snowboarding is not allowed, and the mountain is owned by a member cooperative that strives for low skier density.

MORE INFORMATION

Hedgehog Brook Trail and this section of the Long Trail are on private land. Hikers are allowed to use the trails thanks to the generosity of the landowners. Please stay on the trails and away from buildings. Inconsiderate hiker behavior could lead to trail closures. Camping and fires are not allowed anywhere along Hedgehog Brook Trail or this section of the Long Trail. Both trails are maintained by the Green Mountain Club.

NEARBY

Many sections of the Mad River flowing through Waitsfield, 7 miles southeast, are suitable for swimming and paddling; the multiuse Mad River Path runs parallel to the water. Sugarbush, 14.4 miles south, offers alpine skiing, mountain biking, disc golf, and other outdoor activities. Restaurants and grocery stores are along VT 100 in Waitsfield, 7 miles southeast.

27 CAMEL'S HUMP (EAST AND WEST SIDES)

Visit the craggy, windswept summit of Vermont's most famous peak via one of these two challenging, rewarding loops.

Features

EAST SIDE VIA MONROE, DEAN, AND LONG TRAILS:

Location Duxbury, VT

Rating Strenuous

Distance 7-mile loop

Elevation Gain 2,585 feet

Estimated Time 6 hours

WEST SIDE VIA BURROWS, LONG, AND FOREST CITY TRAILS:

Location Huntington, VT

Rating Strenuous

Distance 5.3-mile loop

Elevation Gain 2,230 feet

Estimated Time 5.5 hours

Maps USGS Waterbury, USGS Huntington; Vermont Department of Forests, Parks, and Recreation: vtstateparks.com/assets/pdf/camels_hump_trails.pdf

GPS Coordinates Monroe trailhead: 44° 18.99′ N, 72° 50.87′ W; Burrows and Forest City trails: 44° 18.30′ N, 72° 54.48′ W

Contact Camel's Hump State Park: Vermont Department of Forests, Parks, and Recreation, District 3, Essex Office; 111 West Street, Essex Junction, VT 05452; 802-879-6565; fpr.vermont.gov; Trails and hiker facilities: Green Mountain Club, 4711 Waterbury–Stowe Road, Waterbury Center, VT 05677; 802-244-7037; greenmountainclub.org

DIRECTIONS

To Monroe trailhead—access to Dean and Long trails

From I-89, Exit 10, go south on VT 100. Exit the rotary to continue on VT 100 south for 0.2 mile. Turn right onto Winooski Street and follow it 0.4 mile to its end. Turn right onto River Road and drive 3.9 miles; then turn left on Camel's Hump Road. Drive 3.5 miles up Camel's Hump Road to a parking lot on the right (space for twenty cars) or straight ahead to the upper lots (space for twenty cars). The upper lots are gated at dusk and reopened at dawn. (The

TRIP 27 // CAMEL'S HUMP (EAST AND WEST SIDES)

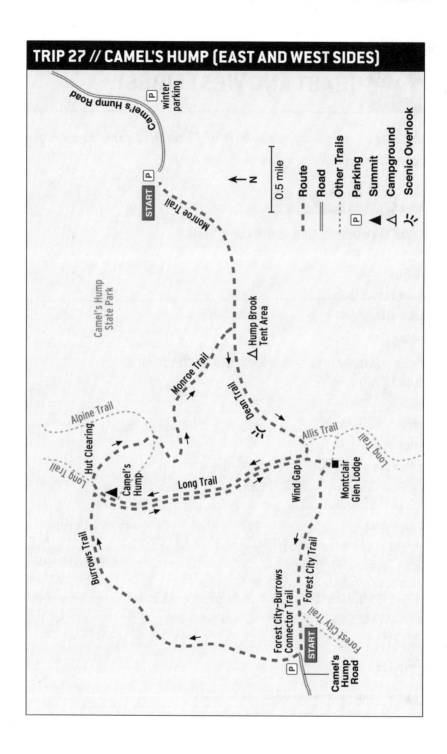

Camel's Hump Road

winter parking

START

Monroe Trail

Camel's Hump State Park

N

0.5 mile

- - - Route
——— Road
······· Other Trails
P Parking
▲ Summit
△ Campground
⚲ Scenic Overlook

Hump Brook Tent Area

Monroe Trail

Dean Trail

Allis Trail

Long Trail

Alpine Trail

Hut Clearing

Camel's Hump

Long Trail

Wind Gap

Montclair Glen Lodge

Long Trail

Burrows Trail

Forest City Trail

Forest City-Burrows Connector Trail

START

Camel's Hump Road

Forest City Trail

final 0.4 mile of Camel's Hump Road is not maintained in winter. Winter hikers: Park in the lot at the end of the maintained road and add 0.8 mile to the hike. This lot also serves as summer overflow parking.)

To Burrows and Forest City trails—access to Long Trail
From Huntington, follow Main Road south 2.5 miles and turn left onto Camel's Hump Road. Drive 3.4 miles (passing the turnoff for Forest City Trail) to the end of the road, at the Burrows Trail parking lot (space for 30 cars).

TRAIL DESCRIPTION
Camel's Hump (4,083 feet) cuts a large profile, literally and figuratively, in Vermont. Its isolated height and distinct shape make it recognizable from great distances. The peak is featured as a symbol of the state in many places, including on the 2001 Vermont state quarter, and it is a National Natural Landmark. One of the first stretches of the Long Trail was built here, and the mountain remains the only undeveloped 4,000-footer in the state. The summit is busy with hikers on most fair-weather days, so go for expansive views, rare plants, and fun rock scrambles but not necessarily for solitude or quiet. Be sure to bring a leash for your dog; it's required above treeline.

East side via Monroe, Dean, and Long trails
This eastern slope lollipop loop can be hiked in either direction. The more scenic and challenging route ascends Dean Trail and scales a steep, rocky ridge on the Long Trail, treating hikers to views early and frequently. Monroe Trail is a steady green tunnel better left for the descent.

Blue-blazed Monroe Trail rises gradually at first and then turns alongside Hump Brook's deep ravine and climbs steadily and moderately to the junction with Dean Trail at 1.3 miles. Turn left onto Dean Trail (also blazed blue, as are all trails connecting to the Long Trail). Pass a short spur path to Hump Brook Tent Area at 1.3 mile and then climb steadily for 0.5 mile and enter a spruce–fir forest. Another spur leads right to wetlands, with a view of the sheer southern face of Camel's Hump above the trees. A closer cliff gives a dramatic preview of the next leg of your hike.

Dean Trail ends 0.2 mile farther, where it meets the Long Trail at Wind Gap. Turn right onto the white-blazed northbound Long Trail. A sign reports that the summit is 1.7 miles ahead, but you'll be heartened to know it's actually only 1.5 miles. A steep rock scramble brings you to a clifftop with a view northeast to the Worcester Range Skyline (Trip 38) and south to Mount Ethan Allen (3,670 feet).

Atop the ridge, clamber up several steep pitches and squeeze through a jumble of giant boulders before the Long Trail descends into the trees. Occasional glimpses of the towering summit appear as you hike through the forest and up switchbacks to the base of the cliff. Alpine Trail heads right here and can be used as a bad-weather bypass to Monroe Trail. (Some remains of a 1944 B-24 bomber crash are flung across the mountainside along Alpine Trail, although most of the wreckage has been removed.) Stay left on the Long Trail, cutting beneath the rock face and climbing its western side. Take care to avoid trampling delicate mountain sandwort, Bigelow's sedge, and bilberry; leash your dog and step only on rocks.

A clear day on the summit of Camel's Hump is a visual feast, with New Hampshire's White Mountains and New York's Adirondacks backing rows of the Green Mountains and

Above treeline, the Long Trail is marked by white blazes painted on the open rock. Whichever routes you follow on majestic Camel's Hump, you're sure to have an adventure.

the shining expanse of Lake Champlain. Whether it is sunny or not, be prepared for wind and cool temperatures.

Follow the Long Trail's white blazes north, descending 0.2 mile to junctions at Hut Clearing. This grassy, flat spot and trail hub was once the site of a mid-nineteenth-century hotel that hosted adventurous guests for about 15 years until it burned down. Turn right onto Monroe Trail, descending about 0.3 mile of moderately steep, rocky trail before the pitch eases. At 0.6 mile from Hut Clearing, Alpine Trail crosses Monroe Trail, and 0.3 mile below that, Monroe Trail swings left and proceeds beneath a cliff band about 0.3 mile before turning downhill again. Two miles below the summit, arrive at the junction with Dean Trail; continue straight down Monroe Trail the way you hiked up.

West side via Burrows, Long, and Forest City trails

The loop on the west side provides a short, steep, and ledgy ascent to the summit followed by a scenic and sometimes scrambly descent via the Long Trail and the lovely, gentle pitches of Forest City Trail.

Blue-blazed Burrows Trail ascends gently for the first mile and then begins power-stepping up ledges. The trees become shorter as you rise along a rocky ridgeline, and the trail climbs steeply before descending a short pitch to arrive at Hut Clearing at 2.1 miles. Follow the Long Trail's white blazes south and uphill from Hut Clearing, and leash your dog for this 0.2-mile leg into the alpine zone, where arctic plants cling tenuously to thin soils and are easily damaged by human or animal footsteps. Round the steep edge of the summit before climbing to the highest point.

The views seem to stretch to eternity from rocky Camel's Hump, but if you focus in closer, you'll see many microenvironments: low pockets, crevasses, tunnels, pools of standing water, and dramatic cliff edges. Mats of krummholz and grasslike sedges anchor the small amount of soil that has developed in this harsh environment. Wherever you go, step only on rock to preserve these delicate patches of vegetation.

If the terrain is slick with rain or ice, consider descending the way you climbed up, as this next stretch of trail is fun only when dry. If conditions are suitable, continue southbound on the Long Trail, following white blazes painted on the rocks to find your way down steep ledges. Scramble over boulders and ledges beneath towering cliffs until you descend past the Alpine Trail junction and into the forest. The next 1.4 miles to Wind Gap are rugged, with rocky descents that occasionally require sitting and scooting.

At 3.8 miles, the trail levels at Wind Gap, and Dean Trail departs to the left. Go 0.1 mile farther on the Long Trail, to the junction of Forest City Trail on your right. Two hundred feet farther south on the Long Trail, on the other side of a small ravine, is Montclair Glen Lodge, an overnight shelter and several tent platforms maintained by the Green Mountain Club.

Turn onto Forest City Trail and enjoy comparatively easy footing and gentle grades for 1.3 miles to Forest City–Burrows Connector Trail, on your right. Turn onto it, cross a wide bridge over a river gully, and proceed 0.1 mile to finish where you began, at the base of Burrows Trail.

DID YOU KNOW?

Camel's Hump has had many names; its current appellation derives from Camel's Rump, the name given to it by Ira Allen, one of the founders of Vermont.

MORE INFORMATION

Trails are closed from snowmelt until Memorial Day weekend. Camel's Hump State Park is managed for multiple uses by the Vermont Department of Forests. Trails and hiker facilities are maintained by the Green Mountain Club.

NEARBY

Backcountry camping is available at Montclair Glen Lodge and Hump Brook Tent Area; fees may be charged. Camel's Hump State Park does not have a developed campground; frontcountry camping is available at Little River State Park in Waterbury (12.7 miles from the Monroe trailhead; 23 miles from the Burrows trailhead). Paddle and swim at Waterbury Center State Park (11.4 miles from the Monroe trailhead) or at Lake Iroquois in Hinesburg (15 miles from the Burrows trailhead). Mountain biking is plentiful in Hinesburg and in the Waterbury–Stowe area (see appendix on page 258). Restaurants are in Waterbury, Hinesburg, and Richmond.

28 BALD TOP MOUNTAIN

Experience a stretch of the 36-mile Cross Rivendell Trail as you climb from the shores of Lake Morey to an open summit on the borderland between the Green and White mountains.

Features

Location Fairlee, VT

Rating Moderate to Strenuous

Distance 6.8 miles round-trip

Elevation Gain 1,320 feet

Estimated Time 4.5 hours

Maps USGS Fairlee; Rivendell Trail Association: rivendelltrail.org

GPS Coordinates 43° 55.27′ N, 72° 09.62′ W

Contact Rivendell Trails Association, P.O. Box 202, Fairlee, VT 05045; rivendelltrail.org

DIRECTIONS
From I-91, Exit 15 (Fairlee), head west on Lake Morey Road for 1.3 miles, rounding the southern end of Lake Morey and heading up the western shore. Trailhead parking is on the left (space for about twelve cars), across the road from the public boat launch.

TRAIL DESCRIPTION
Bald Top Mountain (1,776 feet) is a broad, grassy summit high above the Connecticut River valley—a great place to get perspective on the dense, steep-sided hills that make Lakes Morey and Fairlee so scenic. Multiple paths provide access to the summit. This route, along Cross Rivendell Trail, is not the shortest, but its start and finish on the shore of Lake Morey and its optional short detour to Glen Falls give it additional appeal. There's a fair bit of navigating through a web of old and current dirt roads in the first mile of this trek, but the route becomes simpler as you ascend the ridge. Given the distance and steady climbing, this hike is appropriate for most kids 10 and older.

From a trailhead kiosk with information about the two-state Cross Rivendell Trail, climb steeply into the woods. The path of Old Echo Mountain Road curves left, away from your route; you will cross this woods road several times, but think twice about hiking this steep, eroded treadway instead of the more moderate, switchbacking footpath. The old road is not a pleasant walk in either direction. Blue-blazed Cross Rivendell Trail zigzags up a steep slope through hemlocks and emerges at the top of the hill onto the old road. Follow the road a few

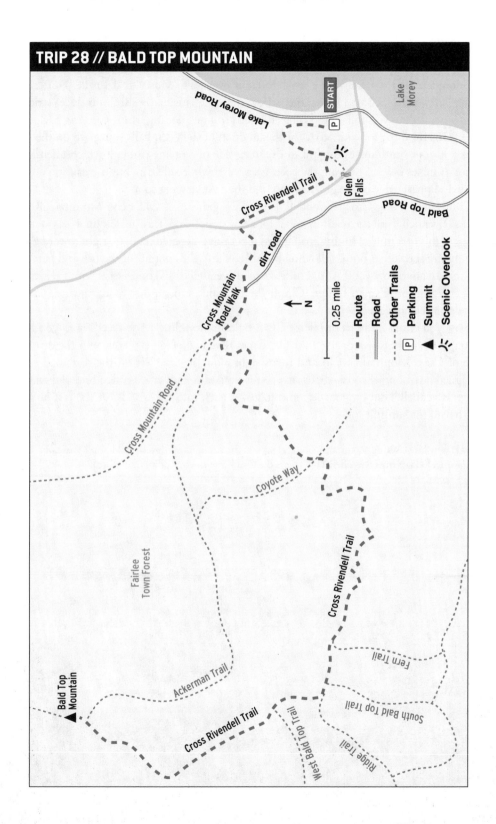

TRIP 28 // BALD TOP MOUNTAIN

Lake Morey Road

START

Lake Morey

P

Cross Rivendell Trail

Glen Falls

Bald Top Road

dirt road

Cross Mountain Road Walk

0.25 mile

N

- - - Route
——— Road
· · · · Other Trails
P Parking
▲ Summit
Scenic Overlook

Cross Mountain Road

Coyote Way

Fairlee Town Forest

Cross Rivendell Trail

Fern Trail

Bald Top Mountain
▲

Ackerman Trail

South Bald Top Trail

Cross Rivendell Trail

West Bald Top Trail

Ridge Trail

steps before the blue blazes lead you left. (To skip the lookout and the side trail to Glen Falls, stay straight on the old road for 150 feet, to where it rejoins Cross Rivendell Trail).

Going left off the road, find a small lookout over Lake Morey at 0.4 mile. Notice the witch hazel, with its broad leaves and yellowish pods. This hardy shrub produces stringy, yellow-petaled flowers in fall and flings its seeds from exploding fruits. Curving back into the woods from the lookout, arrive at the junction of the Glen Falls spur path on the left. This 200-foot spur crosses the hill to the steep side of a ravine through which Glen Falls Brook tumbles before reaching the lake. It's a worthwhile side trip, but use caution on the eroded, slippery edge of the gully as you find the best viewing spot.

Continuing along Cross Rivendell Trail, you again meet Old Echo Mountain Road; Cross Rivendell Trail turns left to join it for a few steps before turning left off it. (Two more times in this first mile of hiking, you'll pass junctions where old roads go right toward Echo Mountain; stay left at both, following blue blazes and the contour of the hill and paralleling the stream below you.) At 0.8 mile, Cross Rivendell Trail comes level with the stream and crosses it on a small bridge. Climb the far bank, cross a dirt road, and reenter the woods on the far side.

Now you climb away from Glen Falls Brook, its tumbling noise receding as you hike through mixed hardwoods. At 1.0 mile, Cross Rivendell Trail emerges onto the dirt surface of Cross Mountain Road and turns right along it. Stay left on the dirt road at an unsigned junction; when the dirt road crosses a broad stream at 1.2 miles, find blue-blazed Cross Rivendell Trail on your left and follow it back into the woods for the rest of your journey to the summit.

New Hampshire's White Mountains loom large from the summit meadow of Bald Top Mountain. Time permitting, follow Cross Rivendell Trail across the Connecticut River valley into those high peaks.

Cross Rivendell Trail begins to climb in earnest now, entering a quieter, more open forest. At 1.8 miles, traverse a stream and Coyote Way. Then, after a slight descent, the trail levels where logging opened the forest on the right. Meet a woods road here and follow Cross Rivendell Trail markers to turn right onto it. From this point, follow the woods road the rest of the way to the summit, passing various other old tracks and adjoining trails, all well signed. The woods road has some steep hills as it rolls up the ridgeline, occasionally with a filtered view of the White Mountains across the Connecticut River. You're close to the summit when you come upon some big, old, gnarly pines with multiple thick stems.

Cross Rivendell Trail emerges onto a broad, shrubby meadow with views all around. The White Mountains to the east steal the show, with the higher peaks carrying the Appalachian Trail and providing a backdrop to the lower foothills along the Connecticut River. Cross Rivendell Trail extends east into New Hampshire, crossing Sunday Mountain (1,823 feet), which appears east-southeast from this vantage point on Bald Top, and ending behind it on the tall point of Mount Cube (2,909 feet). From Bald Top west, Cross Rivendell Trail traipses over and around many small Piedmont hills before ending on Flagpole Hill (2,225 feet) in Vershire some 13 miles away.

Descend the way you hiked up.

DID YOU KNOW?

Cross Rivendell Trail was proposed in 1998 as a physical way to connect four towns—Orford in New Hampshire with Fairlee, West Fairlee, and Vershire, all three in Vermont—when the towns banded together to create an interstate school district. The trail is still maintained as an educational resource for the schools.

MORE INFORMATION

Cross Rivendell Trail is maintained by the membership-based Rivendell Trails Association. Before hiking, consult the website for trail conditions and changes. All the other trails you pass on this trip are shown in detail on a map available on Fairlee's town website: fairleevt.gov.

NEARBY

Paddle out onto the clear waters of Lake Morey from a public boat launch across the road from the trailhead. Lake Morey doesn't have a public beach; head to Treasure Island on the north end of Lake Fairlee for beach swimming and a picnic area, 7 miles south. A classic drive-in theater is 3.3 miles east on US 5.

IS IT A SWAMP, A BOG, A MARSH, OR A FEN?

You round a bend on the trail and see an opening in the forest. Shrubby plants grow on hummocks surrounded by still water. A few scraggly tree trunks poke up, and decaying logs lie in the muck. The ground becomes squishy under your boots, and you hear a faint splash as a small animal takes cover. This is clearly a wetlands area, but is it a swamp, a bog, a marsh, or a fen? How can you tell?

"Wetlands" is a general term for the many types of soggy natural communities that exist somewhere between open water and terra firma. Vermont has 300,000 acres of wetlands, including marshes, swamps, bogs, and fens.

Freshwater marshes are wide-open, water-on-the-surface places: They are the grass-choked corridors you paddle through when a slow river spreads over a broad area. They are the reedy edges of ponds and lakes where frogs and dragonflies hang out. Marshes have many herbaceous plants, such as grasses, cattails, and pond lilies, but because water is usually present year-round, no trees grow here.

Swamps are the slightly less wet version of marshes; in a swamp, trees survive seasonal flooding. At lower elevations, swamps have predominantly hardwood trees, such as maple and ash. Higher in the mountains, softwoods are the rule: cedar, tamarack, spruce, and fir.

Marshes and swamps have water flowing through them, but bogs and fens develop where water collects and stagnates. Thick mats of vegetation may cover the entire surface of the water. Bogs and fens differ in the chemistry of their water. Bog water is acidic, with very few dissolved nutrients and very low levels of oxygen. This is a tough place for plants to live, and only a few thrive: sphagnum moss, heath shrubs, and the adaptable black spruce. Fen water is more accommodating to life, ranging from slightly acidic to slightly basic, with more dissolved nutrients, minerals, and oxygen than bog water has. Fens may have some of the same plants as bogs, but they have much more diversity, including goldenrod, red osier dogwood, cattails, and sedges.

All these soupy places are important parts of healthy ecosystems, although this may be difficult to appreciate as you slap at mosquitoes and search for dry footing. Wetlands provide important habitats, and their absorbent soils help recharge water tables, slow floodwaters, and stabilize shorelines; they also filter out sediments, pollutants, and nutrients. (For more details, read *Wetland, Woodland, Wildland* by Elizabeth H. Thompson, Eric R. Sorenson, and Robert J. Zaino, published by The Nature Conservancy and the Vermont Fish and Wildlife Department in 2019.)

29 SPRUCE MOUNTAIN

A historical fire tower offers intimate looks at Granite Hills peaks, as well as longer views of the highest Green and White mountains.

Features 👥 🐕 〰️ 🔍 ❄️ 🗼

Location Plainfield, VT

Rating Moderate

Distance 4.4 miles round-trip

Elevation Gain 1,300 feet

Estimated Time 3.5 hours

Maps USGS Barre East, USGS Knox Mountain

GPS Coordinates 44° 14.10′ N, 72° 22.68′ W

Contact Vermont Department of Forests, Parks, and Recreation, District 4, Barre Office; 5 Perry Street, Suite 20, Barre, VT 05641; 802-476-0170; fpr.vermont.gov

DIRECTIONS

From the blinking light at the junction of US 2 and Main Street in Plainfield, turn downhill onto Main Street. Follow it 0.5 mile and turn right onto East Hill Road. After 3.8 miles, turn left onto Spruce Mountain Road and drive 1.0 mile to the parking lot at the road's end (space for twenty cars).

TRAIL DESCRIPTION

Spruce Mountain (3,010 feet) is on the western edge of a cluster of peaks known as the Granite Hills in 26,183-acre Groton State Forest. Access to the summit, however, is through the abutting 642-acre L. R. Jones State Forest. Spruce Mountain Trail passes through a variety of landscapes before topping out on a forested summit with a sturdy fire tower. The pitches are generally not steep, although the last part of the hike is a sustained climb. The footing is uneven on the upper half of the mountain, making this trail best suited to hikers 10 and older.

Spruce Mountain Trail begins by heading downhill from the parking lot on blue-blazed multiuse Tower Road, which accommodates both forestry vehicles and hikers. For the first few tenths of a mile, the terrain is flat.

At about 0.5 mile, the wide track enters a former log landing, or clearing where loggers piled cut timber before transporting it out of the woods. When this land was purchased to become Vermont's first state forest in 1909, it was mostly open fields. Between 1910 and 1916, some 300,000 trees were planted, many of which since have matured and been harvested. You may see evidence of forestry practices on your hike.

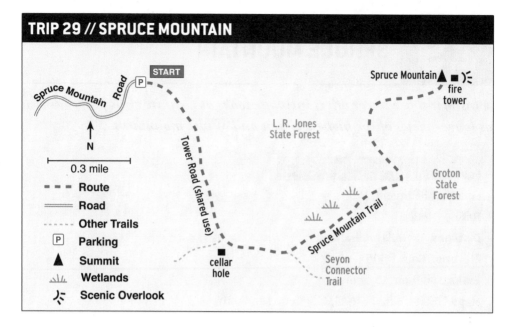

Beyond the former log landing, begin a moderate climb. Where the trail turns east, you may be able to spot a cellar hole (the remains of a farmhouse that predated the state forest) off to the right. Shortly after, pass through a second and larger former log landing, with trees younger than the surrounding forest now growing throughout it. This is the end of the multiuse section of the trail. Stay straight, following Spruce Mountain Trail into a forest with dense conifer walls and a hardwood canopy overhead.

Occasional faded blazes—some white, some blue—mark the route, although it is not difficult to follow Spruce Mountain Trail as it narrows and climbs gradually. At 1.0 mile from the trailhead, Seyon Connector Trail intersects on the right, and rocks soon begin to stud the previously flat dirt trail as it curves northeast. This cobbled path leads past wetlands on the left, where spears of dead trees jab upward.

From here, the almost flat terrain leads toward a sharp left turn to the north, where the character of the hike changes significantly. Spruce Mountain Trail narrows further as it weaves around jumbles of boulders and climbs over angled ledges lying across the slope. The woods shift to a higher-elevation spruce–fir forest, and needles cover the path.

The forest suddenly opens again after Spruce Mountain Trail climbs up and across many stretches of sloped ledge. The final leg of the hike ascends a ridge, with sky visible through the thick forest on either side of the trail. The summit clearing is ringed with tall trees and dominated by the legs of the fire tower. In 1919, a wooden tower was constructed so officials could watch for fires caused by the drying debris remaining from intense forest clearing. The legs of the tower formed the four corners of a caretaker cabin, which squatted beneath an open lookout platform. After a dozen years, a taller wooden tower was constructed, with an enclosed lookout room, called a cab.

Looking east over the trees from high in the tower, you can see a rumpled landscape of peaks and ponds that is largely within the borders of Groton State Forest. Signal Mountain (3,323 feet) is the tallest of the cluster of peaks to the south, with Burnt Rock Mountain

Foxy loves hiking the dog-friendly trails on Spruce Mountain.

(Trip 26) and Butterfield and Knox mountains from left to right beyond it. To the west, the ridge of the highest Green Mountains marches across the horizon: from Killington Peak (Trip 16) in the southwest; across the distinct, two-tiered summit of Camel's Hump (Trip 27) due west; to the long summit ridge of Mount Mansfield (Trips 45 and 46) in the northwest. If you'd rather not climb the tower, you can still enjoy a lovely, but less expansive, outlook from the summit with eastern views. The small body of water is Noyes Pond—known to have some of the best brook trout fishing in Vermont.

Retrace your footsteps to get back to the trailhead.

DID YOU KNOW?

The emerald ash borer is an exotic beetle. Its larvae feed on the inner bark of ash trees, disrupting a tree's ability to transport water and nutrients. This has resulted in millions of dead trees across the Northeast. On Spruce Mountain, a biocontrol project is under way using a parasitoid wasp to help regulate emerald ash borer populations. The wasps are only 3 to 4 millimeters in size and are incapable of stinging humans.

MORE INFORMATION

L. R. Jones State Forest is managed by Vermont Department of Forests, Parks, and Recreation.

NEARBY

The seven state parks within Groton State Forest—New Discovery, Kettle Pond, Big Deer, Boulder Beach, Stillwater, Ricker Pond, and Seyon Lodge—offer many attractions, including campgrounds, backcountry camping, swimming, a rail-trail, boat rentals, fishing, a nature center, and hiking trails, all within 25 miles of the Spruce Mountain trailhead via US 302 or US 2. Plainfield has restaurants and shops along Main Street and US 2. Grocery stores and almost anything else you might want are 15 miles west on US 302 (Barre–Montpelier Road) in Berlin and in downtown Montpelier.

30   OWL'S HEAD

Pass through lovely fern meadows on your way to the open granite summit and unique octagonal stone fire lookout tower at Owl's Head.

Features 🚶 🐕 🔍 ✦ ⛺ $ 🗼

Location Peacham, VT

Rating Easy to Moderate

Distance 3.8 miles round-trip

Elevation Gain 370 feet

Estimated Time 2 hours

Maps USGS Marshfield; Vermont Department of Forests, Parks, and Recreation: vtstateparks.com/assets/pdf/groton_trails.pdf

GPS Coordinates 44° 18.79′ N, 72° 17.26′ W

Contact New Discovery State Park, 4239 Route 232, Marshfield, VT 05658; 802-426-3042; vtstateparks.com/newdiscovery.html

DIRECTIONS

From the junction of US 302 and VT 232 (State Forest Road) in Groton, go north on VT 232 for 9.3 miles (passing Owl's Head Road). Turn right into New Discovery State Park. Pay the day-use fee at the gate and proceed to a fork; go right. Pass through a metal gate and immediately go left at another fork. Owl's Head trailhead parking is a shallow pull-off a short distance down the road on the right (space for about four cars). (Winter hikers: Park at Northern Parking lot on the west side of VT 232, 0.4 miles south of New Discovery, and walk on the Northern Rail Trail Connector to join Owl's Head Trail at the register box, adding 0.2 mile to the hike.)

TRAIL DESCRIPTION

Owl's Head (1,910 feet), a low but prominent peak offering easy access and long views, is the knobby sentinel of Groton State Forest. A mile-long auto road (open during daylight hours when state parks are operating) ascends to within 0.25 mile of the summit and provides a helpful alternative for those who can't walk far. But the beautiful forests and gentle rise of the trail from New Discovery State Park make this one of the most enjoyable hikes in the area, suitable for kids 7 and older.

An old road leads north from the parking area into a shady forest of tall, thin conifers. Follow the road 0.3 mile to the trail register box at a junction just shy of a field with a campground maintenance building behind the Groton State Forest maintenance area. Go left onto blue-blazed Owl's Head Trail, turning almost 180 degrees to head south, parallel

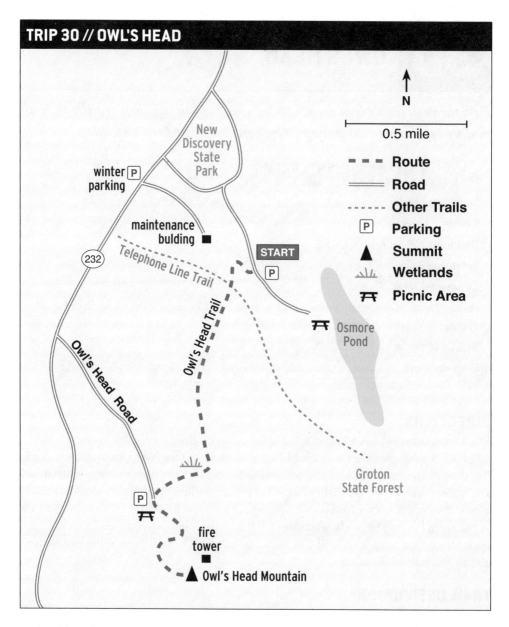

New
Discovery
State
Park

winter P
parking

maintenance
bulding ■

Telephone Line Trail

232

Owl's Head Trail

START
P

Owl's Head Road

🜨 Osmore
Pond

Groton
State Forest

P
🜨

fire
tower
■
▲ Owl's Head Mountain

N

0.5 mile

- - - **Route**
=== **Road**
····· **Other Trails**
P **Parking**
▲ **Summit**
🜄 **Wetlands**
🜨 **Picnic Area**

to the old road. Canada mayflowers and bunchberries sprout amid club moss alongside the path. The flat, rooty trail leaves the conifer forest that dominates the campground, now traveling through beech and maple.

Ascending gradually, arrive at the junction of the nonmotorized multiuse Telephone Line Trail, which heads out toward Peacham Bog. Farming—never easy in the mountains—was especially difficult in Groton, where granite chunks are plentiful, so logging has long been a dominant activity in these woods. Today, the state forest is managed for sustainable forestry, water quality, wildlife, and recreation.

Cross Telephone Line Trail, staying on Owl's Head Trail, and begin a gentle climb. As the route rolls gradually uphill, you are likely to hear white-throated sparrows, ovenbirds, and the distinct fluty calls of wood thrushes, hermit thrushes, and veeries. In light gaps where trees have fallen, the understory grows rapidly, narrowing the trail corridor in places. A series of gentle curves with easy climbing brings you to a remarkable sea of ferns stretching across the forest floor beneath widely spaced trunks, 1.0 mile from the trailhead.

At 1.4 miles, the trail descends slightly to a small wetlands area, studded with ferns growing on hummocks. Owl's Head Trail curves right, crossing a lichen-crusted ledge 5 feet above the wet ground. Beyond the swamp, climb over a low knoll and begin a long, gradual descent into a hollow. A string of bog bridges brings the trail through a low spot, followed by a short climb into another airy fern meadow and the final rise to Owl's Head Road.

Bypassing a parking area, Owl's Head Trail bears left and soon reaches a junction and the busy picnic area with access from the auto road. Ahead, a wide path leads to a toilet building and a picnic pavilion. Turn left onto the summit trail and begin the final 0.2 mile of rocky climbing for the final 100 feet of elevation gain to the summit. Rock steps ascend into a boreal forest of paper birch, spruce, and fir. Blueberry bushes sprout between moss-covered rocks as you round the final curve to the octagonal stone fire lookout tower built on the summit by Civilian Conservation Corps crews in the 1930s (see "From the CCC to the VYCC: Conservation Corps in Vermont," page 249). A granite ledge rolls away below the octagon, giving views west and south, most notably of Kettle Pond, pointing west to the distant peak of Camel's Hump (Trip 27).

Return downhill the way you climbed up.

Hikers who summit Owl's Head can enjoy its unique octagonal stone fire lookout tower.

DID YOU KNOW?

At more than 26,000 acres, Groton State Forest is the second-largest landholding of the state, with only 43,049-acre Mount Mansfield State Forest eclipsing it in size.

MORE INFORMATION

Hiking trails in Groton State Forest (designated with blue blazes) are for foot travel only. Multiuse trails are for foot, horse, or bicycle travel; no motorized vehicles are allowed. State parks within Groton State Forest open for the season on Memorial Day. New Discovery, Kettle Pond, and Ricker Pond state parks are open through Indigenous Peoples' Day; Boulder Beach, Big Deer, and Stillwater state parks are open through Labor Day. Overnight camping and campfires are allowed only at designated remote sites and in the developed campgrounds. Day use of the parks is 10 A.M. to official sunset. Seyon Lodge State Park operates year-round with brief seasonal closures and is open for day use from 6 A.M. to official sunset.

NEARBY

The seven state parks (New Discovery, Kettle Pond, Big Deer, Boulder Beach, Stillwater, Ricker Pond, and Seyon Lodge) in Groton State Forest provide abundant swimming, paddling, camping, and picnicking options, in addition to many more hiking trails. Bike or ski on multiuse Montpelier & Wells River Rail Trail, which hosts the Cross Vermont Trail through Groton State Forest. Limited restaurants and shops are along US 2 in Marshfield, 6 miles northwest, and Plainfield, 12 miles west; more varied choices are in Barre, 22 miles west, and Montpelier, 23 miles west.

QUARRIES AND ROCKFIRE

Have you ever considered what's deep beneath your boots as you scamper up a rocky ledge in the Green Mountains? If you peeled back the dirt, sand, and trees of central Vermont, you would uncover granite that extends miles deep into the earth. A tall, visible example of this rock aboveground is in the Granite Hills of Groton State Forest—specifically, the knobby, granitic summit of Owl's Head (Trip 30).

Nearby in Barre, the miles-deep granite has been quarried for years, with massive blocks hauled up out of the ground and loaded onto trains bound for artists and builders all over the world. Thousands of workers—many of them immigrants from Scotland, Ireland, Italy, and parts of Canada—flocked to central Vermont in the late nineteenth century to excavate the Barre granite plutons, gigantic bodies of igneous rock. They stripped a thousand acres of trees, opened deep holes in the ground with the help of dynamite, and jumbled massive slabs of rock in tall piles around the quarries. Between 50 and 75 individual quarries were operating at the turn of the twentieth century, creating Vermont's largest industrial landscape: a barren, dusty zone of rock, bearing the enormous production of cables, booms, bull wheels, and other machinery used to haul the blocks from their depths.

Today, most of those quarries sit abandoned, filling with water and surrounded by trees. Barre Town Forest and the Millstone Trails Association together maintain a network of multiuse trails around and alongside the now-silent quarries, which provide a unique and curious landscape for hikers, mountain bikers, snowmobilers, and disc golfers. The trail to Grand Lookout in Barre Town Forest is adorned with surprising, sometimes hidden rock carvings: faces, animals, symbols, and other mysterious elements carved into the chunks of granite left behind. Remnants of the extraction industry are visible elsewhere, in rusty cables descending from cliffsides into the watery depths of quarry pools and massive heaps of rock (called grout piles) that issue cool breezes on the hottest summer days. Warning signs and the growl of machinery alert visitors to active quarrying still occurring in some areas.

In Barre, the Vermont Granite Museum has converted a vast, old granite shed into a showcase of the art and industry of quarrying, giving artists and craftspeople studio space and initiating a new class of carvers through its Stone Arts School. One of the most unusual annual events in central Vermont is RockFire, a nighttime celebration of granite heritage, including traditional music, bonfires, and art. Paths lit by luminarias lead attendees to multiple performance locations throughout the woods and to a new appreciation for the varied cultural treasures that quarries provide to central Vermont.

3 // NORTHWESTERN VERMONT

Lake Champlain, one of Vermont's greatest treasures, provides recreation, solitude, and beauty for thousands of visitors and locals each year. This jewel of a lake dominates the landscape in northwestern Vermont, and it supports a range of natural communities with its rocky shoreline (nearly 587 miles long), large tributary deltas, and varied depths and temperatures. It's also home to 318 species of birds, 81 fish species, and (some say) a mysterious monster, affectionately known as Champ. At its widest point, near Burlington, Lake Champlain is almost 12 miles across.

After the last ice age, salt water invaded the basin from the north, creating an inlet of the Atlantic Ocean. As the ocean receded, it left behind deep, fertile clay soils that were prized for agriculture. The Lake Champlain valley has the longest history of human settlement in Vermont. It was first inhabited by indigenous people thousands of years ago and has been settled without interruption since that time. Lake Champlain is called *Bitawbagw*, meaning "the lake between," by the Abenaki people, and it was historically a center of trade and exchange.

Three very large, old rivers flow west through the Green Mountains and spill a constant stream of sediment and water into Lake Champlain: the Missisquoi in the north; the Lamoille, emptying near South Hero; and the Winooski, ending next to Burlington. Their deltas not only provide rich habitats for birds, amphibians, fish, and some mammals but also support rare and uncommon species.

A few of the hikes in this section offer a chance to experience the shore communities along Lake Champlain. Allen Hill in Shelburne (Trip 33) is a steep, rocky knob on the edge of the lake that supports a cedar–pine forest on a limestone bluff. Niquette Bay in Colchester (Trip 35) brings visitors high above the lake on two parallel ridges with opportunities for swimming along the way. Burton Island (Trip 37) can only be reached by boat and is one of more than 70 islands in Lake Champlain.

Burlington and surrounding Chittenden County are densely populated and developed, at least by Vermont standards, but farmland and wooded areas are the norm just a few miles from the city. South of Burlington, the northernmost Taconic Mountains jut from the farmland in small, steep knobs—most notably, Mount Philo (Trip 31), where hikers can enjoy expansive views for very little effort.

31 MOUNT PHILO

Climb through a beautiful hardwood forest to the summit of Mount Philo and admire breathtaking views of the Champlain Valley and surrounding mountains.

Features

Location Charlotte, VT

Rating Moderate

Distance 2.4-mile loop

Elevation Gain 580 feet

Estimated Time 1.5 hours

Maps USGS Mount Philo; Vermont Department of Forests, Parks, and Recreation: vtstateparks.com/assets/pdf/philo.pdf

GPS Coordinates 44° 16.68′ N, 73° 13.32′ W

Contact Mount Philo State Park, 5425 Humphrey's Road, Charlotte, VT 05445; 802-425-2390; vtstateparks.com/philo.html

DIRECTIONS

From the junction of US 7 with Ferry Road and Church Hill Road, travel 2.5 miles south on US 7. Turn left onto State Park Road and follow it 0.6 mile to its end, at Mount Philo Road and the park entrance. Pay a day-use fee in season and park in the parking lot (space for 70 cars).

TRAIL DESCRIPTION

Mount Philo (968 feet) is a small peak packed with pleasant surprises. It rises steeply from gently rolling farmland and is visible for miles across the Champlain Valley. Although the climb is not long, the steepness and the occasionally rough terrain make it most suitable for kids 6 and older. Dogs are welcome but must be always leashed. Scattered picnic tables near the parking lot and many more at the summit make this a great spot to bring lunch for before or after your hike.

House Rock Trail begins where the paved road to the summit leaves the parking lot. The wide, needle-covered path follows blue blazes through hop hornbeam, sugar maple, and tamarack. After a few minutes, the trail's massive namesake boulder looms above a flight of rock steps. House Rock is one of many erratics that traveled south in glaciers during the last ice age and dropped to the ground on Mount Philo when the ice melted, about 11,000 years ago.

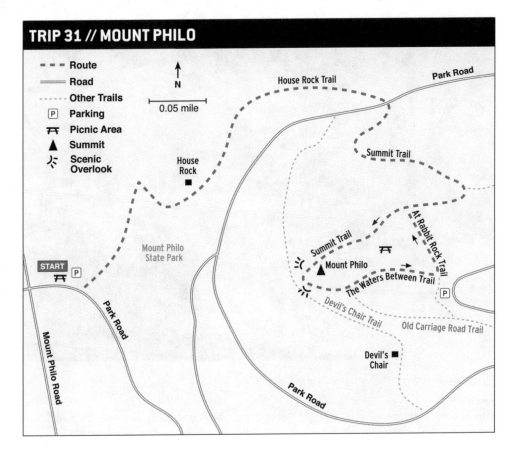

Legend:
- – – Route
- ——— Road
- ········ Other Trails
- P Parking
- ⛱ Picnic Area
- ▲ Summit
- 🔆 Scenic Overlook

N

0.05 mile

House Rock Trail

Park Road

Summit Trail

House Rock ■

At Rabbit Rock Trail

Mount Philo State Park

Summit Trail

⛱

🔆 ▲ Mount Philo

The Waters Between Trail

START ⛱ P

Park Road

Devil's Chair Trail

P

Old Carriage Road Trail

Mount Philo Road

Devil's Chair ■

Park Road

Climb beneath House Rock's shady overhang and skirt its left side. From here the trail climbs steadily on newly built steps, created to reduce erosion on this popular route.

At about 0.4 mile, carefully cross the auto road to continue your climb on Summit Trail. Keep your eyes and ears open for the many bird species that frequent the woods and summit of Mount Philo; 101 species of birds have been observed in the park, including many colorful warblers and the elusive scarlet tanager and indigo bunting. The lovely songs of Philo's resident thrushes provide an ethereal soundtrack for your climb. The beautiful stone steps on this part of the trail make for an easy ascent through a mixed hardwood forest and give hikers an appreciation for the importance of trail design, construction, and maintenance.

At 0.75 mile, Summit Trail intersects with the campground trail on the left, which leads to the park's ten campsites. Turn right to continue on Summit Trail, climbing a sweeping staircase and passing At Rabbit Rock Trail on the left. At Rabbit Rock is also called *Matgwaswabskak*, the Abenaki place name for Mount Philo. Summit Trail continues west, leading to two rocky outcroppings with impressive lookouts toward Lake Champlain and the Adirondacks, as well as a few smaller Vermont peaks. Stretching south in line with Mount Philo, similar lone hills rise from the valley floor: Shellhouse Mountain, Buck Mountain, and Snake Mountain (Trip 23). Along with Mount Philo, these small peaks are

Hikers and picnickers relax on top of Mount Philo.

the northern extent of the Taconic Mountains. Mount Philo's summit area includes restrooms (open in season), several picnic tables, and Adirondack chairs that beg to be enjoyed as you take in the expansive vistas. In September, the summit becomes a lively destination for raptor enthusiasts who come to witness large numbers of migrating hawks on their annual journey to warmer climates.

Continue to loop around the summit toward the parking lot, passing a few private picnic areas tucked into the trees. Follow the short, universally accessible The Waters Between Trail (also *Pitawbagok*, the Abenaki place name for Lake Champlain) until it intersects with At Rabbit Rock Trail. Turn left here to complete your loop around the summit, descending a short stone staircase and turning right to descend on Summit Trail. Follow Summit Trail to House Rock Trail, the same way you walked up.

DID YOU KNOW?

Mount Philo State Park was created in 1924 as Vermont's first state park when it was gifted to the state by Frances Humphreys. Even before its designation as a state park, Mount Philo attracted tourists and locals alike—Mount Philo Inn was built at the base of the mountain in 1896, and a carriage road brought visitors to the summit starting in 1903.

MORE INFORMATION

Mount Philo State Park is open Memorial Day weekend through mid-October, 10 A.M. to official sunset, although hikers can use the trails year-round. A day-use fee is charged when the park is open; a campground with tentsites and lean-tos has a separate fee. Picnic areas, water, and restrooms are available on the summit in season. Dogs must be leashed at all times on state park trails. For campsite reservations, call 888-409-7579 or visit vtstate-parks.com/reservations.html.

NEARBY

Swim and paddle at Kingsland Bay State Park, 10.4 miles southwest. Rokeby Museum, 4.6 miles south on US 7, is a National Historic Landmark with walking trails and one of the country's best-preserved stops on the Underground Railroad. Restaurants can be found along US 7 north into Shelburne and on VT 22A, 7 miles south in downtown Vergennes.

32   RAVEN RIDGE

This fun outing begins in sprawling wetlands and travels through a diverse woodland and along a rocky ridge with beautiful views of the Champlain Valley.

Features

Location Monkton, VT

Rating Moderate

Distance 2.7-mile loop

Elevation Gain 410 feet

Estimated Time 1.5 hours

Maps USGS Mount Philo; The Nature Conservancy: nature.org/content/dam/tnc/nature/en/graphics/maps/vermont-raven-ridge-map.pdf

GPS Coordinates 44° 15.96′ N, 73° 9.22′ W

Contact The Nature Conservancy, 575 Stone Cutters Way, Montpelier, VT 05602; 802-229-4425; nature.org/vermont

DIRECTIONS

From US 7 in Charlotte, drive south for 3.8 miles and turn left onto Old Hollow Road. Continue straight for 1.9 miles and make a slight left onto Rotax Road. The parking area for Raven Ridge is on your right in 2.0 miles (space for about five cars). Raven Ridge Natural Area is a high-usage site, especially on weekends. If the parking lot is full when you arrive, please choose an alternate hike.

TRAIL DESCRIPTION

Raven Ridge Natural Area is a diverse and sensitive wildlife habitat that includes calcareous cliffs and outcroppings, shrub swamps, cattail marshes, and seeps. Stretching from an expansive wetlands complex in Monkton north to Lewis Creek, Raven Ridge's 363 acres are owned and managed by The Nature Conservancy (TNC) and protect numerous wildlife species, including 142 species of birds. A universally accessible boardwalk and packed gravel path provide visitors of all physical abilities with a 0.3-mile trail that leads to a viewing platform on the edge of an attractive beaver pond.

The trail described here is an excellent choice for children, gaining just 410 feet in elevation over 2.7 miles. Due to the sensitive nature of the ecosystem, dogs are not permitted at Raven Ridge.

From the parking area, cross Rotax Road and immediately follow the wide boardwalk through cattail marshes and into wetlands that mark the beginning of the route. In

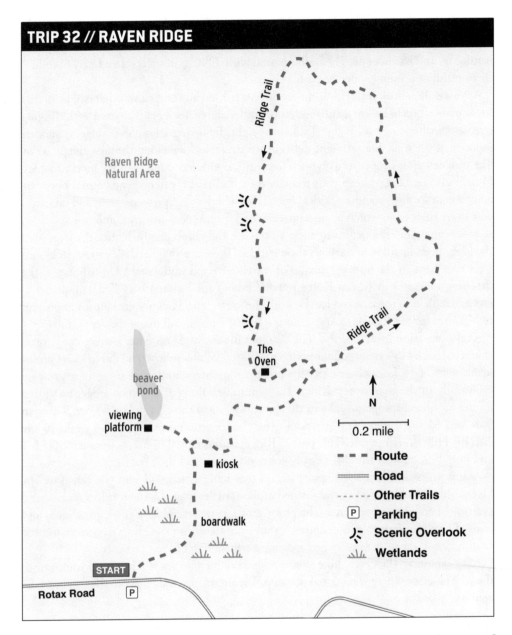

Raven Ridge
Natural Area

Ridge Trail

Ridge Trail

The
Oven

beaver
pond

viewing
platform

■ kiosk

boardwalk

N

0.2 mile

- - - Route
═══ Road
----- Other Trails
P   Parking
)⟨ Scenic Overlook
⫰⫰ Wetlands

START

Rotax Road   P

summer, you will see many types of butterflies, dragonflies, and birds taking advantage of the vast wetlands ecosystem. Marshy sedges and grasses are the most common plants along the boardwalk, but as you meander farther into the wetlands, you will encounter alders, viburnums, dogwoods, white pines, and tamaracks.

Leave the boardwalk and continue on a wide, universally accessible gravel path that leads into a dark evergreen forest of cedars and white pines. Stop at the trail kiosk on the right to read more about Raven Ridge and the work of TNC in Vermont. At 0.25 mile, reach a trail junction; take the short spur path on the left, which crosses a footbridge and leads to a small beaver pond with a viewing platform. Retrace your steps and turn left on Ridge Trail, leaving behind the accessible walkway and climbing into a mixed woodland of white pines, hemlocks, and hardwoods. The trail is blazed with TNC trail markers and easy to follow. Be mindful of poison ivy on the path.

As you walk uphill, you'll leave the evergreens behind and enter a woodland of primarily sugar maple, beech, hickory, and oak. At 0.4 mile, a large, rocky cliff covered with clinging fern rises in front of you. Ridge Trail turns right, following a low, level ridge to another junction at 0.5 mile. Stay straight to begin a counterclockwise loop through the preserve. The trail descends deeper into an open forest thick with ferns and shrubby moose maples. Numerous bog bridges keep your feet dry on a trail that is often soggy. Vernal pools are common in spring, providing critical habitat for wood frogs, spring peepers, and salamanders to lay their eggs, which in turn provide food for raccoons, rodents, and mink.

At 0.8 mile, the trail begins to curve to the left and climb gently. Notice the trees with the long, peeling strips of bark on their trunks? These are shagbark hickories, deciduous trees that grow in the humid climates of the eastern and midwestern United States. The shagbark hickories in Raven Ridge provide homes for Indiana bats (federally listed as endangered), who roost in crevices beneath the loose bark. Hickory nuts are an important food source for black bears, foxes, various rodents, rabbits, and many species of birds.

As the elevation increases, the trail becomes rockier and you enter a more open forest characterized by calcareous outcroppings and cliffs. White, yellow, and red oaks are prominent, with black huckleberry, eastern prickly gooseberry, and wild columbine growing prolifically in the understory. Ridge Trail continues along a long rock ledge, providing numerous spots to stop and take in the western views of the Champlain Valley. Rising to 968 feet, Mount Philo (Trip 31) dominates the foreground, with smaller peaks in the Taconic Hills on either side. This part of Ridge Trail is closed to hikers between March 1 and June 15 to protect the cliff-nesting common ravens and their young.

At 2.0 miles, follow a short spur path on the right, which will lead you down to The Oven. This geological oddity was formed millions of years ago by the continuous heat and pressure of colliding continents. The prominent feature resembles a rustic pizza oven and is also home to a family of porcupines. (You're not likely to meet them in person, but the multitudes of scat under the arched rock are a telltale sign of their presence.)

After exploring The Oven, hike along Ridge Trail for another 500 feet until you come to the trail junction where you started the loop. Turn right and walk back to the trailhead the way you hiked in.

DID YOU KNOW?

A porcupine may have as many as 30,000 quills, which are actually individual hairs with barbed tips. Quills have a hollow shaft and are solid at both ends. It is a myth that porcupines can shoot their quills at potential predators, but when threatened, they will not hesitate to raise their quills and swing their menacing tails at attackers, causing pain and inflammation where the barbed quills become embedded in the skin.

A scarlet tanager on the Ridge Trail.

MORE INFORMATION

Raven Ridge Natural Area is limited to passive recreational activities, such as hiking, snow-shoeing, cross-country skiing, bird-watching, photography, and nature study. Dogs, pack animals, motorized vehicles, bicycles, and camping are not allowed. Do not remove plants, animals, artifacts, or rocks; do not build fires. The trail along the ridge is closed from March 1 to June 15 to protect nesting ravens and bobcats.

NEARBY

Camp and hike at Mount Philo State Park (Trip 31), 6 miles west. Swim and paddle at Kingsland Bay State Park, 12 miles west. Rokeby Museum, 7 miles southwest, is a National Historic Landmark and an excellent place to learn about the Underground Railroad in Vermont. Find restaurants along US 7 in Ferrisburgh, with more options in Vergennes, 11 miles southwest.

33 ALLEN HILL

This hike along Lake Champlain passes through a rare cedar–pine forest on a cliffy hilltop and offers plenty of opportunities for swimming.

Features

Location Shelburne, VT

Rating Easy

Distance 1.9-mile loop

Elevation Gain 120 feet

Estimated Time 1.5 hours

Maps USGS Burlington; Town of Shelburne: vt-shelburne.civicplus.com/DocumentCenter/View/5133/Shelburne-Bay-Park-Trail-Map--Brochure

GPS Coordinates 44° 24.00′ N, 73° 14.23′ W

Contact Town of Shelburne's Parks and Recreation Department, P.O. Box 88, 5420 Shelburne Road, Shelburne, VT 05482; 802-985-9551; shelburnevt.org

DIRECTIONS

From the traffic light at US 7 in Shelburne, go west on Harbor Road 1.6 miles and turn right onto Bay Road. Drive 0.5 mile to Shelburne Bay Park on the left. The parking lot closest to the road provides access to Shelburne Recreation Path, an alternate route. Continue toward the lake and park where the road ends (space for about 50 cars).

TRAIL DESCRIPTION

Allen Hill (270 feet) is a steep, rocky knob on the edge of Lake Champlain that supports a cedar–pine forest on a limestone bluff—a rarity in Vermont. Three parallel trails in Shelburne Bay Park lead to the hill, making hiking loops possible. Shelburne Recreation Path begins from the parking lot closest to Bay Road and meanders through woods and fields for 1.4 miles to end at Harbor Road. It has a wide, hardened surface, and except for some bumpy culvert crossings and two short, steep hills (one near the beginning, one at the end), the path is mostly flat and suitable for outdoor wheelchairs. (An extension of the path called Ti-Haul Trail is across Bay Road and extends south toward Shelburne.) An unnamed middle trail explores the woods in the center of the park. The most scenic route, described below, follows Clarke Trail along the lakeshore to the Allen Hill Trail loop and returns via Clarke Trail. Cross-country skiers and hikers of all ages will enjoy the combination of woods and shore along 0.5-mile Clarke Trail; kids 4 and older will be able to

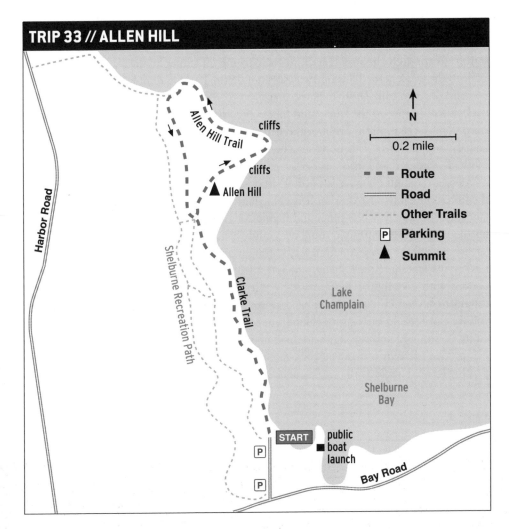

complete the 0.9-mile loop over Allen Hill. In winter, the loop is better suited to snowshoes than to skis. Lookout ledges are near the summit perch on tall cliffs; use caution. Dogs must be leashed in the park.

Clarke Trail begins where the parking area and grassy lawn border the woods. It initially follows a wide gravel path through a dark stand of cedar, hemlock, and white pine. Numerous short side paths lead to smooth rock ledges that slide gently into Shelburne Bay. After the third side path to the lake, Clarke Trail becomes narrower and more rugged. Bog bridges over a damp area lead to a short climb up slanted bedrock, followed by more bog bridges. Walk north along the shoreline through open, grassy areas, dark conifer stands, and muddy spots where water trickles from the ledgy hillside. Almost 2 miles of water stretch across Shelburne Bay on your right, and the tall ridge of 4,393-foot Mount Mansfield (Trips 45 and 46) and tiered top of 4,083-foot Camel's Hump (Trip 27) rise above the Champlain Lowlands.

Descend from the bluff onto a shaded, gravelly beach where a stream enters the lake; then climb through red oaks and trout lilies to a five-way junction on the hillside. The left trail leads through the woods back to the parking lot. Straight ahead, a connector trail leads to the wide, graded Shelburne Recreation Path. The two right legs are the beginning and end of Allen Hill Trail. Take the first right turn—which is actually a couple of steps back downhill toward the lake—and follow the east leg of Allen Hill Trail 0.2 mile up a steep slope to the summit. Trillium and hepatica grow between oaks on the dry, rocky sides and flat top of Allen Hill. Look for chestnut oaks, with their deeply grooved bark and toothed—rather than lobed—leaves.

Leaving the high point, Allen Hill Trail descends gradually, skirting the cliffy edge of the limestone bluffs; use caution here. Northern white cedars line the top of these headlands, giving way to white pines and hemlocks as you drop to lake level. Rounding the northern tip of this peninsula, you'll see a sandy beach on your right. Allen Hill Trail turns left where a short connector trail leads straight ahead to the recreation path. Turn left, leaving the lakeshore for a shady pine forest full of big old trees, some hollow and some pocked with rectangular holes made by pileated woodpeckers. A short climb over the shoulder of Allen Hill brings you beneath steep, mossy cliffs. Look up to see the summit you were just on. In early spring, bloodroot blooms in these woods, opening its white petals in the sunlight and closing them up at night.

A gradual descent brings you back to the five-way junction. Go left, returning to the parking lot via Clarke Trail.

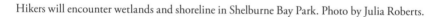

Hikers will encounter wetlands and shoreline in Shelburne Bay Park. Photo by Julia Roberts.

DID YOU KNOW?

Northern white cedars (also called arborvitae, or "tree of life") dominate in environments with difficult living conditions: coniferous swamps and dry, rocky cliffs. Although challenging habitats keep them from growing large, they can live a long time. The oldest-known individual is more than 1,100 years old.

MORE INFORMATION

Shelburne Bay Park is managed by the Town of Shelburne Parks and Recreation Department.

NEARBY

An interpretive water trail exploring Shelburne Bay begins at the boat launch next to Shelburne Bay Park; a brochure guide is available through the Lake Champlain Basin Program, lcbp.org/wp-content/uploads/2013/03/ShelburneBayBrochure.pdf. Shelburne Farms is an education center, a 1,400-acre working farm, and a National Historic Landmark open to the public, 0.5 mile west. Restaurants and shops are in Shelburne, 2 miles southeast.

34 COLCHESTER POND

Walk through open farm fields and shady woods as you circle the quiet waters of this mile-long pond.

Features

Location Colchester, VT

Rating Easy to Moderate

Distance 3.2-mile loop

Elevation Gain 150 feet

Estimated Time 2 hours

Maps USGS Essex Center; USGS Colchester; Winooski Valley Park District: wvpd.org/colchester-pond

GPS Coordinates 44° 33.05' N, 73° 07.50' W

Contact Winooski Valley Park District, 1 Ethan Allen Homestead, Burlington, VT 05408; 802-863-5744; wvpd.org

DIRECTIONS

From the junction of US 2 (also US 7) and VT 2A in Colchester, drive east on VT 2A for 0.8 mile to the center of Colchester. Turn left onto East Road, proceed 1.0 mile, and then turn right onto Depot Road. Drive 2.3 miles to a fork and bear left onto Colchester Pond Road. In 2.2 miles, bear right into the Colchester Pond parking area (space for eighteen cars).

TRAIL DESCRIPTION

Colchester Pond Natural Area is a quiet refuge in a busy part of Vermont. With Indian Brook Reservoir Park on its eastern border and Milton Town Forest to the north, the pond lies within a tract of more than 1,600 acres of contiguous forest. Walking the circumferential trail brings you through different stages of land use and forest succession, from shoreline hayfields and abandoned orchards to young forests growing over old pastures. This is a good exploratory hike for kids 6 and older.

Colchester Pond's unnamed loop trail begins next to a kiosk. Head down the grassy slope, past the boat launch for paddle craft on the water's edge. The trail, marked by white diamond blazes, turns left and follows the shoreline north. Pass through small stands of shagbark hickory, basswood, and sumac between hayfields that rise to a scenic barn on your left. Sections of bog bridges keep your feet out of the soggy soil.

The trail enters woods halfway up the length of the pond. It stays close to the shore, curving through white pines and passing clearings with access to the water for swimming

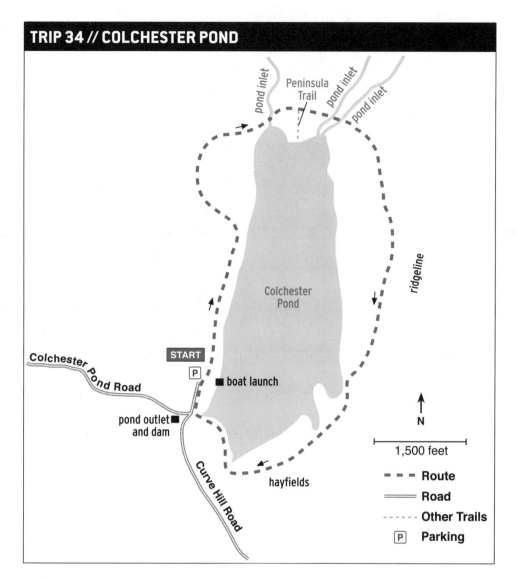

pond inlet

Peninsula
Trail

pond inlet

pond inlet

ridgeline

Colchester
Pond

START
P

■ boat launch

Colchester Pond Road

pond outlet ■
and dam

Curve Hill Road

hayfields

N

1,500 feet

- - - **Route**
════ **Road**
----- **Other Trails**
P **Parking**

or fishing. Then it begins a gentle climb into a mixed hardwood forest, staying high on the hillside for a short time before descending again to water level. As you approach the top of the pond, a rocky opening in the trees reveals a picturesque view south across the water, providing an opportunity to see ducks swimming or, if you're lucky, a bald eagle soaring. Colchester Pond attracts many species of birds and has been designated an Important Bird Area by Vermont Audubon. Canada geese, mallards, great blue herons, and common and hooded mergansers are some of the more frequent visitors. If you are hiking at dusk, you may be treated to barred owls calling *who-cooks-for-you?*

The trail rounds the damp north end of the pond on a series of step stones and bog bridges; it then climbs a small hill to the junction of Peninsula Trail. This path leads south 425 feet down a gentle slope to a clearing and a promontory that provides the last good

Jack-in-the-pulpits are elusive wildflowers that grow in damp areas. Look for them in early May around Colchester Pond.

swimming opportunity until you return to the trailhead. Continue straight on the main trail, descending to cross several threads of inlet streams.

After this soggy section, clamber up rocky ledges and switchbacks on the steep hillside. By the time you mount the ridge that follows the eastern side of the pond, thick woods prevent any views of the water below. Walk south along the relatively flat height-of-land on the remains of a narrow road. This area was once cleared of woods and used agriculturally, probably as pasture, but it's difficult to imagine a farmer driving anything with wheels across this rough, rocky road. Watch for red efts (the juvenile stage of the eastern, or red-spotted, newt), which gravitate to these muddy, mossy areas.

The trail becomes smoother and the woods drier as you descend to walk a long string of bog bridges and emerge in a meadow with views of the pond. Cross several hayfields on your way to the marshy south end of the pond, where the trail returns to the shoreline. As the trail curves northward over bog bridges, tall cattails sprout up amid thick shoreline vegetation on one side, and a fence, grown over with honeysuckle and raspberries, lines the other. At the end of this verdant corridor, the trail hits dirt again and climbs to a road next to the pond's outlet. Turn right on the road and walk onto a bridge. Look down from its left side to see the 25-foot-tall dam controlling the pond's water level. Continue across the bridge to the trailhead parking area.

DID YOU KNOW?

Invasive plant species, such as common buckthorn, aren't eaten by the wildlife in Colchester Pond Natural Area, so they have an advantage over species that are sources of food. As invasive species overtake habitats, animals in search of food are displaced, and entire food chains are disrupted. The Winooski Valley Park District actively removes invasive species to encourage native plants and animals to thrive here.

MORE INFORMATION

Colchester Pond Natural Area is open dawn to dusk. Dogs must be leashed. Motorized boats, motorized vehicles, bicycles, and campfires are not permitted.

NEARBY

Some dining options are available on Main Street and Blakely Road (VT 127) in Colchester, with more south in Winooski. Niquette Bay State Park, 7 miles west on US 2, has a sandy swimming beach. Camping is available near Mallets Bay in Colchester and at North Beach in Burlington, 9 miles south.

35 NIQUETTE BAY

Hike through a diverse forest and several natural communities along two ridges near Lake Champlain and head down to a sandy beach for swimming.

Features

Location Colchester, VT

Rating Moderate

Distance 3.8-mile loop

Elevation Gain 480 feet

Estimated Time 2.5 hours

Maps USGS Colchester; Vermont Department of Forests, Parks, and Recreation: vtstateparks.com/assets/pdf/niquette.pdf

GPS Coordinates 44° 35.37′ N, 73° 11.39′ W

Contact Niquette Bay State Park, 274 Raymond Road, Colchester, VT 05446; 802-893-5210; vtstateparks.com/niquette.html

DIRECTIONS
From the junction of US 2 (also US 7) and VT 2A in Colchester, go north on US 2 West for 2.9 miles. Turn left to remain on US 2 West for another 1.1 miles. Take a slight right toward Raymond Road, and then turn left onto Raymond Road, crossing US 2 West. In 0.5 mile, turn left into Niquette Bay State Park. Stop at the park entrance and pay the day-use fee, and then follow signs to the parking area (space for 40 cars). Once the parking area is full, cars are turned away from the park entrance. (Winter visitors can park outside the gate and walk into the park to get to the trail.)

TRAIL DESCRIPTION
Located on the shores of Niquette Bay in the larger Malletts Bay on Lake Champlain, Niquette Bay State Park is characterized by two long, forested ridges and a sandy terrace, which encompass numerous natural communities and a sandy beach for swimming. Several trails loop through the park, offering hiking opportunities for those of various abilities, but the loop described below travels along the high points of each ridge with overlooks to the south, east, and west. Children older than 6 will enjoy exploring the rocky, wooded trails, especially if they are enticed with the prospect of a swim afterward.

From the parking area, pass the trail kiosk and nature library and turn left to begin your hike on Ledges Trail. Follow the blue blazes into a forest of mixed hardwood and softwood trees, many of which are labeled with their common and Latin names for easy

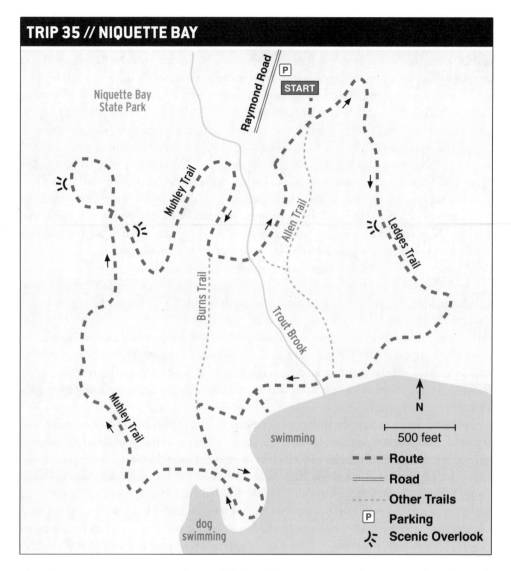

Niquette Bay
State Park

Raymond Road

P

START

Muhley Trail

Allen Trail

Burns Trail

Trout Brook

Ledges Trail

Muhley Trail

swimming

dog
swimming

N

500 feet

- - - Route
═══ Road
----- Other Trails
P   Parking
⟩⟨ Scenic Overlook

identification. Pay attention to the tree labels and you will notice three types of maples (red, sugar, and silver), three types of oak (red, chinkapin, and white), and three types of birch (paper, gray, and yellow). The trail climbs moderately, crossing a mossy stone wall from the 1800s and turning sharply to the right at about 0.1 mile. Climb a series of stone steps as you pass the oldest tree in the park, an impressive 250-year-old northern red oak.

Ledges Trail travels along the edge of a limestone bluff, and you begin to see more cedar and pine trees, with an understory of ferns. In April and May, enjoy the spring wildflowers: small, white bloodroot flowers, wild ginger, blue cohosh, dutchman's breeches, red and white trilliums, trout lilies, and hepatica grow along the trail.

Climb a stone staircase and turn right at 0.3 mile. The trail levels off here, but the terrain is rocky and rooty, requiring careful footwork. A bench and overlook on the right provide your first views of the bay and a nice spot for a water break.

As Ledges Trail brings you closer to the water, descend into an open red maple–green ash swamp, an area with rich, organic soil that experiences extended periods of spring flooding. It may or may not be soggy as you pass through, but a boardwalk ensures that your feet stay dry regardless. Climb a set of stairs and reenter the woods. Now you're on a cedar bluff, which makes for easy walking, and the path is covered with evergreen needles, cushioning your steps. Another bench with a wooded view is followed by an opening leading to a single picnic table; if you packed a lunch for your hike, this is a quiet, shady place to enjoy it.

Pass the junction to Allen Trail (the quickest way back to your car from this point) and stay straight to remain on Ledges Trail. A spur path leads to a sandy, protected beach. The eastern side of the beach is undeveloped to help protect critical habitat for wildlife and rare plants. Dogs are not permitted here, but otherwise, this location is perfect for a midhike swim, as well as a chance to look for shorebirds and resident turtles. Four species of turtles live near Niquette Bay, including painted turtles, snapping turtles, map turtles, and rare northern musk turtles, which are affectionately known as a "stinkpots," thanks to a foul, musky odor that they release from their scent glands when threatened.

Climb the stairs and hike along the 0.3-mile beach bypass trail before turning left on blue-blazed Burns Trail. Pass the intersection with Muhley Trail on your right and continue to the spur path, also on your right, that descends to Calm Cove. This is a beautiful rocky cove surrounded by steep cliffs and open to both human and canine swimmers. After checking out Calm Cove, return to Burns Trail and turn right to meander around the cedar bluff on the 0.1-mile loop through woods of primarily northern white cedar. Some peekaboo views of Lake Champlain appear through the trees, and a few spots provide access to the water.

Complete the loop, pass the spur path to Calm Cove, and turn left on blue-blazed Muhley Trail to begin climbing the second ledge. The trail passes through a mixed forest interspersed with large, mossy rocks and a lush understory of ferns. Pass an intersection on the left where Muhley Trail leaves the ledge, and continue straight, following a sign to Island Loop Trail. Take the left fork and follow blue-blazed Island Loop Trail clockwise. The highlight of this 0.4-mile loop is a western view of the Colchester Causeway, a narrow strip of land that carries a bike path across Lake Champlain from Colchester to the island of South Hero. A feature known as "the Cut" allows boats to pass through, and a seasonal bike ferry ensures that bicyclists can reach the Lake Champlain islands.

Return to the intersection with Muhley Trail and turn left, following the trail over a small, rocky ledge and descending a short distance. A last viewpoint on your left is perhaps the most iconic of all: To the east, 4,393-foot Mount Mansfield (Trips 45 and 46), Vermont's tallest peak, is artfully framed by an opening in the woods. Relax on the single bench and enjoy the scene before descending steeply, entering a dark ravine, and climbing down a set of stairs that leads to another trail intersection.

Despite a sign directing hikers left to the parking area, turn right at the bottom of the staircase, and hike for 0.1 mile before turning left onto blue-blazed Burns Trail. Cross a footbridge over a small stream and climb four sets of sturdy steps as the trail heads north. Pass another intersection with Allen Trail on your right. Continue straight, past a pollinator hotel to attract bees and other beneficial insects, and several trail junctions until you reach the parking area.

A hiker enjoying the wooded trails at Niquette Bay State Park.

DID YOU KNOW?

Niquette Bay and the Champlain Valley support a diverse collection of plants, thanks in part to the underlying bedrock of quartzite and dolomite that provides the calcium that plants need to thrive. Spring ephemerals are abundant in Niquette Bay State Park beginning in mid-April. These fleeting, perennial wildflowers (see "Stalking Vermont's Elusive Spring Ephemerals," page 150) start to grow in early spring, racing to complete their life cycle before the trees leaf out and rob them of needed sunlight.

MORE INFORMATION

Niquette Bay State Park is a day-use park that is open between early May and mid-October, from 8 A.M. to official sunset. Winter visitors can park outside the gate to use the trails. Dogs must be leashed and are only permitted to swim at Calm Cove.

NEARBY

Camping is available near Malletts Bay in Colchester and at Grand Isle State Park, 12.5 miles northwest. Bike the Colchester Causeway starting from Causeway Park, 12.5 miles west. Find dining options along US 2 in Colchester, as well as on US 7 in Milton, 7 miles northeast.

STALKING VERMONT'S ELUSIVE SPRING EPHEMERALS

Nobody appreciates spring quite as much as a Vermonter who has lived and worked through six months of snowpack and icy roads in too many layers of clothing—nobody, that is, except the spring wildflowers that blanket Vermont's forests with bursts of color during April and May. These small woodland plants are spring ephemerals, and while their appearance may suggest fragility, they have found a niche within the ecosystem that makes them incredibly resilient.

A spring ephemeral is a plant that lives under the canopy of hardwood forests. Because very little sunlight reaches the forest floor in summer, spring ephemerals must complete their entire life cycle, from new vegetative growth to producing flowers and seeds, before the trees leaf out. In Vermont, this short window happens during April and May, when the buds of the hardwood trees are just starting to swell.

While much of Vermont is still brown and gray, and mud season is in full swing, spend some time among last year's fallen leaves, and you'll find a variety of spring wildflowers. Due to their brief life cycle, these elusive jewels of the forest rely on a variety of strategies to survive on the edge of spring. For example, as many as 30 percent of spring ephemerals, such as trillium, dutchman's breeches, bloodroot, and hepatica, rely on ants to disperse their seeds in spring, a process called myrmecochory. To do this, the plants attach a structure made of lipids, called an elaiosome, to their seeds. Ants, attracted to the high-energy food source, haul away the seed and eat the elaiosome; the seed eventually grows into a new plant.

Spring ephemerals also must use strategies to get a jump start on their short growing season. Bloodroot, so named because of the reddish sap that exudes from its stem and root, is one of the first spring ephemerals to make an appearance in April. The large, round leaf wraps itself around the early blossom on the stem, keeping it warm as it develops into a beautiful white flower with a showy orange center. Hepatica, a small woodland flower that grows in shades of white, pink, and lavender, has a stem covered with dense hairs to protect it from the cold. Bloodroot and hepatica flowers both open in full sun and close at night to conserve their pollen for times when pollinators are more likely to be flying.

Spring ephemerals prefer calcium-rich soil with lots of nutrients; the more calcium in the soil, the greater the variety of plant life. Areas with an underlying bedrock of limestone, dolomite, or marble provide the soil with plenty of calcium to support wildflower growth. In Vermont, you'll find stellar spring wildflower displays in Niquette Bay State Park (Trip 35) and on Eagle Mountain (Trip 36) in the Champlain Valley. Another great place to see spring ephemerals is in the Taconic Mountains, where limestone bedrock is prevalent. Look for wildflowers on Mount Equinox (Trip 8) in Manchester and Gettysburg Quarry and Owl's Head (Trip 9) in Dorset. Another great spot is Mount Zion Major and Minor in Hubbardton (Trip 19).

When the snow in Vermont finally begins to melt away, and you breathe a sigh of relief as you shed layers and head outside with your face to the sun, think of the tiny spring ephemerals, which are doing the same in a nearby forest—a most welcome event after a long Vermont winter.

36 EAGLE MOUNTAIN

A peaceful hike through woods rich with wildflowers leads to the highest point on the Vermont side of Lake Champlain's shoreline and a broad view of islands and the Adirondack Mountains.

Features 🚶 🐕 🔍 🎿 🌟

Location Milton, VT

Rating Easy

Distance 2.1 miles round-trip

Elevation Gain 200 feet

Estimated Time 1 hour

Maps USGS Georgia Plains; Milton Conservation Commission: miltonvt.gov/DocumentCenter/View/147/Eagle-Mountain-Natural-Area-Map-PDF?bidId=

GPS Coordinates 44° 40.28′ N, 73° 12.08′ W

Contact Lake Champlain Land Trust, One Main Street, Suite 205, Burlington, VT 05401; 802-862-4150; lclt.org

DIRECTIONS
From I-89, Exit 17, go west on US 2 for 2.4 miles. Turn right onto Bear Trap Road and drive 1.8 miles to a fork. Bear left toward a barn and then turn left at the T intersection onto Cadreact Road. Follow Cadreact Road 2.0 miles to a stop sign. Go straight onto Beebe Hill Road and drive 0.9 mile. Turn left onto Henry Road and drive a little more than 0.1 mile to the parking lot, at the road's end (space for ten cars).

TRAIL DESCRIPTION
The land on Eagle Mountain (578 feet) was a pasture and a sugar bush, or source for maple syrup 70 years ago, but today it is a forest of rich variety. The type of limestone bluff and cedar–pine forest found here is increasingly rare in Vermont, and the 226-acre Eagle Mountain Natural Area protects a remarkable diversity of wildflowers, including trillium, hepatica, false Solomon's seal, jack-in-the-pulpit, bloodroot, white baneberry, and blue cohosh. Eagle Mountain's trails are appropriate for hikers of all ages. Hoyt Lookout is a good destination for cross-country skiers, while the summit's slightly steeper, rockier slope may be more easily traveled by snowshoers.

From the parking area, blue-blazed Hoyt Lookout Trail follows diamond-shaped markers across a field, bears left between two rows of trees, and climbs gradually to arrive at the edge of the woods at 0.25 mile. Enter a forest of cedar, maple, and hop hornbeam, with large, blocky, moss-covered rocks. Curving left, cross an old stone wall. At 0.3 mile, arrive

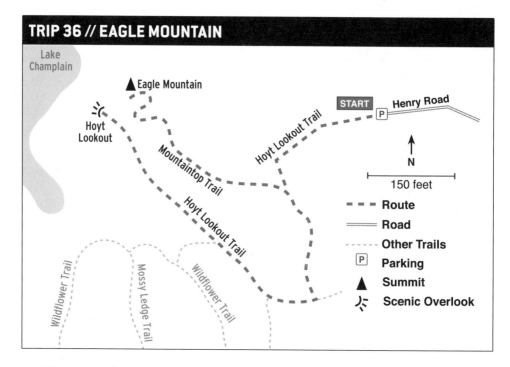

at a T junction where Hoyt Lookout Trail descends left toward Hoyt Lookout, and 0.2-mile Mountaintop Trail (yellow blazes) goes right to the summit. Turn right onto Mountaintop Trail and ascend a moderate pitch. Look for the red-and-black segmented bodies and tiny red legs of millipedes crawling across rotting birch trunks and decaying leaves.

In a short distance, follow Mountaintop Trail when it turns sharply right where a discontinued trail heads straight. Traverse a rocky hillside and curve left up the hill. In spring, this slope supports a patch of large-flowered trilliums, which blossom white and then turn pink as they age and wither. When Eagle Mountain was farmed, this wooded hillside sheltered animals such as the horses that helped with maple sugar production. Today, white-tailed deer, porcupines, mink, fishers, foxes, and bobcats have replaced farm animals. At 0.5 mile, arrive on the thickly wooded summit, which is marked by four rock cairns and is the highest point along Vermont's Lake Champlain shoreline. The scenic views are not at Eagle Mountain's summit, despite its elevation, but a little farther down the trail at Hoyt Lookout.

Return down Mountaintop Trail to the junction with Hoyt Lookout Trail and continue straight, descending on Hoyt Lookout Trail to a T junction in a clearing. The discontinued trail to Cold Spring Road is on the left. As you turn right, staying on Hoyt Lookout Trail, look for a large rock outcropping on your right. This dolomite bedrock leaches calcium into the soil, part of the reason these woods are so hospitable to a wide variety of wildflowers and plants. Walk through a large, flat field of goldenrod, milkweed, and Queen Anne's lace to reenter the woods. Climb gradually for about 0.3 mile to Hoyt Lookout and its tree-framed view west.

Lake Champlain's Inland Sea—its eastern arm—opens in front of you. The small Lower and Upper Fishbladder islands are centered in your sight; Savage Island stretches to the north; Cedar Island is just visible to the south. What looks like the mainland behind these islands is actually the broad expanse of another island: Grand Isle. Slivers of Main Lake can be seen beyond it. Lyon Mountain (3,820 feet), the tallest peak in the northern Adirondack Mountains, rises in the distance, and turkey vultures frequently soar overhead in wide, slow circles, searching for food.

Return to the parking lot the way you hiked in.

DID YOU KNOW?
The dolomite bedrock underlying Eagle Mountain was once the floor of an ocean. The calcium it provides to the soil comes from seashells slowly dissolving.

MORE INFORMATION
Lake Champlain Land Trust donated Eagle Mountain Natural Area to the town of Milton and retains a conservation easement.

NEARBY
The town of Milton maintains several trail systems, including the Lamoille River Walk and a circuit in the woods and wetlands around Milton Pond (maps at miltonvt.org). Swim and picnic on the shore of Lake Champlain at Sand Bar State Park, 7 miles southwest. Camp at Grand Isle State Park, 15 miles west. Dining options are along US 7 in Milton, 7 miles southeast; around Colchester, 12 miles south; or along US 2 in South Hero, 11 miles west.

Large-flowered trilliums thrive on Eagle Mountain. Petals start white and grow rosy pink with age.

37 BURTON ISLAND

This island hike passes through woods and fields teeming with wildflowers, travels along rocky shorelines with astounding views, and offers plenty of swimming opportunities.

Features

Location Saint Albans, VT

Rating Easy

Distance 2.8-mile loop

Elevation Gain Minimal

Estimated Time 2 hours

Maps USGS Saint Albans Bay; Vermont Department of Forests, Parks, and Recreation: vtstateparks.com/assets/pdf/burton.pdf

GPS Coordinates 44° 46.74′ N, 73° 10.89′ W

Contact Burton Island State Park, 2714 Hathaway Road, Saint Albans, VT 05481; 802-524-6353; vtstateparks.com/burton.html

DIRECTIONS

From US 7 (South Main Street) in downtown Saint Albans, turn west onto Lake Street (VT 36). Drive 2.9 miles (Lake Street becomes Lake Road) to Saint Albans Bay and stay on Lake Road as it swings right, along the bay. After crossing the bay's inlet, turn left onto Hathaway Point Road. After 2.8 miles, Hathaway Point Road leads directly into Kill Kare State Park's parking area (space for about 100 cars). Ferry service runs in season from Kill Kare to Burton Island ($8 per person round-trip), or you can boat the approximately 0.8 mile in your own craft. Winter explorers will need a dependable craft before freeze or certainty of reliable ice thickness after freeze to get to Burton Island.

TRAIL DESCRIPTION

Burton Island comprises 253 acres of nearly flat woods, fields, and marshes ringed by rocky Lake Champlain shoreline. A campground, swimming beach, and marina are at the north end, but most of the rest of the island is undeveloped. Several trails link to make a beautiful 2.8-mile hike around the perimeter of the island. Kids 4 and older will have fun exploring the varied shoreline and identifying wild strawberries, raspberries, and thimbleberries as they hike.

From the marina, follow the campground road along the north shore, keeping right at all junctions to stay near the water. Where the road ends, North Shore Nature Trail departs into a tunnel of staghorn sumac. The trail winds generally along the water's edge, the forest

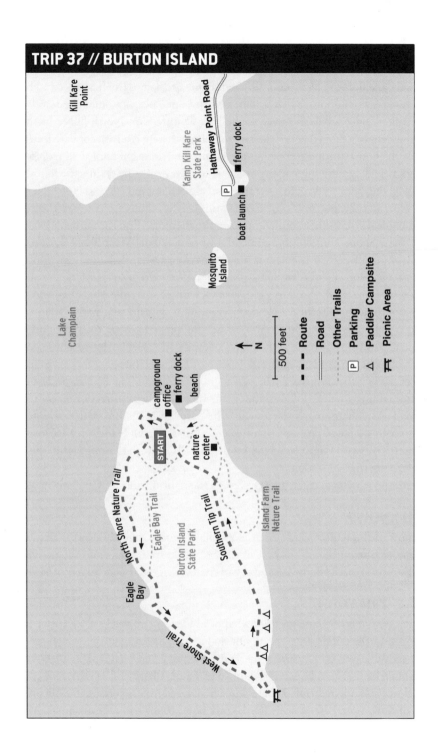

Kill Kare Point

Kamp Kill Kare State Park

Hathaway Point Road

■ ferry dock

P boat launch ■

Mosquito Island

Lake Champlain

← N

500 feet

- - - Route
——— Road
········· Other Trails
P Parking
△ Paddler Campsite
⊼ Picnic Area

campground office ■ ■ ferry dock
beach

START

nature center

North Shore Nature Trail

Eagle Bay Trail

Burton Island State Park

Southern Tip Trail

Island Farm Nature Trail

Eagle Bay

West Shore Trail

△ △
△
△ △

⊼

shifting between dark, dry cedar and hemlock stands (common on rocky, thin-soiled shores) to lighter, greener stands of poplar, paper birch, and ash (where farm fields stood not long ago). Canada anemone, goldenrod, milkweed, dame's rocket, daisy fleabane, and bedstraw are just a few of the wildflowers that sprout in sunny, open places around the island.

At 0.3 mile, Eagle Bay Trail leaves to the left. Continue on North Shore Nature Trail through the trees to a curved cove. The rare sandy beach here is a treat for bare feet, making this one of the best swimming spots on the island. Startling spikes of wild red columbine sprout from pebbly ground high on the beach. A narrow peninsula defines the southern edge of the cove, giving wide views across the lake's Inland Sea. Grand Isle and North Hero Island lie to the west, and the low profiles of Woods and Knight islands are visible to the north.

Passing Eagle Bay, continue southwest along the shore and find the fainter, unsigned and unblazed West Shore Trail climbing into the woods. Follow West Shore Trail as it stays mostly within the trees for the next 0.5 mile, passing wetlands before emerging on the rocky shore near the island's southern tip. Walk along the water and, where the rocky beach gives way to a bluff, climb to a grassy lawn with picnic tables, benches, and spectacular views south to the distant Adirondack Mountains beyond nearby Ball Island.

On the eastern side of the promontory, find the mowed woods road of Southern Tip Trail, which leads 0.7 mile back to the island's developed east side. An outhouse perches in the woods on your left, and a boardwalk leads past paths to four paddler campsites on the right. After passing the campsite paths, wide, grassy Southern Tip Trail meanders through sumac until ending in a field. Continue in the same northeast direction to join a campground road. As you approach the marina, the path to the nature center diverges to the right across a grassy lawn. From the nature center, Island Farm Nature Trail leads through a pretty marsh of sweet flag; a brochure guide is available at the campground office if you decide to explore this short loop.

Return to the marina to catch a ferry back to the parking area at Kill Kare State Park.

DID YOU KNOW?

During most of the 8,000 years since the Abenaki people moved into this area, the lake was lower, and Burton Island was part of the peninsula stretching from the mainland. By the time Europeans arrived, the lake level had risen enough to isolate this spot as an island.

MORE INFORMATION

Burton Island State Park operates from Memorial Day to two weeks after Labor Day; the island is open to the public year-round, but no facilities are available in the off-season. Bicycles are only allowed on Southern Tip Trail. The ferry and boat launch are operated by Kill Kare State Park, 2714 Hathaway Point Road, Saint Albans, VT 05481; 802-524-6021; vtstateparks.com/killkare.html. A day-use fee is charged unless you're camping on Burton Island. Kill Kare State Park is open for day use only, 10 A.M. to official sunset, Memorial Day to two weeks after Labor Day. Pets are permitted at both Kill Kare and Burton Island.

Burton Island's shoreline leads from one fabulous view to the next with plenty of swimming options.

NEARBY

Camp and swim on Burton Island or at state parks on the more remote Woods and Knight islands. A small store and a grill provide food near the marina; more dining options are in Saint Albans, 6 miles east. Paddling on the lake can be difficult due to wind and waves, but Missisquoi National Wildlife Refuge, 13 miles north, has a slow river and excellent opportunities for wildlife watching.

4 // NORTH-CENTRAL VERMONT

The northern Green Mountains tower over most of north-central Vermont with their buckled and crevassed landscape of dark forests, imposing rocky peaks, alpine lakes, and swift-flowing streams and rivers. The Long Trail passes through the northern Greens, providing a challenging route and dramatic scenery for hikers, and the Catamount Trail leads skiers on equally challenging terrain at lower elevations. Between the western-flowing Winooski and Lamoille rivers, the northern Green Mountains encompass the highest-elevation peaks in Vermont.

With cold winters and a short growing season, the northern Green Mountains have historically been one of the least populated regions of Vermont. Recreation and tourism have increased the pace of development in the last 75 years, with four ski resorts and their associated collection of hotels and restaurants dramatically expanding the number of visitors and residents. Despite the

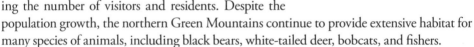

population growth, the northern Green Mountains continue to provide extensive habitat for many species of animals, including black bears, white-tailed deer, bobcats, and fishers.

The long, windswept ridge of Mount Mansfield (Trips 45 and 46), Vermont's highest mountain at 4,393 feet, rises dramatically at Smugglers' Notch in Stowe, appearing from many places in northern Vermont as the profile of a face gazing toward the sky. Mount Mansfield's rocky summit supports vestiges of alpine tundra that were prevalent during the last ice age. Rare, fragile arctic plants hug the ground, clinging to life in soil that is thin and nutrient poor. Jay Peak (Trip 51), 3,862 feet, is one of the northernmost peaks in the Green Mountains of Vermont, and with an average snowfall of 359 inches a year, it's also one of the snowiest places in Vermont.

The Worcester Range runs parallel to and just east of the main range of the Green Mountains, and while the peaks are smaller, they are plenty steep, providing hikers with a hearty challenge. The most well-known, 3,570-foot Mount Hunger (Trip 40), features a craggy, domed top with unsurpassed views of Mount Mansfield and the high peaks of the

Green Mountains. The main ridge of the Worcester Range can be tackled on a day hike, the longest in this guidebook (Trip 38), traversing four peaks over the course of 10.5 miles on beloved Skyline Trail.

From the Lamoille River north to the Missisquoi River along the Canadian border, the mountains are a little lower and more spread out. The Lowell Mountains begin near 25-mile-long Lake Memphremagog, which straddles the Canadian border, and extend southwest to the town of Eden. Their relative isolation gives places like Devil's Gulch and Big Muddy Pond (Trip 49) a feeling of remoteness despite their locations along the popular route of the Long Trail.

38 WORCESTER RANGE SKYLINE

This rugged ridgeline hike traverses four peaks and winds through remote, moss-covered woods for a full day on one of Vermont's most beautiful and challenging trails.

Features

Location Worcester and Middlesex, VT

Rating Strenuous

Distance 10.5 miles one-way

Elevation Gain 3,350 feet (cumulative over four peaks)

Estimated Time 8 hours

Maps USGS Worcester, USGS Stowe

GPS Coordinates 44° 25.31' N, 72° 34.44' W

Contact C. C. Putnam State Forest, Vermont Department of Forests, Parks, and Recreation; fpr.vermont.gov. Green Mountain Club, 4711 Waterbury–Stowe Road, Waterbury Center, VT 05677; 802-244-7037; greenmountainclub.org

DIRECTIONS

From VT 12 in the village of Worcester, head west on Minister Brook Road 1.5 miles to Hampshire Hill Road. Turn right onto Hampshire Hill Road, travel 2.3 miles, and turn left onto Mountain Road where Hampshire Hill Road bends sharply to the right. Follow Mountain Road 0.1 mile to its end at the trailhead parking area for Mount Worcester (space for twelve cars).

For directions to this hike's end point in Middlesex, see Trip 39 directions to White Rock Mountain's trailhead.

TRAIL DESCRIPTION

The Worcester Range is home to the well-loved Mount Hunger (Trip 40), Elmore Mountain (Trip 41), and Stowe Pinnacle (Trip 44), as well as the less frequently visited gems of White Rock Mountain (Trip 39) and 3,225-foot Mount Worcester. All these rocky high points give perspective over the big mountains and picturesque valleys of northern and central Vermont, so their appeal to hikers is understandable. But the range also harbors a more remote and meditative hiking experience along Skyline Trail, which traverses two tall, forested peaks between the bookends of Mount Worcester in the north and Mount Hunger in the south. Looking at a satellite map, you could be lured in to thinking the

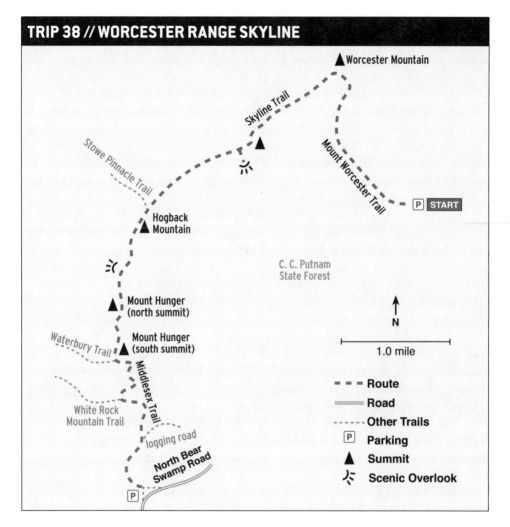

Worcester Mountain

Skyline Trail

Stowe Pinnacle Trail

Mount Worcester Trail

P START

Hogback Mountain

C. C. Putnam State Forest

N

1.0 mile

Mount Hunger (north summit)

Mount Hunger (south summit)

Waterbury Trail

Middlesex Trail

White Rock Mountain Trail

logging road

North Bear Swamp Road

P

- - - Route
=== Road
····· Other Trails
P Parking
▲ Summit
⅍ Scenic Overlook

ridgeline has less elevation drop and gain than it does, but this is a rigorous 10.5 miles. The 3,350 feet of elevation gain is the sum of ascending four peaks along Skyline Trail, starting in the north and heading south as described below, which has most of the elevation gain in the beginning and less as you get farther along and more tired. A shorter alternative is the more popular southern segment of Skyline Trail, reachable from the western side by connecting Stowe Pinnacle to Mount Hunger for a 6.8-mile hike with a healthy 2,780 feet of climbing when hiked north to south one-way. No matter how you approach Skyline Trail, you'll need to either spot a second car at the other end of your point-to-point hike or plan to turn around and hike back to your starting point.

Mount Worcester Trail begins on the west side of the parking area as a blue-blazed woods road, ascending at a measured pace for the first mile and then becoming increasingly steep. At 1.8 miles, climb a rocky, narrow, conifer-lined gully and arrive at the open pitches leading to Worcester's summit. Thick bands of quartz contrast brightly with the gray summit ledges, and their slick, white surfaces make precarious footing. The summit of Worcester doesn't have much flat ground, but you will find a view of what lies ahead: distinct peaks stacked up to the south. Follow the sign to Skyline Trail, which begins with a steep drop off the summit into dark green woods, zigzagging down the ridge through moss-covered humps and bumps, brushing past thickly needled boughs of balsam fir and red spruce. Cross a saddle and begin climbing. Infrequent use can cause the route to be easily disguised by a windblown pile of birch leaves, so watch for blue blazes in some less obvious spots, although Skyline Trail never wanders far from the crest of the range. At 4.0 miles, cross an unnamed, wooded summit (3,470 feet). At 4.2 miles, a spur path leads left a short distance (there are no long spurs when you're walking such a narrow spine) to a small window in the trees, which gives a view southeast.

Upon returning from the spur path, follow Skyline Trail as it continues gently downhill and across a saddle for the next mile, and then begins climbing the next peak, the tallest one in the Worcester Range at 3,600 feet. It is known sometimes as Hogback Mountain, sometimes as Putnam Mountain, and sometimes, oddly, as an unnamed mountain. Log ladders assist your ascent over ledges with sheets of moss blanketing the rock and hanging off the edges. The ladders and a wider, more obvious trail are the first signs you're approaching the more frequently visited southern half of Skyline Trail. Sure enough, at 5.8 miles, you arrive at a T junction, with the trail downhill to Stowe Pinnacle (also blazed blue) on your right and the continuation of Skyline Trail heading left. Go left and uphill on Skyline Trail, reaching the forested height-of-land at 5.9 miles. From here, the ridgeline rolls along its highest stretch, passing an opening on the western rim with views of Mount Mansfield's skyward-facing profile and the bumpy line of peaks to its south: Dewey Mountain (3,323 feet), Mount Clark (2,970 feet), Mount Mayo (3,110 feet), and Bolton Mountain (3,690 feet), the latter recognizable by a wind tower rising from a divot in its summit ridge. Waterbury Reservoir reflects the sky in the southwest, with the two-tiered top of Camel's Hump (Trip 27) beyond it.

Skyline Trail descends to the 7-mile mark, at which point it begins to climb Mount Hunger. Reach Hunger's north summit (3,570 feet) at 7.3 miles and continue another 0.6 mile in and out of woods as the trail undulates over big rocks and down slabby ledges to Hunger's south summit (3,539 feet). In addition to views of Mount Mansfield and the Stowe Valley, Mount Hunger's broad, bald top gives a magnificent vantage point east to the Granite Hills of Groton State Forest; south to the Northfield Range and the tall peaks of Monroe Skyline stretching south from Camel's Hump; and west, where the Winooski River cuts a deep cleft in the main chain of the Green Mountains, opening a view to Lake Champlain and the distant Adirondacks.

Two trails lead off the south dome of Mount Hunger: Waterbury Trail heads west and blue-blazed Middlesex Trail—our route—goes east. Middlesex Trail's descent is very steep and exposed for the first 0.3 mile. Footing on the open slabs can be tricky in dry conditions and dangerous when wet or icy. If conditions make Middlesex Trail risky, or if you simply want to visit one more excellent Worcester Range peak, you can descend instead via White

A broad stripe of brilliant white quartz in Mount Worcester's summit ledges alerts hikers they're nearing the top of the first peak on magnificent Worcester Range Skyline Trail.

Rock Mountain (3,150 feet) on a slightly less steep, somewhat less exposed route that rejoins Middlesex Trail after 1.6 miles, adding 0.6 mile to your total hike. (For this option, head west on blue-blazed Waterbury Trail 0.1 mile, dropping to the junction of White Rock Mountain Trail on your left. Follow White Rock Mountain Trail 0.8 mile to the open shoulder of White Rock Mountain [Trip 39] and blue-blazed Bob Kemp Trail, which descends east to meet Middlesex Trail.)

From the summit of Mount Hunger, go east on Middlesex Trail and follow blue blazes painted on the open rock, clambering downhill on wide slabs with little to grab for handholds. You may want to sit and scoot a lot of it, preferring a hole in your pants to a tumble. The steepest final pitch usually has ropes you can grab to slow your descent into the forest. When you put your boots back on dirt at the base of the ledges, the going is still rugged and rocky for another 0.7 mile until you reach the junction of Bob Kemp Trail on your right at 8.9 miles. Turn left, continuing down Middlesex Trail on an old woods road with easy footing and a gentle pitch. After crossing a wide stream, the trail reverts to single-track and passes a register box just before descending onto a wide logging road at 9.7 miles. Turn right and follow the logging road 0.7 mile, watching for a spur path on the right shortly after passing a metal gate (which may be open or closed). The spur ducks through dense woods for 0.1 mile to the trailhead parking lot.

39 WHITE ROCK MOUNTAIN

The rugged spire of White Rock provides an adventurous hike and exhilarating views.

Features

Location Middlesex, VT

Rating Moderate to Strenuous

Distance 4.6 miles round-trip

Elevation Gain 1,558 feet

Estimated Time 3.5 hours

Maps USGS Middlesex, USGS Stowe

GPS Coordinates 44° 22.31′ N, 72° 38.41′ W

Contact C. C. Putnam State Forest, Vermont Department of Forests, Parks, and Recreation; fpr.vermont.gov. Green Mountain Club, 4711 Waterbury–Stowe Road, Waterbury Center, VT 05677; 802-244-7037; greenmountainclub.org

DIRECTIONS

From downtown Montpelier, follow VT 12 north 5.3 miles and turn left onto Shady Rill Road. Go 2.1 miles and turn right onto Story Road. At 0.5 mile, stay straight onto Nellie Chase Road; 0.1 mile farther, bear left onto North Bear Swamp Road. Drive 1.9 miles to the parking lot on the right (space for fifteen cars).

TRAIL DESCRIPTION

White Rock Mountain (3,150 feet) is a ledgy peak off the south shoulder of Mount Hunger. Open, flat terraces with panoramic views circle its summit, and the hand-over-hand scrambling required to get to the very top makes this one of Vermont's more exciting peaks to attain. The top third of the trail up White Rock Mountain is particularly rugged, steep, and often wet, but the payoff is worth muddy feet.

From the parking lot, Middlesex Trail follows a 500-foot, blue-blazed connector trail to a dirt road; turn left, continuing to follow blue blazes north past a metal gate. Martin's Brook gurgles mostly unseen on the left as the road climbs gradually through a mixed hardwood forest. At 0.8 mile, just after a cascade tumbles out of the woods, turn left off the road onto a footpath marked by a small sign ("Trail"). The footpath climbs moderately, curving through birches and maples and traversing occasional rock steps. After crossing a wide brook on rocks, Middlesex Trail becomes wider, reminiscent of its early days as a carriage road. After a gradual climb, the trail levels. A logged clearing can be seen through

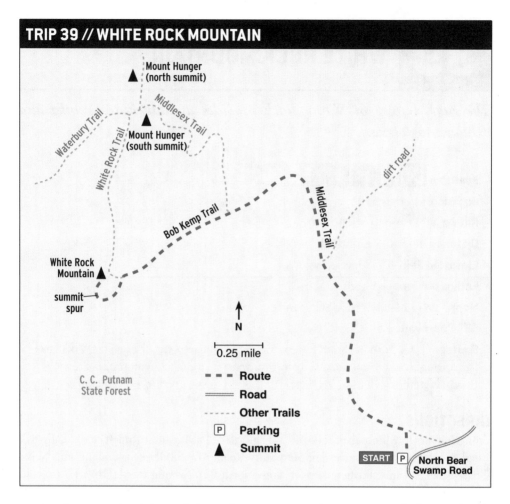

a strip of trees on the right, and the trail curves west and enters a tunnel of young beech trees.

The trail alternately crosses and climbs a damp, ledgy hillside. At 1.6 miles, a small clearing marks a junction. Middlesex Trail turns right here, toward Mount Hunger. Do not follow it; instead go straight onto blue-blazed Bob Kemp Trail. The next 0.5 mile is steeper and more rugged than Middlesex Trail, with numerous ledges and rock steps to mount and muddy saddles to traverse. After two stream crossings, arrive at a long rock escarpment that slices down through the forest. Follow the trail up into a cleft in the cliff and then climb through an airy stand of paper birch with long, slightly obstructed views as the mountainside drops away on the right. The trail ascends steeply into balsam firs, where thick mosses blanket the forest floor.

After a short scramble that requires hands as well as feet, cross two log bridges over a foamy, copper-colored pool. Tannic acid from decomposing conifers gives the water its unusual color. A short distance above the pool, Bob Kemp Trail climbs a bare rock slope into a gully and emerges onto flat, open rock with views eastward. The bald summit of

Mount Hunger (Trip 40) rises behind you to the north. Although these views are magnificent, they get better as you circle and ascend the peak. Weave through small clumps of trees, across broad terraces of rock, and climb to a trail junction. Bob Kemp Trail, also called White Rock Trail on the Waterbury side, heads right here to meet Waterbury Trail just below the summit of Mount Hunger. Go left on the 0.1-mile spur to White Rock Mountain's summit.

Cross an open, rocky area with a view of 4,083-foot Camel's Hump (Trip 27) and then climb a tricky rock pitch, where a long crack makes the best toeholds. Ascending this kind of slab using a combination of friction and balance is characteristic of hikes in the Worcester Range. Around the next curve, dramatic western views appear. The dark waters of Waterbury Reservoir snake through the hills, and the notch of the Winooski River valley points west to distant Adirondack peaks. As you continue around the curve, the profile ridge of Mount Mansfield (4,393 feet) and the pointed summit of Whiteface Mountain (3,714 feet) come into view. Hoist yourself through a crack in the boulders to clamber onto the little bare summit of White Rock Mountain.

Return the way you came up.

DID YOU KNOW?

When settlers cleared farmland in Middlesex in the 1760s, White Rock Mountain and Mount Hunger were covered with trees. Forest fires left the peaks in their current bald state.

Climbing to the tip-top of White Rock Mountain is a fun scramble over rugged outcrops. For easier destinations with the same great views, opt for the rock terraces surrounding the summit.

MORE INFORMATION

White Rock Mountain is within C. C. Putnam State Forest, managed by the Vermont Department of Forests, Parks, and Recreation. There are no managed campgrounds, but primitive camping is permitted below 2,500 feet. To minimize erosion along fragile, high-elevation terrain, the state closes Worcester Range trails between mid-April and Memorial Day. The Green Mountain Club helps maintain trails in the Worcester Range.

NEARBY

Swimming holes along Shady Rill Road are well marked by a dirt road pull-off with picnic shelters, 4 miles southeast. Wrightsville Reservoir has a public beach and boat launch, 5.2 miles southeast. Grocery stores, shops, and restaurants are in Montpelier, 10 miles southeast.

VERMONT'S ANCIENT, ILLOGICAL RIVERS

Logic says that water takes the path of least resistance: Rain and snowmelt flow downhill off mountains and continue to the sea. The ridge of highest mountains divides the watersheds. As in the Continental Divide in the Rocky Mountains, the Green Mountains' high peaks shed water from their east side easterly and from their west side westerly. Why, then, do some rivers start on one side of a mountain range and, instead of continuing downhill to the ocean, cut through those high hills to drain on the other side?

Look at three of Vermont's big rivers: the Missisquoi, the Lamoille, and the Winooski. Each rises on the eastern side of the Green Mountains and slices through the highest ridgeline to empty into Lake Champlain on the western side. How did the water end up on such an illogical path?

The simple answer is that these three rivers have been flowing since before the Green Mountains were born. Their ancient routes were established and continued as continental plates crashed into one another and thrust up mountains around them. The Acadian orogeny—the mountain-building period in which the Greens arose—was immensely disturbing to the landscape but also took 40 million years. During this time, the rivers continued down their paths and cut into the new mountains as the peaks heaved upward.

Ancient rivers that predate and cut through mountain ranges are known as antecedent drainages, and many exist across North America and in other parts of the world. In the Appalachian Mountains, the Potomac and Delaware rivers are prime examples. Both have water gaps, or places where the rivers slice through a ridge. The Columbia River similarly cuts a deep canyon through the Cascade Mountains on the Washington–Oregon border as it flows westward to the Pacific.

Because antecedent rivers provide passage through steep terrain, they are natural routes for people finding their way through the mountains. The Abenakis used the relatively slow flow of the Missisquoi River for upstream canoe travel into the Green Mountains and the more rollicking descent of the Lamoille River to return through the mountains to Lake Champlain. Today, four parallel roads and a railroad take advantage of the Winooski River's mighty erosive power as it plows its illogical route through the Green Mountains' highest peaks.

40 MOUNT HUNGER

"The mountaintop is one of the pleasantest places of earth, and will be visited so long as people inhabit the country." Mount Hunger's rocky, domed top was a favorite with hikers even before Middlesex resident William Chapin penned this thought in 1880, and it has remained so ever since.

Features

Location Waterbury Center, VT

Rating Moderate to Strenuous

Distance 4 miles round-trip

Elevation Gain 2,290 feet

Estimated Time 3.5 hours

Maps USGS Stowe

GPS Coordinates 44° 24.14′ N, 72° 40.52′ W

Contact Vermont Department of Forests, Parks, and Recreation, District 4, Barre Office; 5 Perry Street, Suite 20, Barre, VT 05641; 802-476-0170; fpr.vermont.gov. Green Mountain Club, 4711 Waterbury–Stowe Road, Waterbury Center, VT 05677; 802-244-7037; greenmountainclub.org

DIRECTIONS

From I-89, Exit 10, follow VT 100 (Waterbury–Stowe Road) north 1.2 miles and turn right onto Guptil Road. Travel 2.0 miles to the town green in Waterbury Center and bear right onto Maple Street. Go 0.2 mile and turn right onto Loomis Hill Road. Drive up Loomis Hill Road 1.9 miles; here it curves left and becomes Sweet Farm Road. Go 1.5 miles north on Sweet Farm Road to the trailhead parking lot on the right (space for about twenty cars). Overflow parking is along the far side of Sweet Farm Road, but be sure to leave space for emergency vehicles to pass.

TRAIL DESCRIPTION

Mount Hunger (3,570 feet at its forested north summit, although the south summit, where most hikes end, is 3,539 feet) is a rounded bald spot at the southern end of the Worcester Range. Its rocky top is a fun place to explore, in addition to providing expansive views. Waterbury Trail is moderate, but the final 0.5 mile becomes progressively steeper, with ledges to scramble up. Most kids 8 and older will enjoy this hike if they're prepared for the distance and steepness. Dogs and winter hikers may struggle to climb the steep slab.

TRIP 40 // MOUNT HUNGER

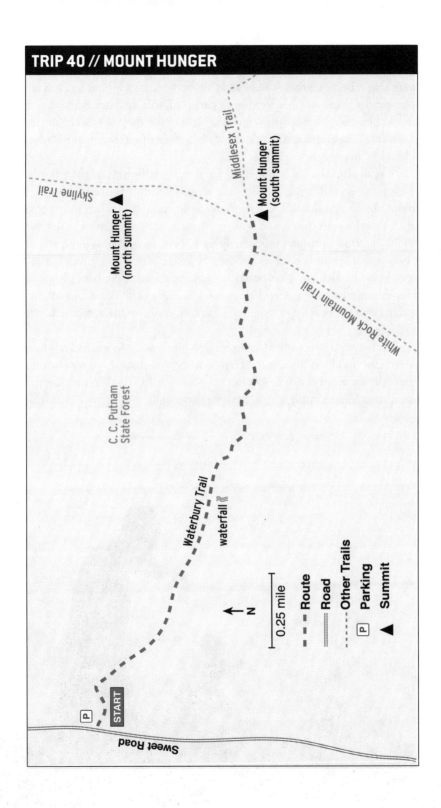

Rocky, rooty, blue-blazed Waterbury Trail leads east from the parking lot into a hard-wood forest sprinkled with a few hemlocks. The climb begins gently, although as the trail curves southeast, it becomes more moderate. Pass between mossy boulders and climb rock steps. Listen for the hermit thrush, Vermont's state bird, trilling short, ethereal phrases that almost sound like they have their own echo. Named for their shy behavior, these little brown-and-white songbirds are difficult to spot in a thick forest, but their haunting song is the soundtrack of many summer hikes.

Waterbury Trail climbs steadily but easily for about a half-mile and then descends grad-ually to traverse two small streams. After the second stream, the trail becomes steep and climbs to the edge of a boulder-filled stream. A scenic waterfall tumbles from above during wet weather. Continue up the eroded slope on the left side and cross the streambed above the waterfall. The trail continues moderately up a rocky slope that is loose and eroded in places. Following a streambed, enter the boreal forest of the upper mountain. Canada mayflowers, bunchberries, and blue-bead lilies cover the forest floor beneath spindly sprigs of hobblebushes, and the first steep ledge appears. Zigzag up it and continue to ascend another 0.2 mile to the next set of ledges. Climb cautiously on this steep rock, which may be especially slick on wet or humid days.

At 1.9 miles, between two vertical scrambles, White Rock Mountain Trail heads right. Continue straight uphill on Waterbury Trail, skirting small stands of wind-stunted trees, to arrive on Mount Hunger's rock summit. Skyline Trail (Trip 38) leads north into the trees, passing over Mount Hunger's forested north peak. (The south peak was also forested

The views from Mount Hunger's bare summit reward hikers willing to scale its ledges.

before a fire left the rock bare.) Middlesex Trail leads straight ahead, down the eastern side of the mountain, joining the trail from White Rock Mountain (Trip 39).

Views from Mount Hunger are vast and unencumbered, justifying this small peak's popularity. To the south, along Mount Hunger's descending ridgeline, are the rocky terraces and pointy summit of White Rock Mountain. To the west, the long ridge of the Green Mountains' highest peaks stretches as far as you can see south and north. The Winooski River cuts a deep gouge between Camel's Hump (Trip 27) and Bolton Mountain. Waterbury Reservoir shines in the foreground, and the craggy profile of Mount Mansfield (Trips 45 and 46) dominates the ridgeline heading north. The eastern side of the Worcester Range is mostly low foothills, with the exception of the Granite Hills in the southeast. This cluster of tall peaks is related geologically to the White Mountains in New Hampshire, which are also visible from the summit of Mount Hunger on a clear day.

Retrace your steps to the trailhead.

DID YOU KNOW?

In 1878, a road ascended the eastern side of Mount Hunger. It was broad and smooth enough to accommodate six horses pulling a carriage of twenty people to within a half-mile of the summit.

MORE INFORMATION

Mount Hunger is within C. C. Putnam State Forest. To minimize erosion along fragile, high-elevation terrain, the state closes the upper mountain trails in the Worcester Range between mid-April and Memorial Day; lower Waterbury Trail is open as far as the waterfall during mud season (see Introduction, page xviii). The Green Mountain Club helps maintain trails in the Worcester Range.

NEARBY

Waterbury Center State Park, 4 miles west, offers swimming and boating on Waterbury Reservoir; the Winooski River also has good paddling. Camp on the reservoir at Little River State Park, 12 miles west, or at Smugglers' Notch State Park, 12.5 miles northwest. The Green Mountain Club Visitor Center is along VT 100 in Waterbury Center, 4.5 miles west. Restaurants are on VT 100 in Waterbury, 7 miles south, and in Stowe, 7 miles northwest.

41 ELMORE MOUNTAIN

Elmore's loop hike explores many facets of the mountain: multiple outlook points, a historical fire tower, a ridgeline walk, and an unusual balanced boulder.

Features 🏃 👤 🐕 📍 ❄ $ ⛏

Location Lake Elmore, VT

Rating Moderate

Distance 4.5-mile loop

Elevation Gain 1,145 feet

Estimated Time 3 hours

Maps USGS Morrisville; Vermont Department of Forests, Parks, and Recreation: vtstateparks.com/elmore.html

GPS Coordinates 44° 32.38′ N, 72° 32.17′ W

Contact Elmore State Park, 856 VT Route 12, Lake Elmore, VT 05657; 802-888-2982; vtstateparks.com/elmore.html

DIRECTIONS
From the junction of VT 12 and Beach Road in Elmore, head north on VT 12 for 0.2 mile. Turn left into Elmore State Park, where a day-use fee is charged in season. Follow the road through the campground to a parking area by a metal gate (space for about fifteen cars). (Winter hikers: Follow Beach Road 0.1 mile from VT 12 to the park's day-use parking lot on the right. Walk through the campground to the trailhead, adding 0.7 mile to the hike.)

TRAIL DESCRIPTION
Elmore Mountain (2,590 feet) is a low peak at the north end of—and slightly detached from—the higher peaks of the rugged Worcester Range. Elmore's solitary location and many ledgy outlooks afford spectacular views in all directions, a plus for hikers who prefer to keep their boot soles on the ground rather than ascend to the windy, swaying cab of a fire tower. Formerly an out-and-back hike, Ridge Trail now connects Balancing Rock with Fire Tower Trail, creating a loop. At the foot of the mountain's forested slopes, the sparkling waters of 219-acre Elmore Lake top off the list of reasons why this mountain is a favorite. The hike is appropriate for kids 7 and older.

From the parking area, walk past the metal gate to head uphill on Fire Tower Trail, a multiuse dirt road. The road climbs gradually as it heads first west and then south, paralleling the ridge of the mountain high above. The long-distance Catamount Trail shares this route along

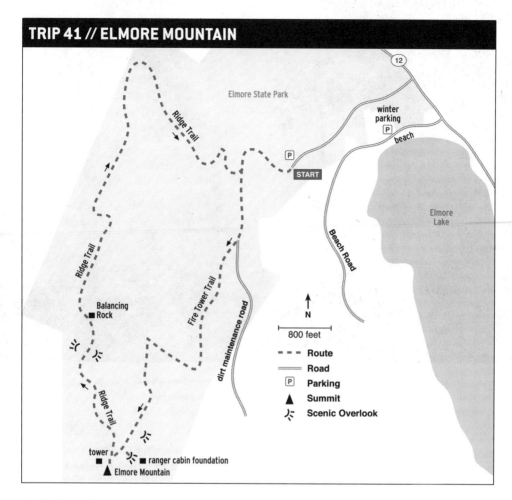

the flank of the mountain. At 0.3 mile, Ridge Trail departs right; this is the bottom of your return route. Stay straight and continue climbing the wide track of Fire Tower Trail.

At 0.6 mile, follow Fire Tower Trail when it turns right off the road and climbs rock steps into the forest. Blue blazes mark the route through hobblebushes and ferns as it continues southward along a stream. Climbing moderately, the trail crosses patches of bare bedrock and occasional step stones. A switchback to the right leads onto a rugged, rocky path through a tall maple forest. After several more switchbacks, Fire Tower Trail flattens, and the forest becomes noticeably shorter due to the elevation and exposure. At 1.6 miles, where the trail bends right, an opening straight ahead beckons. Follow this short side path onto a rocky outcropping with an old ranger cabin foundation and a view east. Look up to the ridgeline to spot the 60-foot fire tower above the trees. From 1938, when the present tower was erected to replace one destroyed by that year's infamous hurricane, through 1974, a fire lookout lived in a cabin here on the ledge and hiked each day to work.

Return to Fire Tower Trail and go left, continuing uphill. This final 0.2 mile to the summit is steep, with scrambles through rooty sections and on steps blasted into the bedrock. A T intersection marks the top of the climb; go left to the fire tower (1.8 miles), which

Canine hikers are welcome on Elmore Mountain. The long ridge features several rock outcrops, providing plentiful views east over Elmore Lake and west to Vermont's tallest peak, Mount Mansfield.

provides extensive views over the treetops. The spine of the Worcester Range snakes south, and the tallest Green Mountains lie to the west, including Mount Mansfield's 4,393-foot Chin (Trip 45), the highest point in Vermont. Lamoille River valley farmland spreads across the landscape north of Elmore, and boats are visible on Elmore Lake beneath the eastern slope.

Return to the T intersection and turn left, following blue-blazed Ridge Trail north. Rocky outcroppings provide views east and west from this high spine. At 2.4 miles, a killer-whale-sized boulder raises its mighty bulk from a precarious-looking perch on a bed of ferns. Known as Balancing Rock, this glacial erratic was left here when the glacier transporting it melted about 11,000 years ago.

Follow the blue blazes, heading west across a level area before continuing north another mile along the ridge. At 3.4 miles, a long U-turn steers you off the ridge and south through a hollow between the main ridgeline and a lower, parallel ridge. Ridge Trail continues generally southeast for its final 0.5 mile, descending through mixed hardwoods and alongside tall walls of mossy rock before crossing a depression and climbing back onto Fire Tower Trail. Turn left and return downhill 0.3 mile to the trailhead parking lot.

DID YOU KNOW?

A hotel hosted guests on the eastern slope of Mount Elmore at the turn of the twentieth century. It was removed when the Civilian Conservation Corps developed the recreational area that became Elmore State Park in 1936.

MORE INFORMATION

Elmore State Park is open for day use from 10 A.M. to official sunset, Memorial Day through Indigenous Peoples' Day. Dogs are allowed except on the beach; bring proof of rabies vaccination.

NEARBY

Swimming, paddling, and camping are at the base of the mountain in Elmore State Park. The Lamoille River has good paddling as well, and mountain-bike trails can be found in Morrisville, 4.5 miles west, and Stowe, 13 miles southwest. A small general store is on VT 12 next to Elmore Lake; head to Morrisville or Stowe for dining options.

42 WIESSNER WOODS

Tall hemlocks and bubbly brooks characterize this leisurely loop walk to a lookout point with a quintessential Vermont view.

Features

Location Stowe, VT

Rating Easy

Distance 1.5-mile loop

Elevation Gain 100 feet

Estimated Time 1 hour

Maps USGS Stowe, USGS Sterling Mountain; Stowe Land Trust: stowelandtrust.org/fileadmin/slt/maps/WiessnerWoodsMap.pdf

GPS Coordinates 44° 29.81′ N, 72° 43.62′ W

Contact Stowe Land Trust, 6 Sunset Street, P.O. Box 284, Stowe, VT 05672; 802-253-7221; stowelandtrust.org

DIRECTIONS

From the junction of VT 100 and VT 108 in the town of Stowe, take VT 108 (Mountain Road) 3.3 miles and turn right onto Edson Hill Road. Drive 0.5 mile and, just past the Stowehof (an inn), turn right into a drive. Parking is in a lot on the left (space for eight cars).

TRAIL DESCRIPTION

Wiessner Woods is a lovely, shady forest sprawling over 79 acres near Stowe. Its network of wide trails is inviting for hikers of all ages as it ambles across rolling ground, passing through stands of mature trees and crossing small brooks.

From the parking area, cross a private driveway and a grassy meadow to a kiosk at the trailhead. Enter Wiessner Woods on a broad dirt path and immediately cross a wide bridge over a stream. Blue paw-print trail markers let you know you're on a section of the Catamount Trail, a 300-mile cross-country ski and snowshoe trail that extends the length of Vermont. Follow the flat path through birch, maple, and broad patches of jewelweed, a native plant that sends up soft, leggy stems in spring and dangles a small orange or yellow open-mouthed flower between June and September.

Around a bend, white pines surround the Four Corners junction at 0.1 mile. Meadow Trail, your return route, rises gently to the left; Main Street continues straight ahead. Go right, following the Catamount Trail, also called Hardwood Ridge Trail here. The path narrows and traverses a long line of bog bridges before entering a lovely, mature hemlock forest. The thick canopy of these large trees blocks so much sun that few plants grow in the

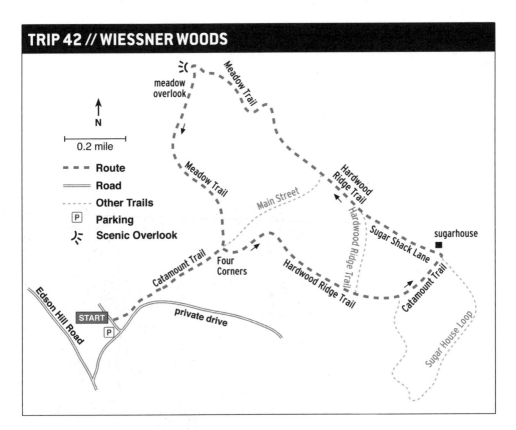

understory; the ground is covered with copper needles and the soft, mossy remains of rotting logs. Dip through a stream valley before climbing out of the conifers. At 0.4 mile, Hardwood Ridge Trail goes left; stay straight on the Catamount Trail. Pass the junction for Sugar House Loop on your right and reach the boundary of Wiessner Woods. The large, metal-roofed sugarhouse (now a privately owned warming hut) stands in a clearing.

Just before the sugarhouse, reenter Wiessner Woods and turn left, following Sugar Shack Lane—blazed with orange diamonds—over bog bridges along a wide, rolling trail. As you pass through this moist area, watch for patches of wood sorrel, which looks like clover growing low to the ground. Its heart-shaped leaves have a thirst-quenching, lemony flavor, but don't overdo it; the sourness comes from oxalic acid, which is toxic in large amounts. Delicate white flowers veined with dark pink bloom above the leaves between June and August.

After crossing a footbridge, Sugar Shack Lane turns into Hardwood Ridge Trail, continuing in the same northwesterly direction. Pass several junctions, where private trails lead to the right and Main Street departs left (returning to Four Corners). After the junction with Main Street, Hardwood Ridge Trail is called Meadow Trail, and it passes into a stand of relatively young conifers. Unlike more mature forests, these smaller trees let some sunlight through to the forest floor, encouraging thick undergrowth. Meadow Trail dips through a stream valley and climbs out the other side to a wooden bench alongside a stone wall. A large field rolls away on the far side of the wall beyond a stand of trees, toward gently rounded Dewey Mountain (3,323 feet).

From this wooded viewpoint, follow Meadow Trail downhill through a mixed hardwood forest. After crossing a stream, enter the widely spaced pine forest once again and soon arrive at Four Corners. Turn right to follow the Catamount Trail out to the trailhead.

DID YOU KNOW?

Jewelweed is also commonly called spotted touch-me-not for its tendency to burst and fling seeds when disturbed late in the season. The juice from the stem has traditionally been used to soothe itch and irritation from poison ivy, poison oak, and stinging nettle.

MORE INFORMATION

Wiessner Woods is for day-use hiking, skiing, and snowshoeing only; no camping, fires, mountain bikes, horses, or hunting are permitted. Please respect surrounding private property by parking in the designated lot and observing No Trespassing signs. Keep dogs under control and clean up after them. Please stay on the marked trails to protect plants, nesting sites, and fragile habitats. Wiessner Woods is owned and managed by Stowe Land Trust.

NEARBY

Swim and paddle at Waterbury Center State Park, 11 miles south. The Winooski and Lamoille rivers both have whitewater and flatwater paddling. Camp near a scenic waterfall and swimming hole at Smugglers' Notch State Park, 4 miles northwest. Restaurants and shops are along VT 100 and VT 108 in Stowe, 4 miles southeast.

Catamount Trail, a long-distance cross-country ski trail stretching the length of Vermont, uses the gentle paths of Wiessner Woods on its route through Stowe. Photo courtesy of Stowe Land Trust.

43 BARNES CAMP LOOP

This fun loop features an accessible boardwalk through wetlands with dramatic views of Smugglers' Notch and provides an opportunity to explore sections of the Long Trail without a major time commitment.

Features

Location Stowe, VT

Rating Moderate

Distance 1.5-mile loop

Elevation Gain 390 feet

Estimated Time 1 hour

Maps USGS Stowe

GPS Coordinates 44° 31.97′ N, 72° 47.22′ W

Contact Mount Mansfield State Forest: Vermont Department of Forests, Parks, and Recreation; fpr.vermont.gov. The Long Trail: Green Mountain Club, 4711 Waterbury–Stowe Road, Waterbury Center, VT 05677; 802-244-7037; greenmountainclub.org

DIRECTIONS

From the junction of VT 100 (Main Street) and VT 108 (Mountain Road) in Stowe, head north on VT 108 for 7.7 miles. Park in the hiker parking area on the left (space for more than 100 cars), which is maintained by Stowe Mountain Resort.

TRAIL DESCRIPTION

Barnes Camp Loop was created in 2018, when a mile-long section of the Long Trail was re-routed to travel past the historical Barnes Camp building, which more closely coincides with its original route. Featuring a universally accessible boardwalk, excellent views of Smugglers' Notch, and a steep woodland climb, this loop may be a quick afternoon jaunt, but it's certainly no stroll in the park. The route is best hiked clockwise for a steep ascent and more gradual descent back to your car. Barnes Camp Loop is suitable for kids 6 and up.

From the parking area, carefully cross VT 108 to Barnes Camp Visitor Center. This structure was built 1927 to replace an older logging camp that was destroyed by a fire. At various points, it has been used as a ski dormitory, housing for Green Mountain Club caretakers, and a lodging house for hikers. The visitor center is currently open on weekends and run by Green Mountain Club volunteers.

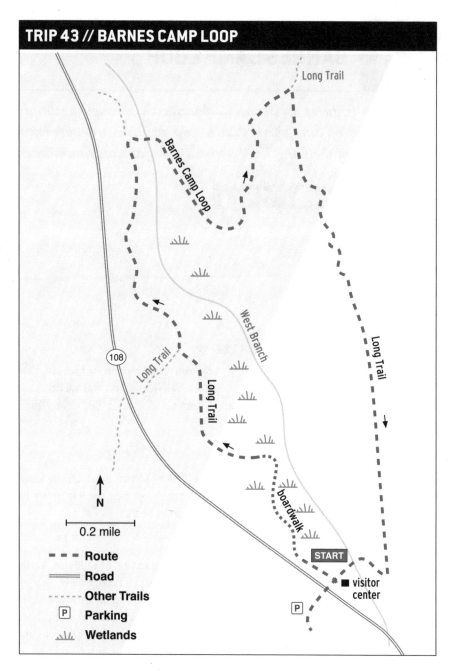

Long Trail

Barnes Camp Loop

West Branch

Long Trail

Long Trail

Long Trail

108

boardwalk

START

visitor center

N

0.2 mile

- - - Route
═══ Road
- - - Other Trails
P Parking
Wetlands

Follow the signs directing you to Long Trail South past a kiosk and onto a universally accessible boardwalk through wetlands along Notch Brook, headwater for the West Branch of Little River. Look for evidence of the many beaver that live and work here; they have shaped a vibrant community of water-loving plants and animals while at the same time protecting the valley from flood damage. Interpretive signs tell you more about the role

One of the authors crosses Little River's West Branch while hiking Barnes Camp Loop.

beaver play in landscaping the valley, and if you're lucky, you may see the industrious critters sliding through the water.

The Barnes Camp boardwalk runs parallel to VT 108 as it travels north into Smugglers' Notch, and the views are worth admiring before heading into the woods. After approximately 600 feet, the boardwalk gives way to a traditional woodland path, part of the 272-mile Long Trail, which is marked by white blazes. The young hardwood forest here is populated with lanky birch, beech, and cherry trees, as well as a lush undergrowth of ferns and hobblebush.

At 0.3 mile, the Long Trail veers left, continuing toward Mount Mansfield's supine ridgeline. Continue straight on Barnes Camp Loop, now blazed with blue. Another trail intersection at 0.5 mile leads to the Smugglers' Notch picnic area with picnic tables, cement fireplaces, and vault toilets. Barnes Camp Loop curves to the right, almost immediately descending a wide wooden ladder and crossing Little River's West Branch. In summer and fall, you can usually rock-hop easily across the stream; use caution when the water is high.

After crossing the stream, the trail ascends steeply, climbing almost 400 feet in a quarter-mile. Catch your breath at 0.8 mile, where blue-blazed Barnes Camp Loop connects once again with the white-blazed Long Trail. Turn right to begin a more gradual descent on gentle switchbacks back to the visitor center. Ignore a short spur that leads to Spruce Peak Resort and follow the trail as it curves right. The narrow path becomes a wide gravel treadway and crosses a footbridge to the back of Barnes Camp Visitor Center.

DID YOU KNOW?

Between 1807 and 1809, the United States outlawed trade with Britain and Canada, eventually leading to the War of 1812. This negatively affected Vermonters whose livelihoods depended on commerce with their Canadian neighbors. Illicit trade continued between Vermont and Canada, and the network of caves through the narrow passageway of the notch here made ideal hiding places for contraband, earning it the name Smugglers' Notch. In later years, Smugglers' Notch hid fugitive slaves en route to freedom in Canada and illegal liquor during Prohibition.

MORE INFORMATION

Mount Mansfield State Forest is managed by the Vermont Department of Forests, Parks, and Recreation. The Green Mountain Club maintains the Long Trail.

NEARBY

Camp at Smugglers' Notch State Park, 1 mile south on VT 108. Swim and paddle at Waterbury Center State Park, 14 miles south. Restaurants and shops are along VT 100 and VT 108 in Stowe, 8 miles southeast.

44 STOWE PINNACLE

Stowe Pinnacle's rocky knob provides dramatic, close-up views of the Worcester Range, Mount Mansfield, and the pastoral Stowe Valley.

Features 🐕 📍 ❄️

Location Stowe, VT

Rating Moderate

Distance 2.8 miles round-trip

Elevation Gain 1,520 feet

Estimated Time 2.5 hours

Maps USGS Stowe

GPS Coordinates 44° 26.19′ N, 72° 40.04′ W

Contact C. C. Putnam State Forest, Vermont Department of Forests, Parks, and Recreation; fpr.vermont.gov. Green Mountain Club, 4711 Waterbury–Stowe Road, Waterbury Center, VT 05677; 802-244-7037; greenmountainclub.org

DIRECTIONS

From the junction of VT 100 (Main Street) and VT 108 (Mountain Road) in Stowe, head north on VT 100 and take the third right onto School Street. After 0.2 mile, when Taber Hill forks left, bear right onto Stowe Hollow Road. After 0.8 mile, at the junction with Covered Bridge Road, go left to stay on Stowe Hollow Road. After another 0.7 mile, when Stowe Hollow Road turns right, stay straight onto Upper Hollow Road. Follow this road 0.6 mile to the parking lot on the left (space for about nine cars), just past Pinnacle Road (also on the left).

TRAIL DESCRIPTION

Stowe Pinnacle (2,610 feet) is a rocky bald spot poking out of the side of the Worcester Range, giving hikers unrivaled views of the high peaks of north-central Vermont. The steepness of the climb makes the short hike vigorous, and the open summit is a good picnic spot. This is a popular outing in a popular resort town, so don't expect solitude, but you can look forward to the wide-open skies and long views usually reserved for higher summits.

From the parking area, Stowe Pinnacle Trail proceeds through an overgrown field before entering woods. Blue blazes mark the route as it ascends gradually over bog bridges and large step stones through maples, white pines, and paper birches. An overgrown rock cairn, continuously built by hikers over the years, sprawls in the middle of the trail at the point where the climb becomes more sustained.

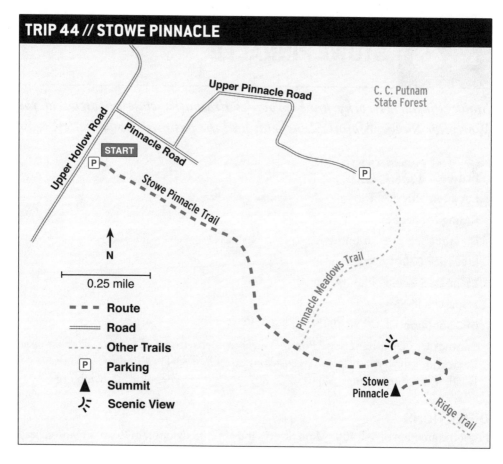

Stowe Pinnacle Trail takes the most direct route up a steep, wooded ridge between two stream valleys. Rock staircases provide a relatively flat treadway on this highly angled route; they prevent erosion and gullying of the trail. At 1.0 mile, catch your breath in a clearing where Pinnacle Meadows Trail leaves to the left. Climb rock steps out of the clearing and follow the blue blazes for Stowe Pinnacle Trail to the right, where an old footpath veers left.

More climbing, and flight after flight of rock steps lead, finally, to a small saddle between two steep slopes. A spur path heads up the left slope to a view of the ridgeline between 4,083-foot Camel's Hump (Trip 27) and 4,393-foot Mount Mansfield (Trips 45 and 46) and of the farm fields and rolling hills of Stowe. Stowe Pinnacle Trail continues straight ahead, curving through beech, hobblebush, and striped maple as it circles behind Stowe Pinnacle. Rock steps lead down briefly before the trail levels across the contour of the hill and then begins to climb again. A hard right turn brings you into woods full of fragrant balsam fir. Wide wooden ladders help with the scramble up vertical ledges. Just before the summit, Ridge Trail (also called Hogback Trail) departs left. Stay on Stowe Pinnacle Trail as the trees open and the views take center stage.

The long ridge of summits before you includes, from south to north, Monroe Skyline, Camel's Hump, Bolton Mountain, Mount Mansfield, Whiteface Mountain, and Belvidere Mountain, as well as Jay Peak on the Canadian border.

Looming to the east, the steep ridge of the Worcester Range (Trip 38) stretches 18 miles between the Lamoille River to the north and the Winooski River to the south. Elmore Mountain (Trip 41) is the somewhat isolated peak on its northern end. Rising steeply from there, the rocky tip of Mount Worcester is one end of the high, densely forested Skyline Trail, which traverses the spine of an unnamed peak before climbing Hogback Mountain and traveling from the wooded north summit of Mount Hunger (Trip 40) to Hunger's bald south summit, not visible from Stowe Pinnacle. A short distance south of Mount Hunger, a thrust of rocky ledges makes up White Rock Mountain (Trip 39). The Worcester Range's large tracts of red spruce and balsam fir subalpine forest support the inconspicuous spruce grouse, the elusive Bicknell's thrush, and one of the boreal forest's savviest hunters, the fisher. On lower slopes, red oak forests feed black bears, and the dense cover of mixed hardwoods provides protection and food for breeding neotropical songbirds, such as wood thrushes.

Follow the trails back downhill to reach your starting point.

DID YOU KNOW?

Gold Brook Covered Bridge, just down the slope from Stowe Pinnacle's trailhead, is reportedly haunted by the ghost of a lovelorn nineteenth-century girl. Read Tim Simard's *Haunted Hikes of Vermont* (PublishingWorks, 2010) for the spooky details.

Stowe Pinnacle offers dramatic views of the Stowe Valley.

MORE INFORMATION

C. C. Putnam State Forest is managed by the Vermont Department of Forests, Parks, and Recreation. To minimize erosion along fragile, high-elevation terrain, the state closes trails in the Worcester Range between mid-April and Memorial Day. The Green Mountain Club helps maintain trails in the Worcester Range.

NEARBY

Swim and paddle at Waterbury Center State Park, 8 miles south. The Winooski and Lamoille rivers have popular whitewater and flatwater paddling. Camp near a scenic waterfall and swimming hole at Smugglers' Notch State Park, 9.5 miles northwest. Restaurants and shops are along VT 100 and VT 108 in Stowe, 4 miles northwest.

45 MOUNT MANSFIELD'S CHIN

The exceptional Sunset Ridge hike to Vermont's highest summit quickly rises above treeline for spectacular vistas and includes a visit to the remarkable Cantilever Rock.

Features ❋ 🏃 🚶 🐴 🔍 ❀ $

Location Underhill, VT

Rating Strenuous

Distance 6.2 miles round-trip

Elevation Gain 2,543 feet

Estimated Time 4.5 hours

Maps USGS Mount Mansfield; Vermont Department of Forests, Parks, and Recreation: vtstateparks.com/assets/pdf/underhilltrails.pdf

GPS Coordinates 44° 31.78′ N, 72° 50.52′ W

Contact Underhill State Park, 352 Mountain Road, Underhill, VT 05490; 802-899-3022; vtstateparks.com/underhill.html. The Long Trail: Green Mountain Club, 4711 Waterbury–Stowe Road, Waterbury Center, VT 05677; 802-244-7037; greenmountainclub.org

DIRECTIONS

From VT 15 east in Underhill Flats, bear right onto River Road, following the sign for Underhill State Park. After 2.7 miles, go straight at the stop sign in Underhill Center onto Pleasant Valley Road. In 0.9 mile, turn right onto Mountain Road and ascend 2.5 miles to the entrance of Underhill State Park. The parking area can accommodate 60 day-hiker vehicles in addition to overnight campers. (Winter hikers: Park at a plowed area partway up Mountain Road and add 3.0 miles to the hike, making this a full-day adventure.)

TRAIL DESCRIPTION

Mount Mansfield's easily recognizable summit ridge looks like a profile in repose. From the Forehead (3,940 feet) at the south end, over the craggy Nose (4,060 feet) dotted with transmitter towers, to its highest point at the Chin (4,393 feet), and down to the Adam's Apple (4,060 feet) at the north end, the ridge stretches 2.5 miles. The high-elevation ridgeline supports the biggest patch of rare alpine tundra in Vermont (see "The Sparse Tundra of Vermont," page 197), but to the peril of those delicate plants, more than 40,000 visitors explore Mount Mansfield each year.

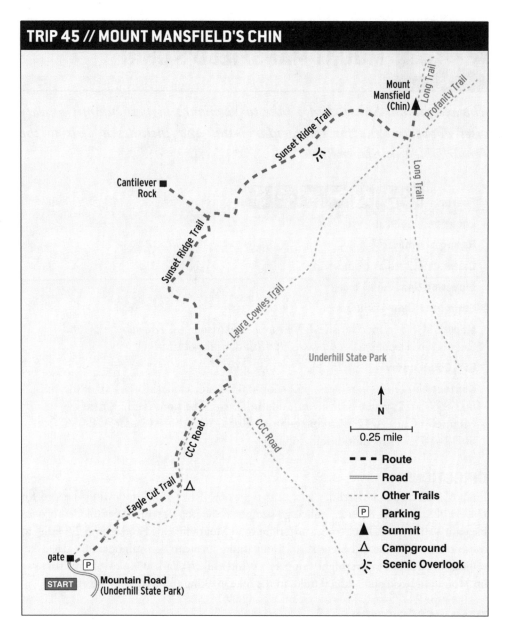

Sunset Ridge, which ascends from the valley to Mount Mansfield's Chin, is a favorite of day-hikers for good reasons: it is one of the easier ascents (its strenuous rating comes more from overall distance and time than from hiking difficulty), and its relatively quick arrival on open rock means the awe-inspiring views are part of the journey, not just the reward at the summit. While this trek may be too ambitious for kids younger than 10, the shorter trips to Cantilever Rock or onto the open rock of lower Sunset Ridge are excellent destinations on their own merits.

After paying a day-use fee and getting the day's high-elevation forecast at the ranger station, follow blue-blazed Eagle Cut Trail up a gentle pitch for 0.3 mile, crossing CCC Road three times before turning left onto it at the fourth encounter. Follow CCC Road for 0.4 mile to a clearing with a kiosk; turn left and cross a bridge to begin ascending blue-blazed Sunset Ridge Trail. After 0.1 mile, Laura Cowles Trail departs to the right; stay left on Sunset Ridge Trail. The wide, rocky treadway heads north across the flank of the mountain, climbing moderately. After a small clearing, the trail gets steeper, passing cascades and an elephant-sized glacial erratic.

At 0.7 mile, the spur path to Cantilever Rock heads left. Follow it into a damp, dense conifer forest, scrambling between moss-covered boulders. In 0.2 mile, a cliff towers over a narrow canyon. Stuck in a high crack, Cantilever Rock juts 30 feet into open air above your head (thus the name). This schist column likely ended up here due to ice and water eroding fractures in the cliff, causing occasional and sometimes drastic movement. Climb the huge boulder beneath the rock to get a view of Camel's Hump (Trip 27).

Return to Sunset Ridge Trail and continue climbing through a more challenging section weaving through boulders and rocky gullies. The fragrance of balsam fir marks your arrival in the primarily coniferous forest above 2,700 feet.

Climb from a narrow gully onto open rock. The view is incredible, especially the long ridge of Mount Mansfield looming steeply above. Minuscule hikers pick their way across the rocks between the Nose and the Chin. A large bulb of rock ahead appears to be the top of Sunset Ridge. This is the West Chin, which is closed to hiking for alpine revegetation; the summit proper is behind it. Crossing bands of rock and stunted, bent trees, you may notice lengths of thin, white string at ankle height. These subtle guides help define the route and keep boot soles off fragile vegetation; please respect the tenuous existence of rare alpine plants by stepping only on rock.

After traversing beneath the West Chin, Sunset Ridge Trail passes the top of Laura Cowles Trail and continues to the ridgeline, ending at the Long Trail. Turn left, following the white blazes of the Long Trail north. Pass Profanity Trail—a steep, 0.5-mile bad-weather bypass of the Chin—on your right and climb a rock gully to the summit. The views from here are panoramic, as you might expect when standing on the highest point in Vermont. The Adirondacks cut a jagged line across the western horizon, high above Lake Champlain. Camel's Hump (4,083 feet) is the tallest point in a sea of high peaks to the south. The Worcester Range (Trip 38) stretches across the valley to the east, while just north of the Chin, across the rugged gap of Smugglers' Notch, Spruce Peak leads your gaze northward over Madonna Peak to Whiteface Mountain.

Return the way you came up.

DID YOU KNOW?

You may hear occasional loud booms while hiking here. Some say that's the wampahoofus, a legendary creature that lives on Mount Mansfield and whose legs evolved to be shorter on one side of its body than the other due to always walking across the steep hillside. (Others say that the booming is from the Ethan Allen Firing Range in nearby Jericho.)

Hikers crossing Mount Mansfield's long, rugged, above-treeline ridge help protect delicate, rare tundra plants by walking only on rocks and plank bridges.

MORE INFORMATION

In the alpine zone, walk only on rock and keep dogs leashed. The Underhill State Park office is open from Memorial Day to mid-October, 9 A.M. to 9 P.M. daily; use self-pay envelopes before 9 A.M. The Long Trail is maintained by the Green Mountain Club.

NEARBY

Underhill Center has a small store; dining options are on VT 15 in Jericho, 10 miles west. The Bentley Museum in Jericho exhibits some of the 5,000 snowflake photographs made by Wilson "Snowflake" Bentley after 1885, when he discovered how to photograph a single snow crystal.

46 MOUNT MANSFIELD'S FOREHEAD

Mount Mansfield's craggy Forehead requires hikers to slither through cracks and scramble along the edges of cliffs, rewarding bravery and agility with access to this special rocky dome.

Features

Location Underhill and Stowe, VT

Rating Strenuous

Distance 5.2-mile loop

Elevation Gain 2,520 feet

Estimated Time 4.5 hours

Maps USGS Mount Mansfield; Vermont Department of Forests, Parks, and Recreation: vtstateparks.com/assets/pdf/stevensville-trail.pdf

GPS Coordinates 44° 30.34′ N, 72° 50.83′ W

Contact Vermont Department of Forests, Parks, and Recreation (fpr.vermont.gov). Green Mountain Club, 4711 Waterbury–Stowe Road, Waterbury Center, VT 05677; 802-244-7037; greenmountainclub.org

DIRECTIONS

From VT 15 east in Underhill Flats, bear right onto River Road. After 2.7 miles, go straight at the stop sign in Underhill Center onto Pleasant Valley Road. In 0.3 mile, turn right onto Stevensville Road and drive 2.6 miles to its end in the trailhead parking lot (space for twenty cars).

TRAIL DESCRIPTION

Mount Mansfield's Forehead (3,940 feet) is at the southern end of the 2.5-mile-long ridge of Vermont's tallest mountain. This mound of ledges and krummholz provides technically challenging hiking and sometimes requires steel nerves. Although leashed dogs are allowed, think twice before inviting four-legged friends along, as the trail includes ladders, steep slabs, and sheer dropoffs. This is not a route for children. A bad-weather bypass trail avoids the hairiest parts of the Forehead via a more typical woods route without exposure, but it passes 0.3 mile beyond the Forehead and the downhill route used in this description. That bypass on the east side of the ridge and Wampahoofus Trail on the west side are the best choices in wet or icy weather, as well as smarter routes for hikers with dogs, big backpacks, a fear of heights, or a lack of interest in crawling and scooting as part of their outing. The rewards of making it up the Forehead on a nice day are an exhilarating view and the adrenaline rush of a thrilling climb. Check the summit weather forecast before you go; the

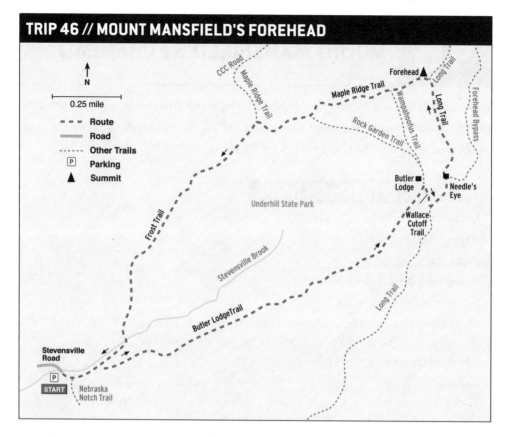

air will be cooler, winds stronger, and chance of precipitation greater on the ridgeline than in the valley. This lollipop route can be taken in either direction, but whichever way you choose has steep ascents and descents on open slabs.

From the parking area, pass a kiosk and the beginning of Nebraska Notch Trail, which heads off to the right, and follow signs for Butler Lodge Trail. Walk on a woods road alongside Stevensville Brook, going around a metal gate and over a bridge before following markers to the left, leaving the old road and arriving at the junction of Frost Trail and Butler Lodge Trail at 0.3 mile. Go right to stay on blue-blazed Butler Lodge Trail, climbing away from the stream through hardwoods, ferns, and hobblebushes. The trail ascends steadily up a gentle ridgeline, occasionally providing glimpses of the looming spine of the Green Mountains through gaps in the canopy. At 1.1 miles, the woods shift to higher-elevation spruce and fir, and the trail becomes rocky and climbs several ledges. At 1.9 miles, arrive at Butler Lodge, a Green Mountain Club cabin in a dramatic setting beneath the cliffs of the Forehead. This is the last water source until almost the end of the hike.

Wampahoofus Trail cuts west behind the cabin, providing a 0.6-mile alternate route to Maple Ridge Trail by crossing beneath the Forehead on a scramble around boulders. To continue uphill to the Forehead, backtrack 75 feet on Butler Lodge Trail and find Wallace Cutoff on your left (on the right, coming uphill into the lodge clearing). Follow blue-blazed

Wallace Cutoff 0.1 mile through open, pretty balsam fir woods up to the ridgeline, meeting the white-blazed Long Trail and turning north (left) onto it.

At 2.2 miles, squeeze through a low tunnel between two boulders—a tight spot called the Needle's Eye—and arrive at the Forehead Bypass junction on your right; this is the east side bad-weather route that ends on the Long Trail 0.3 mile north of the Forehead. Go left, continuing on the Long Trail northbound and climbing the first of numerous ledges in the next 0.5 mile to the top of the Forehead.

Just 0.1 mile past the Needle's Eye, the Long Trail traverses boulders along the edge of a steep drop directly above Butler Lodge, requiring some scrambling, squeezing, and bravery. This is the most exposure on the hike, and once you're past it, climbing ladders and steep slabs feels almost tame. Views extend east and west, as well as south behind you, as you climb northward. The open rock faces and low vegetation on the Forehead's south side feel as remote and wild as it's possible to get on this popular and developed mountain. Enjoy a break here before reaching the highest point of the Forehead at 2.8 miles, which is anticlimactic, with views of cell towers and a cluster of summit signs, and the lack of a 360-degree view.

Turn left down Maple Ridge Trail from the summit, and quickly descend from the ridgeline on a steep, open slab. Take in the stunning views of Mount Mansfield's ridge, extending north to the massive Chin, and the expansive west shore of Vermont along the shining waters of Lake Champlain in front of you. Maple Ridge Trail drops precipitously at times and can be

The hike to Mount Mansfield's Forehead is not for everyone: Ladders and precipices require steel nerves, agility, and a backpack small enough that it won't throw you off-balance.

as tricky as the Forehead in bad weather. (Wampahoofus Trail heads left to Butler Lodge just 0.2 mile below the Forehead, or 3.0 miles into the hike, providing a less exposed alternate route downhill. Rock Garden Trail does the same 0.4 mile below, but by that time, you've covered the steepest downhill terrain.) Continue on Maple Ridge Trail over alternately open and forested stretches, sometimes zigzagging across the ridge, sometimes climbing into and out of gullies. At 3.6 miles, turn left onto Frost Trail, continuing through open terrain and low trees until finally dropping into the forest. Come alongside the wide Stevensville Brook and then cross it and return to the junction of Butler Lodge Trail at 4.9 miles. Descend from the woods on Butler Lodge Trail (a woods road) and return to the trailhead the way you came.

DID YOU KNOW?

New England's famously changeable weather is due to many storm tracks that cross North America, west to east and south to north, and converge over the Northeast, creating turbulent and quickly changing conditions. Mountains amplify the effect, obstructing the airflow and increasing its speed, the same way rivers become rapid when constricted. Mount Mansfield's ridgeline shows the impact of these high winds in its flag trees, with branches that grow only on the leeward side.

MORE INFORMATION

In the alpine zone, walk only on rock and keep dogs leashed. These trails are maintained by the Vermont Department of Forests, Parks, and Recreation and by the Green Mountain Club.

NEARBY

Underhill Center has a small store; dining options are on VT 15 in Jericho, 8 miles west, and in Essex Junction, 15 miles west. VT 108, 12 miles north, is a twisty, wildly scenic, seasonal drive through Smugglers' Notch on the north side of Mount Mansfield (not for RVs or vehicles pulling trailers due to its very tight switchbacks around boulders). On the east side of the mountain, Stowe, 31 miles east via VT 108 (closed in winter), or 38.4 miles in winter via VT 15, has many shops and restaurants, including Vermont-style fine dining in the summit building under Mount Mansfield's Chin, reachable by gondola ride or by hiking. Essex and Stowe offer excellent mountain-bike trails. Swim in Jeff Falls or Bingham Falls, both along VT 108 on either side of Smugglers' Notch. Camp at Underhill State Park, 4.4 miles away.

THE SPARSE TUNDRA OF VERMONT

Most hikers know that climbing a mountain is similar to traveling north: the air gets cooler, the winds get stronger, and the trees get shorter and then disappear altogether as the tundra begins. The word *tundra* conjures images of arctic places—Alaska, perhaps, or Canada. But peaks that rise higher than 4,000 feet in New England exhibit the same extreme conditions. Vermont has three of these special arctic alpine zones: one each on Mount Mansfield, Camel's Hump, and Mount Abraham.

The plants you most often see on Vermont's highest windswept peaks are grassy-looking sedges and lichens spreading over the rocks. In spring, dwarf wildflowers add splashes of color. The word *krummholz*, meaning "crooked wood," refers to the dense mats of stunted, bent spruce and fir trees on these peaks that look more like creeping shrubs than proper trees.

Some of the plants that live above treeline in New England are arctic plants that don't occur anywhere else in the contiguous United States. They are therefore designated rare and, in some cases, threatened or endangered. These plants are adapted to the harsh life above treeline: they grow low to the ground in clusters that are designed to retain warmth and moisture; they absorb water from fog as well as from precipitation; and they photosynthesize in low light to make the most of the brief season when they aren't under a cap of snow and ice.

That these plants are hardy is obvious; what isn't so easily observed is how fragile they are. While tundra plants have adapted to withstand harsh conditions, they are not equipped to survive being trod on by people wearing hiking boots. Imagine a lawn of Bigelow's sedge, a grassy alpine plant that forms appealing meadows across open summits. When a patch of sedge is killed, its roots no longer stabilize the thin soil, and strong summit winds blow the soil away. This hole in the vegetation is now susceptible to further erosion at its exposed edges, and what started as a small patch of damage can spread quickly.

Be sensitive to the challenges of life on these harsh summits and keep your feet on the rocks or the trail. If you're hiking on Mount Abraham (Trip 25), Camel's Hump (Trip 27), or Mount Mansfield (Trips 45 and 46), take time to speak with the Green Mountain Club's summit caretakers to learn more about the fragile natural communities on the summits.

47 STERLING POND

This scenic hike leads around a high mountain lake perched above the steep cliffs of Smugglers' Notch.

Features

Location Cambridge, VT

Rating Moderate

Distance 3.3-mile loop

Elevation Gain 1,320 feet

Estimated Time 3 hours

Maps USGS Mount Mansfield; Vermont Department of Forests, Parks, and Recreation: vtstateparks.com/assets/pdf/smuggstrails.pdf

GPS Coordinates 44° 33.39′ N, 72° 47.63′ W

Contact Green Mountain Club, 4711 Waterbury–Stowe Road, Waterbury Center, VT 05677; 802-244-7037; greenmountainclub.org.

DIRECTIONS

From the junction of VT 100 and VT 108 (Mountain Road, closed in winter) in Stowe, turn onto VT 108. Go 9.5 miles to the visitor center parking area on the left (space for twenty cars), just beyond the height-of-land in Smugglers' Notch. (The final mile is a narrow roadway with switchbacks around enormous boulders and is not passable by recreational vehicles or buses. VT 108 is closed beyond the ski area in winter; add 4.0 miles for a 7.3-mile winter hike.)

TRAIL DESCRIPTION

Sterling Pond rests in a thickly forested alpine basin between Spruce Peak (3,330 feet) and Madonna Peak (3,610 feet), both of which host ski areas. The spring-fed pond is a small refuge of beauty between these high-mountain developments. The hike to Sterling Pond Shelter is relatively short and quite popular, but if you loop around the far side of the pond, you are likely to find some solitude on the craggy slopes before descending. Although the destination is appealing to children of all ages, the climb is steep in places and most enjoyable for kids 8 and older.

Sterling Pond Trail begins opposite the visitor center and ascends the east wall of Smugglers' Notch. A steep flight of rock steps climbs directly up and then turns north to cross a gully. Blue blazes lead to a break in the trees and a view of 1,000-foot cliffs across the narrow valley. These awe-inspiring crags were exposed by mile-thick glaciers that plowed

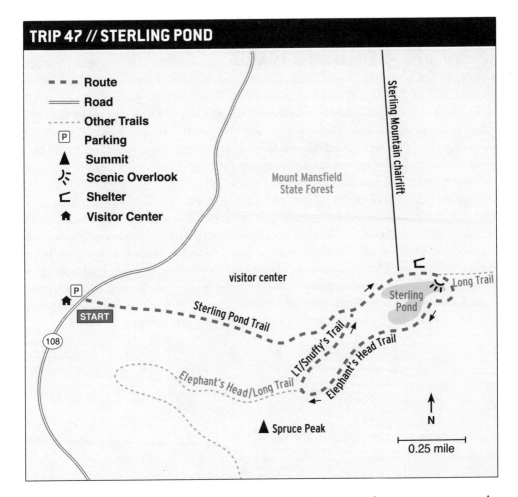

Legend:
- - - Route
===== Road
····· Other Trails
P Parking
▲ Summit
Scenic Overlook
⊏ Shelter
♠ Visitor Center

Mount Mansfield State Forest

Sterling Mountain chairlift

visitor center

Sterling Pond Trail

Sterling Pond

Long Trail

LT/Snuffy's Trail

Elephant's Head Trail

Elephant's Head/Long Trail

108

START

▲ Spruce Peak

N

0.25 mile

through the notch for thousands of years, gouging and scraping their massive way southward. Today, landslides and toppling rocks are part of the normal geomorphic activities shaping the notch.

Sterling Pond Trail traverses the steep hillside above the notch for a short distance and then turns up a drainage. Moderate pitches of the rooty dirt trail are interspersed with sections of steep rock steps and stream crossings. In the dense spruce–fir forest on the upper section of Sterling Pond Trail, look and listen for high-mountain inhabitants. Red squirrels erupt in sudden annoyed chatter and leave piles of plucked spruce-cone scales; white-throated sparrows call *old Sam Peabody-Peabody-Peabody*. In winter, snowshoe hares leave oblong tracks in the snow, and fisher prints show five distinct toes.

At 1.0 mile, Sterling Pond Trail tops out at a wide swath of cleared forest. This is Snuffy's, a service road and ski trail, as well as part of the Long Trail. Turn left, following the Long Trail's white blazes north 0.1 mile to Sterling Pond. Rock-studded soil rims the western shore, giving an open view across the water to the ridge of Madonna Peak. Be sure dogs are leashed in this sensitive area.

Continue north on the Long Trail, crossing a log bridge at the pond's outlet and climbing onto a ridge above the water. The trail weaves through thick shoreline woods and then ascends from the pond to traverse a wide, grassy opening. Stay straight, reentering the woods and climbing to the top of the Sterling Mountain chairlift. Find white blazes on the opposite side of the lift and continue through the woods to Sterling Pond Shelter at 1.3 miles. From the shelter's southeast corner, pick up blue-blazed Elephant's Head Trail and follow it downhill to a fork. Turn right for a view across the pond to Mount Mansfield's steep ridge, and then return and take the left fork to continue your hike. (This would be a good turnaround point for hikers who are losing steam, as there is a fair bit of climbing in the next 0.7 mile to rejoin the Long Trail.)

Elephant's Head Trail circles the eastern end of the pond and follows the southern shore over rough, rooty terrain before ascending from the pond, weaving through huge, mossy boulders, and crossing slabs with footholds chipped into the rock. After a scramble beneath an overhang and through a narrow notch of rock, the ascent finishes steeply. This is the highest point of the hike. Pass through a hollow before meeting the Long Trail again. Elephant's Head Trail continues straight and descends steeply into Smugglers' Notch. Go right, following the Long Trail north and downhill for 0.3 mile of easy walking to the top of Sterling Pond Trail. Turn left here, descending the way you came up.

A hiker relaxes after climbing the steep trail to Sterling Pond.

DID YOU KNOW?

Stands of paper birch often indicate old debris slides because these trees colonize disturbed soil. Sterling Pond Trail passes through an evenly aged white birch stand that is believed to have taken root after a destructive 1938 storm.

MORE INFORMATION

Sterling Pond's trails and shelter are maintained by the Green Mountain Club.

NEARBY

Camp at Smugglers' Notch State Park, 3.1 miles south, across the road from scenic Bingham Falls, which is a good location for a picnic and a swim. The Lamoille River, 8 miles north, has whitewater and flatwater paddling options. Shops and restaurants are along VT 108 south and on VT 100 in Stowe, 9.5 miles south.

48 PROSPECT ROCK

This small cliff provides panoramic views of the Lamoille River's braided channels and the high peaks rising steeply beyond them.

Features

Location Johnson, VT

Rating Easy to Moderate

Distance 3 miles round-trip

Elevation Gain 540 feet

Estimated Time 2 hours

Maps USGS Johnson

GPS Coordinates 44° 38.70′ N, 72° 43.70′ W

Contact Green Mountain Club, 4711 Waterbury–Stowe Road, Waterbury Center, VT 05677; 802-244-7037; greenmountainclub.org

DIRECTIONS

From downtown Johnson, follow VT 15 west 2.7 miles to the Long Trail parking lot on the right (space for about fifteen cars).

TRAIL DESCRIPTION

Prospect Rock is an open ledge jutting out of the trees above the pastoral Lamoille River valley. This hike passes through a lovely, diverse forest, and the rock is broad enough to accommodate numerous picnic blankets. The ascent is vigorous but short enough for kids 8 and older to accomplish. Because you need to cross a side channel of the Lamoille River 0.4 mile into the hike, where high water could stop you in your tracks, check the river level before hiking by driving to the Long Trail crossing on Hogback Road (which meets VT 15 about 1 mile east of the parking area). There used to be trailhead parking here, at the Hogback Road/Long Trail crossing, but parking is discouraged on the shoulders here.

Peregrine falcons often nest on Prospect Rock's cliffs. In recent years, the overlook has been closed between April 15 and August 1. Check with Audubon Vermont (vt.audubon.org) or the Vermont Fish and Wildlife Department (vtfishandwildlife.com/watch-wildlife/tips-for-protecting-wildlife/cliffs-closed-to-protect-peregrine-falcons) for up-to-date trail closings before planning your hike.

From the parking area alongside VT 15, head north on the white-blazed Long Trail across a field and into the woods, being mindful of the scattered patches of poison ivy. Walk 0.4 mile on gently rolling terrain to the bank of the Lamoille River. If the water is low enough to cross safely, descend via a short ladder to the first channel and cross to an island where an

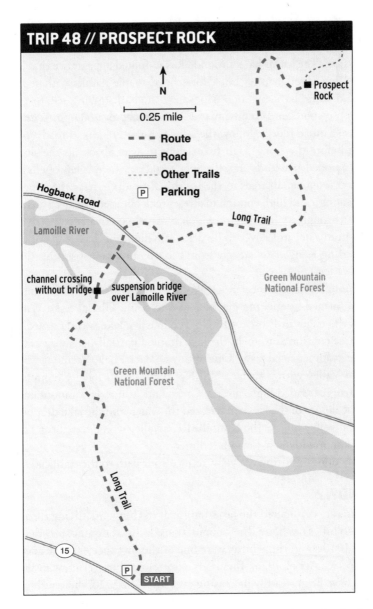

■ Prospect
Rock

N

0.25 mile

- - - **Route**
═══ **Road**
······ **Other Trails**
P **Parking**

Hogback Road

Lamoille River

Long Trail

channel crossing
without bridge ■

suspension bridge
over Lamoille River

Green Mountain
National Forest

Green Mountain
National Forest

Long Trail

15

P START

impressive suspension bridge provides dry footing over the main channel. Climb to Hogback Road and find the continuation of the Long Trail on the opposite side, heading uphill, away from the river. Ascend a steep pitch on a wide path through mixed hardwoods and soft-woods, followed by a couple of switchbacks across the hill and another climb. The Long Trail continues this pattern of climbing steeply, traversing a hill, and climbing again for most of the rest of the 1.5-mile distance between Hogback Road and Prospect Rock.

The craggy, southwestern-facing hillside supports a diverse forest at this elevation: hemlock, red oak, spruce, fir, birch, black cherry, red pine, red maple, and striped maple. Some striped maples have grown large here—to about 8 inches in diameter and 30 feet tall—for a species that grows very slowly. Striped maples are shade tolerant, so they often form the understory in mixed hardwood forests of the Northeast. Because they grow mostly in the shade, their leaves are large, 5 to 7 inches long and wide, allowing them to catch as much sunlight as possible. The leaves have a rounded, web-footed appearance that lends this tree the nickname "goosefoot maple." Look for striped maple trunks with sections of their pretty green-and-white bark missing. Moose eat the bark (giving rise to the additional nicknames "moosewood" and "moose maple"), as do rabbits, porcupines, and deer.

Climbing into a broad saddle, follow the faint remnants of an old road along the side of Prospect Rock before the Long Trail turns right to switchback up the slope onto drier ground. A flat, wooded area leads onto the open terraces, where a view opens broadly to the southwest and through small trees to the south. Use caution near the edges of the rock, which is steep enough and high enough to attract rock climbers. Below, the Lamoille River meanders west through its floodplain, which is largely cultivated. The river extends 85 miles from its headwater in Glover to its delta in Milton, on Lake Champlain. The long ridge of the Sterling Range rises steeply from the river and points southeast to Whiteface Mountain (3,714 feet).

If you were standing on Prospect Rock about 13,000 years ago, you would have looked out over a lake formed by melting glaciers. At one point, Glacial Lake Winooski would have lapped at the edges of Prospect Rock. The massive lake was dammed by retreating glaciers; as the ice continued to melt, the lake drained partially, creating a series of subsequently lower-elevation glacial lakes. One of these, Glacial Lake Vermont, stretched across the Champlain Valley with a surface 500 feet higher than Lake Champlain's is today. Long, watery arms extended high into the Green and Adirondack mountains until a sudden catastrophic failure of the ice dam released the water, and the lake dropped 300 feet in just a few days, possibly hours. The Lamoille River valley would have been revealed at that time, covered with muddy lake-bottom sediment.

When you are done admiring the view, retrace your path to the trailhead.

DID YOU KNOW?

Peregrine falcons are considered the fastest animals in the world, diving through the air at speeds up to 240 miles per hour. Their populations declined significantly due to DDT use beginning the 1940s, and these birds were one of the first species to be added under the Endangered Species Act of 1973. They were reintroduced to Vermont in the 1980s, and their numbers have been steadily increasing ever since. In 2020, there were more than 55 nesting pairs of peregrine falcons in Vermont. During the falcon breeding season, between April 15 and August 1 each year, cliff access for visitors at Prospect Rock and other sites is restricted to ensure the success of peregrine falcon families.

MORE INFORMATION

The Long Trail is maintained by the Green Mountain Club.

Prospect Rock overlooks the valley floodplains of the Lamoille River and the mountains of Sterling Range.

NEARBY

The Lamoille River is popular for paddling, and the multiple waterfalls along the Gihon River in Johnson, 2.5 miles east, give steep-creek kayakers a wild run. Jeff Falls on the Brewster River along VT 108 in Jeffersonville, 9 miles west, is a clear, pretty swimming hole (public access on private property). Smugglers' Notch State Park has camping, 16.7 miles southwest. Smugglers' Notch Resort, 13.5 miles southwest, has outdoor activities year-round. Restaurants and shops are along VT 15 in Johnson, 1.5 miles east.

49 DEVIL'S GULCH AND BIG MUDDY POND

Two beautiful ponds, a boulder-strewn ravine, and a camp on a high perch keep this hike varied and interesting from beginning to end.

Features 🧍💧🛶📐❄️

Location Eden, VT

Rating Moderate

Distance 5.2-mile loop

Elevation Gain 1,000 feet

Estimated Time 4 hours

Maps USGS Hazens Notch, USGS Eden

GPS Coordinates 44° 45.84′ N, 72° 35.27′ W

Contact Long Trail and Spruce Ledge Camp: Green Mountain Club, 4711 Waterbury–Stowe Road, Waterbury Center, VT 05677; 802-244-7037; greenmountainclub.org. Babcock Trail: Babcock Nature Preserve, Northern Vermont University, 337 College Hill, Johnson, VT; 800-635-2356; northernvermont .edu/student-life/activities-and-events/outdoors/johnson-outdoor-adventures

DIRECTIONS

From the junction of VT 100 and VT 118, go north on VT 118 for 4.6 miles. Just after a left curve, turn right into the Long Trail State Forest parking lot (space for about twelve cars).

TRAIL DESCRIPTION

The Green Mountains landscape on the southwest side of Belvidere Mountain is rumpled and gullied, with pockets of water between steep-sided hills and heaps of boulders beneath the cliffs that calved them. The Long Trail and Babcock Trail make a lollipop loop through this enchanting location, navigating boulders in Devil's Gulch, climbing to a lovely camp and overlook on Spruce Ledge, and traversing the shoreline of Big Muddy Pond (more scenic than it sounds). With a lot to see in a relatively short distance, this is a fun hike for kids 8 and older. The rolling route has multiple ascents and descents, and the overall elevation gain is about 1,000 feet, but it comes in small chunks. Although many Long Trail thru-hikers have scrambled through Devil's Gulch with their canine companions, the slippery rock pile at the head of the ravine is challenging for most dogs.

From the parking lot, climb a short trail to VT 118 and cross carefully on this blind curve, heading slightly left to find the white-blazed continuation of the southbound Long

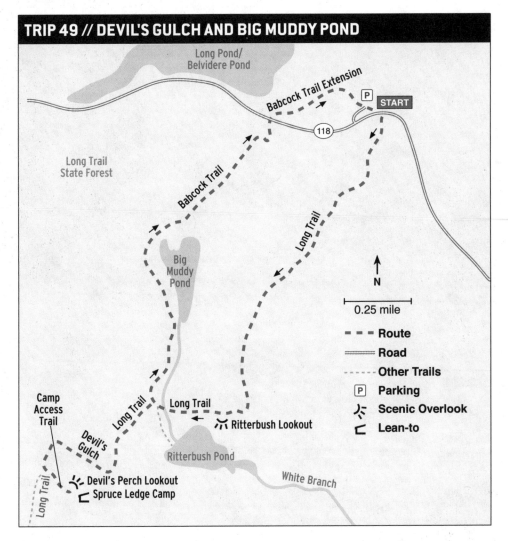

Trail. The path rises for 0.4 mile and then meanders along a pleasant wooded ridge for 0.5 mile, eventually descending along the right side of a stream ravine. As the trail begins a more noticeable descent, Ritterbush Lookout appears at 1.3 miles, with a view of Ritterbush Pond beneath a steep, wooded hillside. From here, the Long Trail descends steeply on multiple sets of rock steps, dropping to the hike's lowest point (1,100 feet) at the junction with Babcock Trail at 1.7 miles. The Long Trail continues straight across this intersection, with Babcock Trail rising to the right. An unidentified extension of Babcock Trail drops down a gully to the left.

Continue on the Long Trail across the hillside, where the landscape gets really interesting. Approaching a stream plummeting from a mossy gully, the trail bends right and ascends a log ladder. The path snakes between boulders and ledges to the entrance of Devil's Gulch at 2.1 miles, where enormous slabs of rock lean against one another like a massive

A backpacker traverses the top of the rock pile at the head of Devil's Gulch, a narrow, craggy canyon that is one of several highlights on this hike through varied terrain. Photo by Jerry Monkman.

house of cards. Pass under this rock A-frame and enter a mossy, drippy canyon. Sheer rock walls soar up to 70 feet high, undercut in large arcs where chunks of rock fell to the damp floor of the ravine. A line of bog bridges leads to the head of the short gully, which is choked by rockfall. Navigate the boulders, taking care on their slick surfaces. Suddenly, about 0.1 mile after entering the gulch, you are out of it and climbing gradually along the left side of a gentle valley.

Curving left, the trail steepens and follows a stream up to a junction. Turn left onto the spur path to Spruce Ledge Camp, climbing a ridgeline before dropping to an attractive little cabin at 2.6 miles. Just beyond, a log bench perches atop a steep drop—watch children and dogs carefully here—giving a broad view of Belvidere Mountain and a slice of Ritterbush Pond.

From Spruce Ledge Camp, retrace your steps 0.9 mile back through Devil's Gulch to the Babcock Trail/Long Trail junction. Go left on Babcock Trail, climbing steadily northward out of the valley along a rocky, blue-blazed path. The outlet of Big Muddy Pond appears through the trees 0.4 mile from the junction. As you skirt the western shore, look for signs of beaver. At the far end of the pond, Babcock Trail climbs out of the basin and traverses a narrow height-of-land. From here, 0.7 mile of mostly moderate descent leads to VT 118. Cross the road and continue northeast on the 0.4-mile Babcock Trail Extension, which passes a cellar hole and briefly follows a dirt road before returning to a footpath. The trail rises to parallel the dirt drive and then climbs to the parking lot.

DID YOU KNOW?

In the hollows deep under the boulders of Devil's Gulch, winter ice is sheltered and melts slowly through spring and early summer, keeping the ravine pleasantly ventilated. You may even feel cool breezes.

MORE INFORMATION

The Long Trail and Spruce Ledge Camp are maintained by the Green Mountain Club. Babcock Trail is within Babcock Nature Preserve, owned by Northern Vermont University.

NEARBY

Paddle on Long Pond (also called Belvidere Pond), 0.5 mile west. Camp, paddle, and swim at Green River Reservoir State Park, 20 miles southeast. A general store is on VT 100 in Eden, 4.6 miles southeast, and restaurants and shops are in Johnson, 14 miles south.

50 LARAWAY LOOKOUT

Dramatic rock overhangs, multiple stream crossings, and stunning southwest views make this secluded hike delightful in both summer and winter.

Features

Location Johnson, VT

Rating Moderate

Distance 3.9 miles round-trip

Elevation Gain 1,400 feet

Estimated Time 2.5 hours

Maps USGS Johnson

GPS Coordinates 44° 42.50′ N, 72° 42.80′ W

Contact The Long Trail: Green Mountain Club, 4711 Waterbury–Stowe Road, Waterbury Center, VT 05677; 802-244-7037; greenmountainclub.org. Long Trail State Forest: Vermont Department of Forest, Parks, and Recreation, District 4, Barre Office; 5 Perry Street, Suite 20, Barre, VT 05641; 802-476-0170; fpr.vermont.gov

DIRECTIONS

From downtown Johnson, follow VT 15 west for 1.6 miles and turn right onto Hogback Road. Drive 4.6 miles to the end of Hogback Road and turn right at the stop sign onto VT 109. In 2.2 miles, turn right onto Codding Hollow Road and follow it for 2.5 miles. A parking lot is on the right (space for fifteen cars). An overflow parking area sits 0.1 mile farther on Codding Hollow Road. The trail is plowed for winter use.

TRAIL DESCRIPTION

Unlike most mountain hikes, where the summit is the star, the summit of Laraway Mountain (2,795 feet) is not the main attraction here. Instead, this trek brings you just shy of the summit to a rock outcropping with far-reaching mountain vistas. The hike to Laraway Lookout on the Long Trail is a delight for the senses. The trail crosses several symphonic streams, climbs through a mixed hardwood forest carpeted with wildflowers, and hugs several imposing cliffs decorated with wild columbines in summer and massive ice formations in winter. The climb ends with a dramatic southwest vista that you'll likely have all to yourself. Kids older than 8 will enjoy the interesting features of this climb.

Turn right out of the parking area and walk along a rutted dirt road. Pass the junction with the southbound Long Trail on the right and follow the signs to the Long Trail north

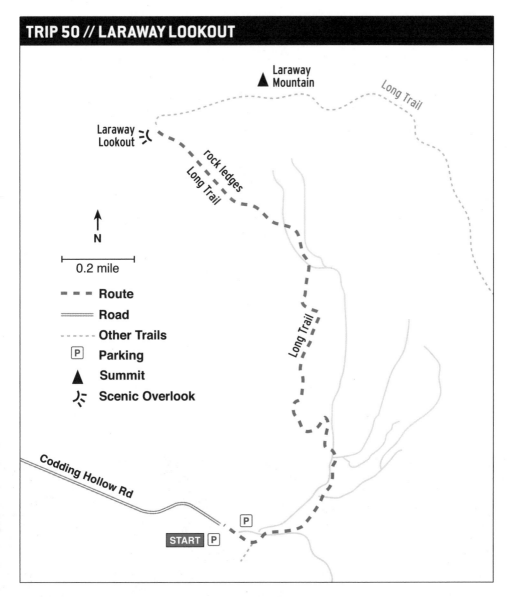

through the overflow parking area and into the woods. The trail begins on an old logging road in a dark, open hemlock forest interspersed with sugar maples, beeches, and yellow birches. Shade-tolerant hemlocks happily live under the canopy of hardwoods for decades or more before overtaking them as the dominant species. Because of their adaptability, hemlocks can live up to 1,000 years.

Follow white blazes as the trail begins to climb gently, traversing small, picturesque streams on well-placed rocks. It zigzags a bit as it gains in elevation, leaving the hemlocks behind and entering a hardwood forest dominated by beeches and sugar maples. In late spring, the ground is carpeted with wildflowers—yellow violets, trout lilies, red trillium, common wood sorrel, foamflower, and wild columbine.

The ascent is interspersed with short, flat sections, giving you ample time to enjoy the peaceful surroundings as you walk up the side of the ridge. Make the fifth and final stream crossing at 1.3 miles before climbing to a wooded ridge. From here, the trail levels off again and the surroundings become more dramatic: massive, overhanging cliffs drip with moisture in summer and immense collections of glistening icicles in winter. Indeed, this is one of those rare hikes that can be busier in the winter months, as hikers gather to check out the fascinating ice formations that look different from day to day.

After admiring the last massive rock formations, climb the short distance to Laraway Lookout to enjoy views to the west and south. This small rock outcropping is framed with fragrant spruce and balsam trees, with room for six happy hikers. On a clear day, you can see Lake Champlain sparkling in the distance, with the Adirondacks rising from the western shore. Prominent peaks include New York's tallest mountain, Mount Marcy (5,343 feet); Algonquin Peak; and Whiteface Mountain. Southwestern views feature Mount Mansfield, Spruce Peak, and Madonna Peak.

If peak-bagging is important to you, continue on the Long Trail north for another 0.4 mile to the wooded summit of Laraway Mountain. Otherwise, retrace your steps to return to the trailhead.

DID YOU KNOW?

Laraway Mountain is part of Long Trail State Forest, which was established in 1996 primarily to protect the Long Trail. Known as the "footpath in the wilderness," the Long Trail is the oldest continuously used hiking trail in the United States. While hundreds of

Hikers walking near the cliffs on the Long Trail near Laraway Mountain.

hikers tackle the 272 miles in one go each year, most visitors are day-hikers. According to the Trust for Public Land, this historic landmark attracts an average of 200,000 visitors from across the country each year.

MORE INFORMATION

The Long Trail is maintained by the Green Mountain Club. Long Trail State Forest is managed by the Vermont Department of Forest, Parks, and Recreation.

NEARBY

Lamoille Valley Rail Trail is New England's longest rail-trail for walking, hiking, cycling, horseback riding, snowshoeing, cross-country skiing, and snowmobiling. A trailhead is in Johnson, 11 miles south. Numerous sites are available to launch a canoe or swim in the Lamoille River or Gihon River, both near Johnson. Camping is available at Smugglers' Notch State Park, 20 miles south.

51 JAY PEAK

This boreal forest hike to the summit of Vermont's northernmost ski area features sweeping vistas of northern Vermont, New Hampshire, and New York, as well as southern Quebec.

Features 🐕 📍 ⌐ ☀

Location Westfield, VT

Rating Moderate

Distance 3.4 miles round-trip

Elevation Gain 1,638 feet

Estimated Time 3 hours

Maps USGS Jay Peak

GPS Coordinates 44° 54.77′ N, 72° 30.24′ W

Contact Jay Peak: Jay State Forest, Vermont Department of Forests, Parks, and Recreation, District 5, Saint Johnsbury Office; 375 Emerson Falls Road, Suite 4, Saint Johnsbury, VT 05819; 802-751-0110; fpr.vermont.gov. The Long Trail: Green Mountain Club, 4711 Waterbury–Stowe Road, Waterbury Center, VT 05677; 802-244-7037; greenmountainclub.org

DIRECTIONS

From its junction with VT 101 in Jay, take VT 242 west 6.5 miles, driving through the town and passing the entrance to the ski area. At the height-of-land, the Long Trail crosses VT 242. Park on the southern shoulder of the road (space for about fifteen cars).

TRAIL DESCRIPTION

Jay Peak (3,862 feet) is a quintessential peak: high and solo, with a distinct profile and incredible summit views. Its ardent fans are numerous, from skiers and snowboarders who cherish its rugged terrain and famously deep snowfalls to Long Trail hikers for whom the singular summit is a milestone at the beginning or end of their journeys. The trek from Jay Pass is short and steep, rocky and beautiful. Snowshoers can expect to share some of their trip with skiers on the upper mountain.

Find the trailhead on the north side of VT 242, where the white-blazed Long Trail enters the trees and immediately encounters Atlas Valley Shelter. (This roofed resting area was built in 1967 by a plywood company and is not intended for overnight use. For campers, the Jay Loop spur path departs on the left here, leading to the bunks at Jay Camp, and rejoins the Long Trail 0.2 mile uphill.) The climb begins gradually through a deciduous

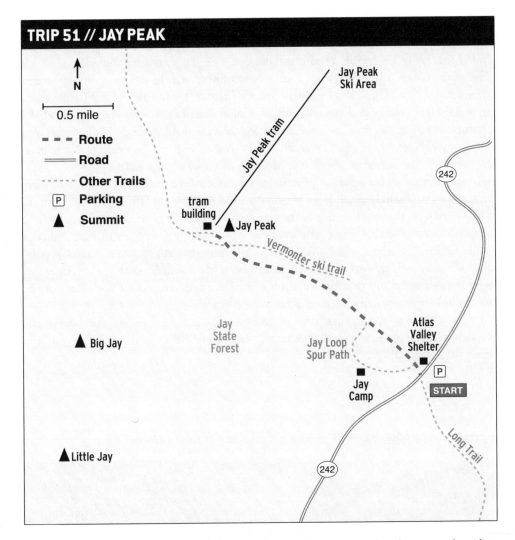

forest. By the upper junction with Jay Loop, the trail has narrowed and steepened; within minutes, the forest becomes distinctly more boreal.

The trail rises steadily along the southwestern-facing slope of the ridge. (Where the Long Trail crests the ridge and traverses the top of it, an informal path leads right a short distance onto a ski slope.) The Long Trail curves to the west and continues climbing through a dense conifer forest. Moderate pitches are interspersed with scrambles up rocky ledges, and moss grows thickly on the forest floor. At 1.5 miles, the Long Trail crosses steel snowmaking pipes and emerges from the woods onto the Vermonter ski trail. To the left, the ski tram's summit building is visible a short distance up the open slope. The Long Trail continues directly across the ski slope, climbing steep ledges onto the ridgeline for the final 0.2-mile. Walk on the rocks, weaving between spruce and fir krummholz (trees stunted and deformed by wind and snowpack). Pass a stone bench and arrive at the summit, next to the tram station.

The views from here are unparalleled in north-central Vermont. Big Jay (3,770 feet) hulks close by to the southwest, rising opposite a glacial cirque that connects it with Jay Peak. Little Jay (3,170 feet) is a short distance down Big Jay's southern shoulder. The high ridge of the Green Mountains leads your eyes southwest over the distinct point of Mount Mansfield's Chin (Trip 45) to Camel's Hump (Trip 27), 46 miles away. To the west, beyond the low, rolling landscape of Franklin County's dairy farms, narrow slivers of Lake Champlain reflect the sky. Look southwest for the famed Adirondack High Peaks. You know you're about as far north as you can go in Vermont when the big peaks of the Adirondacks (and, to the southeast, the White Mountains) are south of you.

To the north, Quebec's Sutton Mountains continue where the Green Mountains leave off at the international border. Bear Mountain and Owl's Head (Trip 30)—both with ski trails—perch on the western edge of the transborder Lake Memphremagog. Much of the Sutton Mountain massif due north has been conserved by groups in Canada, such as Ruiter Valley Land Trust, which maintains hiking trails through its property, and Appalachian Corridor, which works with Vermont's Green Mountain Club and other American organizations to ensure that conservation strategies are developed on both sides of the border, linking important ecological areas to each other.

Descend the way you came up, or, to give your knees a brief respite, head down the wooden stairway to the top of Vermonter ski trail and follow its gentle grade downhill to rejoin the Long Trail.

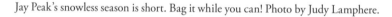

Jay Peak's snowless season is short. Bag it while you can! Photo by Judy Lamphere.

DID YOU KNOW?

The 25-mile-long Lake Memphremagog hides curiosities beneath its surface. At least one car loaded with Prohibition-era whiskey rests in the murky depths, and divers have surfaced with still-corked jugs of hooch. A sea serpent, known as Memphre, has supposedly been spotted numerous times in the lake since 1816.

MORE INFORMATION

Jay Peak is within Jay State Forest, managed by the Vermont Department of Forests, Parks, and Recreation. The Long Trail is maintained by the Green Mountain Club.

NEARBY

The Missisquoi River and Lake Memphremagog are part of the 740-mile Northern Forest Canoe Trail. The multiuse Missisquoi Valley Rail Trail extends 26 miles between Richford and Saint Albans. Big Falls State Park in Troy, with the state's largest undammed cascade and gorge, is a scenic picnic site 10 miles northeast. Jay Peak Resort is a center of recreational activities, including skiing and a popular water park, 2.4 miles northeast. For dining, head to Jay Peak Resort, to Jay (5.5 miles east), or to Newport (21 miles east). The Newport State Office Building on Lake Memphremagog houses an interesting exhibit about the lake's history, and the waterfront area has been nicely developed.

5 // NORTHEASTERN VERMONT

Colder, grittier, and more remote than other regions of Vermont, northeastern Vermont is a land apart from the rest of the state. Its small granite hills and mountains are scattered and have more in common geologically with New Hampshire's White Mountains than Vermont's ancient Green Mountains. The extreme cold, nutrient-poor soil, and short growing season contribute to an area that supports far more forests than farms and more wildlife than people. The landscape is dotted with open bogs and fens, beaver swamps and meadows. Numerous streams and rivers flow either east into the Connecticut River or north into Lake Memphremagog.

The boreal forests of the Northeastern Highlands hold the record for the coldest temperatures in Vermont, and although it is not the snowiest region in the state, snow tends to fall earlier and stay on the ground later than anywhere but the highest peaks.

This sparsely populated part of Vermont has been called the loneliest and loveliest corner of the state, and it is often referred to as the Northeast Kingdom, or simply the Kingdom. The plants and animals that survive on these approximately 600 square miles have adapted to the unforgiving harshness of the land. The region is dominated by black spruce, red spruce, and balsam fir, with hardwood forests at lower elevations.

Large tracts of undeveloped land provide important habitat for solitary mammals such as black bears, moose, lynx, and bobcats. The spruce–fir forests of the lowland basins are home to rare birds, including the spruce grouse, black-backed woodpecker, and Canada jay. Loons are frequent visitors to the glacial lakes, and white-tailed deer, while common throughout the state, use the Nulhegan Basin as one of the largest deer wintering areas in Vermont.

Small, remote lakes and ponds are common throughout the Kingdom, such as Caspian Lake beside Barr Hill (Trip 53), Island Pond below Bluff Mountain (Trip 59), and Little Averill Pond beneath the cliffs of Brousseau Mountain (Trip 60) on the Canadian border. The most dramatic of these lakes is Willoughby—narrow, long, and deep, with precipitous cliffs on either side that give it a fjord-like appearance. Carved by an ancient river and deepened by glacial ice, Lake Willoughby's impressive cliffs can be reached from either side. Mount Pisgah (Trip 54) provides spectacular vistas from its western-facing ledges, and Mount Hor (Trip 55) delivers views of Lake Willoughby and Mount Pisgah. Both are in Willoughby State Forest and part of Willoughby Gap, a National Natural Landmark.

More than anywhere else in Vermont, the Northeast Kingdom is defined by the land—a place where nature prevails over industry, and the outdoors is a way of life.

52 BURKE MOUNTAIN

This remote trail passes through a stand of enormous ash and maple trees on its way to spectacular views from the summit of a popular skiing and mountain-biking destination.

Features

Location Burke, VT

Rating Strenuous

Distance 6.2 miles round-trip

Elevation Gain 2,080 feet

Estimated Time 4.5 hours

Maps USGS Burke Mountain; NorthWoods Stewardship Center: northwoodscenter.org/wordpress/conservation-corps/trails

GPS Coordinates 44° 35.25′ N, 71° 55.08′ W

Contact Darling State Park: Vermont Department of Forests, Parks, and Recreation, District 5, Saint Johnsbury Office; 375 Emerson Falls Road, Suite 4, Saint Johnsbury, VT 05819; 802-751-0110; fpr.vermont.gov. Trails: Burke Mountain Resort; 223 Sherburne Lodge Road, East Burke, VT 05832; 802-626-7300; skiburke.com

DIRECTIONS

From VT 114 in the village of East Burke, follow Mountain Road 1.1 miles to Sherburne Lodge Road on the right. Ample parking for the trailhead is at the far end of the large lower lot.

TRAIL DESCRIPTION

Burke Mountain (3,267 feet) rises steeply from the gently sloping Passumpsic River valley. Its northern slopes and summit are a beehive of activity during ski season, but the challenging hiking trail up its western ridge is surprisingly insulated.

From the trailhead kiosk, red-blazed Red Trail follows a dirt woods road into the forest and curves through tamarack, maple, and overgrown log landings as it gently rises. After 0.6 mile, Red Trail turns left, departing the road. In 500 feet, Red Trail turns right, joining Kirby Connector, a mountain-bike trail. The two trails coincide for 0.2 mile; be aware of bikers and give them room to pass. The open understory here allows for long views beneath the canopy, a rare treat in eastern forests. At a register box, turn left off Kirby Connector and continue up Red Trail, entering Darling State Park.

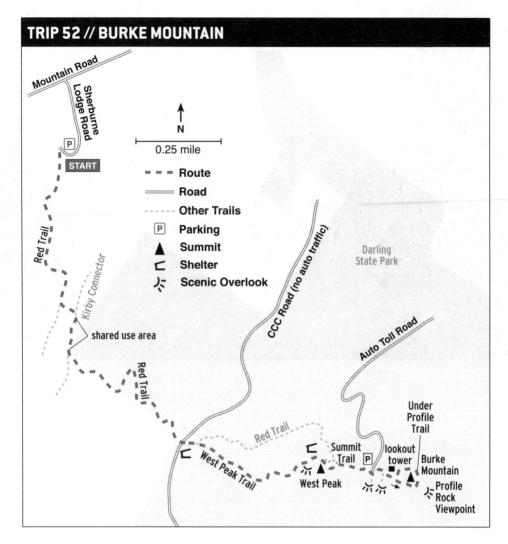

Mountain Road

Sherburne Lodge Road

P

START

Red Trail

Kirby Connector

shared use area

Red Trail

N

0.25 mile

- - - Route
=== Road
---- Other Trails
P Parking
▲ Summit
⊏ Shelter
⅄ Scenic Overlook

CCC Road (no auto traffic)

Darling State Park

Auto Toll Road

Red Trail

West Peak Trail

Summit Trail

P

lookout tower

West Peak

Under Profile Trail

Burke Mountain

Profile Rock Viewpoint

Enormous tree trunks add interest to this section of trail. The largest are ash and maple; larger-than-usual yellow birch and paper birch also make an appearance. Look for jumbo-sized shelf mushrooms growing off the huge trunks. The undergrowth thickens as the slope steepens. Red Trail turns sharply left to climb alongside a steep ravine and then traverses a saddle before ascending onto a maple ridge, heading straight up the fall line. After passing through a dark spruce–fir stand, Red Trail crosses Civilian Conservation Corps (CCC) Road, which no longer bears vehicle traffic, at 1.7 miles. Straight ahead, Red Trail intersects with West Peak Trail in a clearing that's home to a CCC-era lean-to and a stone fireplace still used by campers and skiers. Turn right in this clearing and head up scenic blue-blazed West Peak Trail.

Ascend steeply through paper and yellow birches for 0.2 mile and then enter a shallow ravine, thick with bushy chokecherries and maples. West Peak Trail ascends through stunted

Ski trails on Burke Mountain provide breaks in the treeline that allow hikers to spy Willoughby Gap, a National Natural Landmark made up of Mount Pisgah's cliffs on the east and Mount Hor's on the west.

birches and mountain ashes, traverses the gully, and climbs out. Now on a high ridge, the hiking alternates between scrambling up ledges draped in thick moss and crossing level areas where small pockets of fern glades open between fragrant softwood thickets. After several rising switchbacks, West Peak Trail emerges from the tree canopy, passes along the bottom of a steep rock face, and climbs the far side. On top of this promontory, views extend west across the broad Passumpsic Valley and south over the shoulder of nearby Kirby Mountain (2,750 feet). The wooded summit of West Peak (3,150 feet) is just 0.1 mile farther and is marked by a log lean-to. Go right on West Peak Trail, which ends at a five-way junction.

Stay right at the junction to follow Summit Trail along the undeveloped south edge of the mountaintop, walking by remnants of CCC campsites and shelters. After passing the top edge of a ski trail and a parking lot, reenter the woods and find two successive spur paths leading to outlooks. Summit Trail winds through the forest to the junction with Under Profile Trail (a.k.a. Profile Trail). Summit Trail heads left to the fire tower, but go right, continuing along the ridge to pass beneath the jutting rock overhang before circling to climb on top of Profile Rock (via the Profile Vista spur) for the most expansive views. (*Caution:* Surrounding trees can disguise cliff edges.) To the northeast, East Haven Mountain (3,070 feet) rises in the foreground. Beyond it, an abandoned Cold War–era radar station is visible on East Mountain (3,420 feet).

Leaving Profile Rock, continue on Under Profile Trail west across the rocky, open area of Burke's true summit. Just beyond it, climb the metal fire tower for a 360-degree vista, including Willoughby Gap to the northwest, a remarkable notch formed by Mount Hor to the west, and Mount Pisgah to the east. From the tower, follow Summit Trail downhill and return the way you came. An alternate route down is via Toll Road and Mountain Road, 3.6 miles from the summit to the trailhead.

DID YOU KNOW?

Burke Mountain is one of several Vermont monadnocks, isolated mountains that, due to their erosion-resistant rock, rise abruptly from gently sloping surroundings.

MORE INFORMATION

Darling State Park is managed by the Vermont Department of Forests, Parks, and Recreation. Trails are maintained by Burke Mountain Resort in partnership with the Vermont Department of Forests, Parks, and Recreation and local conservation organizations.

NEARBY

East Burke's Kingdom Trails Association is a renowned mountain-biking center, with trails open to hiking, running, skiing, and snowshoeing. Find groceries and dining options on VT 114 in East Burke or on US 5 in Lyndonville, 5.7 miles southwest.

53 BARR HILL

More of a sightseeing ramble than a hike, this short loop treats walkers to a collection of scenic vistas from several perspectives as it circles the wooded summit of Barr Hill.

Features

Location Greensboro, VT

Rating Easy

Distance 0.8-mile loop

Elevation Gain 120 feet

Estimated Time 45 minutes

Maps USGS Caspian Lake

GPS Coordinates 44° 36.52′ N, 72° 17.27′ W

Contact The Nature Conservancy, 575 Stone Cutters Way, Montpelier, VT 05602; 802-229-4425; nature.org

DIRECTIONS

From the center of Greensboro, follow East Craftsbury Road north 0.2 mile and bear right onto Laurendon Road. Go 0.6 mile and bear left onto Barr Hill Road. Drive 1.7 miles to a circle turnaround at the top of the hill and park alongside the woods (space for six cars). (In winter, expect to park at the end of the plowed section of Barr Hill Road and hike into the trailhead. Follow the signage and do not block the snowplow turnaround.) Parking is limited, and this is a very popular hike. If no parking is available, please consider returning during off-peak hours or choose another hike.

TRAIL DESCRIPTION

Barr Hill (2,110 feet) is a locally loved little bump and a favorite sunset destination with its wide southwestern views and a stone fire ring that encourages visitors to settle down and stay awhile. The 256-acre preserve encompasses woods, fields, ledges, and a ravine, which make the short, undulating loop trail feel chock-full of experiences. You certainly can walk the 0.8 mile in less than 45 minutes, but with so much to see, why hurry? This mellow trail is appropriate for kids of all ages; dogs are welcome but must be leashed. In winter, the nearby Craftsbury Outdoor Center grooms trails into the preserve (although not along this hiking loop), so visitors can ski here from the center.

The parking area has a kiosk with information about the natural area and a trail map. The hilltop is small enough that you're never too far from the trailhead.

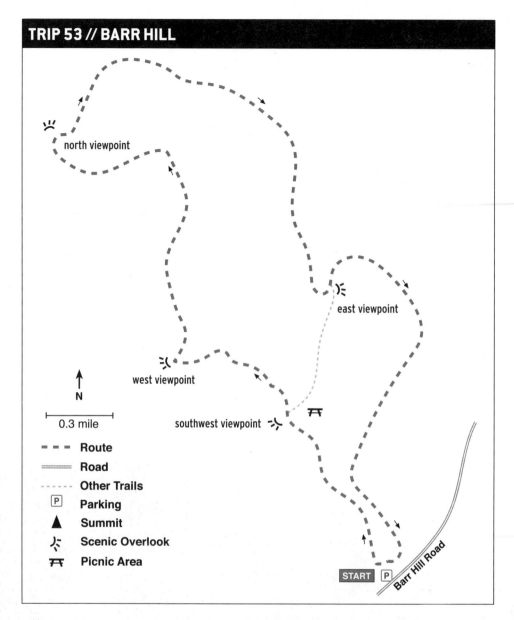

north viewpoint

east viewpoint

N

0.3 mile

west viewpoint

southwest viewpoint

- - - Route
═══ Road
----- Other Trails
P Parking
▲ Summit
ᐳᐸ Scenic Overlook
⊤ Picnic Area

START P

Barr Hill Road

The trail begins at the kiosk on the south side of the parking area and crosses the open hillside to the lookout spot, where a signboard names the many peaks and ranges spread across the horizon. From Spruce Mountain (Trip 29) in the south to the massive, rocky bulk of Mount Mansfield (Trips 45 and 46) in the west, you can pick out Vermont's most recognizable and well-loved peaks—Breadloaf Mountain (3,835 feet), Mount Abraham (Trip 25), Camel's Hump (Trip 27), and Mount Hunger (Trip 40)—and observe some lesser-known summits, such as Woodbury Mountain (2,471 feet) and Mount Worcester (Trip 38).

When you turn away from the view and continue uphill on the path, look for the picnic knoll in the top-right corner of the meadow and the trail loop's departure into the woods on the left (0.1 mile). Follow the trail into the woods and immediately descend a staircase, cross a small ravine, and climb out the other side. Mount a gentle slope through maples to a spur path (0.2 mile) on the left and walk a few steps to a view of Caspian Lake. This 789-acre lake has crystal-clear water—and an active local association working diligently to keep it that way. Loons frequent the lake, as do writers, artists, and others seeking refuge and inspiration. Wallace Stegner set several of his novels here.

Returning to the main trail, bear left and traverse ledges and soft, needle-covered ground as you circle the summit. Chunks of white quartz rest alongside the trail amid patches of thick club moss. Reach the far side of the loop at 0.4 mile, where an opening in the trees affords a view northwest. The chocolate-kiss summit of Jay Peak (Trip 51) perches near the Canadian border, and wind turbines in the foreground spin atop the long ridge of Lowell Mountain (2,641 feet). The trail U-turns at this point, heading north through large spruces before curving east. A stone wall and privately owned camp are visible downhill through the trees.

Continue on the curving, rolling trail, with large patches of moss and fern spreading between the conifer trunks. A small window in the foliage gives a preview of the panorama just around the next bend, where the trail climbs onto a knoll and arrives at a junction, 0.6 mile from the start. Straight ahead, a 200-foot shortcut returns you to the picnic area.

Turn left to stay on the loop trail, entering a clearing that slopes downhill, opening a broad vista east. A signboard provides a guide to the peaks. In the northeast, Mount Pisgah (Trip 54), Mount Hor (Trip 55), and Wheeler Mountain (Trip 56) cluster together around the high, pointy peak of Bald Mountain (3,310 feet) in Westmore (Trip 57). To the

Barr Hill's circumferential trail provides a great opportunity for families to spend time together outdoors. Photo by Kip Roberts.

southeast, Burke Mountain (Trip 52) is recognizable by the towers on its ridge and the north-facing ski trails. Beyond the signboard, follow the rock ledge across the top of the clearing before curving downhill to cross the bottom of the field. The trail curves south and west, descending into a wooded ravine on its final leg before returning to the trailhead.

DID YOU KNOW?

Every summer, circus performers ages 10 to 18 train at the Circus Smirkus campus in Greensboro and then hit the road for a two-month tour of New England. Their amazing stunts will knock your socks off. Make sure to catch a show if you're visiting in season.

MORE INFORMATION

Barr Hill Natural Area is maintained as a sanctuary for all wildlife. Dogs must be leashed and cleaned up after at all times. Camping, biking, hunting, and trapping are not permitted. Please picnic only in the designated area.

NEARBY

Swim in and paddle on beautiful Caspian Lake from the public beach and boat launch at its south end. Lodging and dining are available in Greensboro, with more options in Hardwick, 9 miles south. Craftsbury Outdoor Center maintains cross-country ski trails that extend around Caspian Lake and to Barr Hill. Mountain biking is at Craftsbury Outdoor Center, 9 miles northeast.

54 MOUNT PISGAH

Outlooks atop Mount Pisgah's cliffs, which drop precipitously into scenic Lake Willoughby, provide sweeping vistas across the Northeast Kingdom.

Features

Location Westmore, VT

Rating Moderate

Distance 4.8 miles round-trip

Elevation Gain 1,395 feet

Estimated Time 3 hours

Maps USGS Sutton; Vermont Department of Forests, Parks, and Recreation: fpr.vermont.gov/sites/fpr/files/Forest_and_Forestry/State_Forests/Library/willoughby_trails_2019.pdf

GPS Coordinates 44° 42.65′ N, 72° 01.44′ W

Contact Willoughby State Forest: Vermont Department of Forests, Parks, and Recreation, Saint Johnsbury Office, 374 Emerson Falls Road, Suite 4, Saint Johnsbury, VT 05819; 802-751-0110); fpr.vermont.gov. Mount Pisgah: NorthWoods Stewardship Center, P.O. Box 220, East Charleston, VT 05833; 802-723-6551; northwoodscenter.org

DIRECTIONS

From the junction of US 5 and VT 5A in West Burke, travel north on VT 5A for 5.7 miles. Mount Pisgah's South Trail parking lot is on the right (space for about fifteen cars). An additional parking lot is on the left (space for about twelve cars), at the bottom of the CCC Road. Mount Pisgah's South Trail is a high-use trail. Hikers can avoid crowded parking and trail conditions by timing visits for off-peak periods (midweek, early in the day, or late afternoon). If the parking lots are full, consider an alternate hike, such as Mount Hor (Trip 55) or Wheeler Mountain (Trip 56).

TRAIL DESCRIPTION

Hikers climb Mount Pisgah not for its wooded summit, which you can cross without realizing you're on it, but for the dramatic scenery from its western-facing ledges. The dark, deep waters of Lake Willoughby fill the narrow gap between Pisgah and its cliffy cousin, Mount Hor (Trip 55). Together, these mountains and the lake make up a National Natural Landmark. (*Caution*: Mount Pisgah's cliffs are spectacular, but have no restraints on them—not a railing or even a warning sign.)

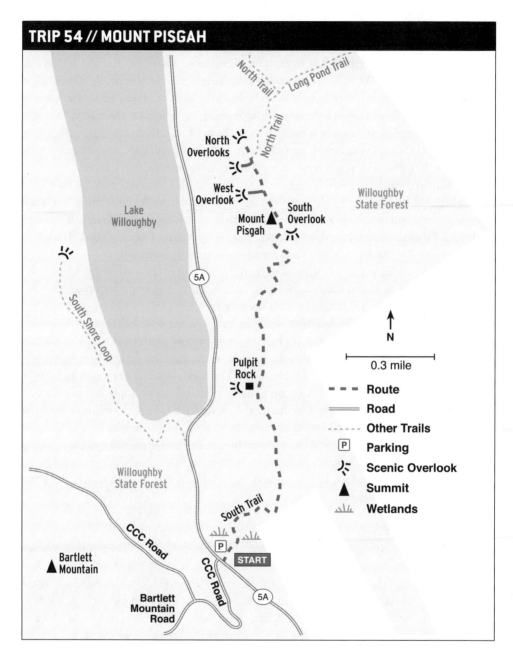

North Trail

Long Pond Trail

North Trail

North Overlooks

West Overlook

Mount Pisgah

South Overlook

Lake Willoughby

Willoughby State Forest

5A

South Shore Loop

N

0.3 mile

Pulpit Rock

- - - Route
= Road
----- Other Trails
P Parking
Scenic Overlook
▲ Summit
Wetlands

Willoughby State Forest

South Trail

P

START

CCC Road

Bartlett ▲ Mountain

Bartlett Mountain Road

CCC Road

5A

Blue-blazed South Trail begins in the far-right corner of the parking lot and descends a gradually sloping hill into the woods. A short distance from the road, reach the first of two wide boardwalks at a beaver pond. Watch for great blue herons standing quietly amid the dead tree trunks and lily pads. Cross the swamp and head north along a low ridge, passing a register box and beginning to climb gradually through a deciduous forest. Purple-flowering raspberry spreads its maple-like leaves alongside the steepening trail. Hobblebush also thrives here, its flexible stems bending and taking root again where they touch the ground.

Glimpses of Lake Willoughby appear as South Trail follows the edge of the steep western hillside. Be wary of this drop when exploring any of the informal footpaths that lead to lookout points alongside the trail. Pulpit Rock, a small overlook almost 700 feet above the lake, appears on your left at 0.9 mile. This popular destination provides a striking, if somewhat limited, view of the south end of Lake Willoughby and the cliffs of Mount Hor. After passing an interesting tangle of two tree trunks leaning toward the precipice, the trail turns away from the ledges and heads into the woods, starting the most sustained part of the climb. The forest changes to firs and short, thick paper birches. As you huff and puff, note the many rock staircases built by the local youth crews of the NorthWoods Stewardship Center.

Just below the summit, South Trail emerges onto South Overlook, a rocky bald spot from which Burke Mountain's ski trails appear to be just a stone's throw away. The trail returns to the woods and, without any fanfare, traverses the summit of Pisgah en route to the ledges. From the summit to the overlooks, you are on Mount Pisgah's North Trail, also blazed in blue. If you haven't already put a leash on your dog, do so now.

Three ledge overlooks provide three slightly different angles from which to admire the surrounding landscape, and each rocky sitting area is a little more spacious than the last. Spur paths to the ledges are marked with brown signs.

Below the ledges, Lake Willoughby stretches long and narrow, its far shore an oddly straight line, lacking coves or inlets. It's easy to imagine how southward-creeping glaciers of the last ice age pushed through this narrow valley, gouging the trough that eventually became the deepest lake (308 feet) entirely within Vermont's borders. Look northwest over the trees to the cliffs of Wheeler Mountain (Trip 56) for another example of that grinding ice sheet's power. Beyond Wheeler Mountain, the spine of the Green Mountains etches the western horizon, with Mount Mansfield (Trips 45 and 46) to the southwest and the distinctive point of Jay Peak (Trip 51) to the northwest. In the far northwest, Lake Memphremagog stretches into Quebec.

Climb back up the overlook spur path and turn right on North Trail to return to the summit. Descend the way you came up.

DID YOU KNOW?

According to the *Northeast Kingdom Mountain Trail Guide* (Luke O'Brien, NorthWoods Stewardship Center, 2010), Mount Pisgah's nineteenth-century name was Mount Annance (or variants of that), after a local Wabanaki chief. When settlers of European descent began hosting tourists on the lake, the mountain was renamed, perhaps as clever marketing, to refer to the biblical promised land. The south side of Pisgah has had a trail since at least 1857, when a local innkeeper cleared a route so visitors could enjoy the views.

MORE INFORMATION

Willoughby State Forest is managed by the Vermont Department of Forests, Parks, and Recreation. Mount Pisgah trails are maintained by the NorthWoods Stewardship Center.

Pulpit Rock, overlooking the south end of Lake Willoughby, provides a scenic rest stop midway up Mount Pisgah or a worthwhile destination on its own merits.

NEARBY

Camping and swimming areas are at both ends of Lake Willoughby. Some dining options can be found along the lake, with many more in East Burke or Lyndonville, each 20 miles south, in or Newport, 20 miles north. Outdoor outfitters are in East Burke and Newport.

THE PSYCHOLOGY OF TRAIL MAINTENANCE

When you pause—panting—at the top of a flight of rock steps, are you more inclined to curse the steps or to appreciate their flat surfaces? Your answer may indicate your awareness of erosion prevention and trail maintenance techniques. Although some trail features are put in place to ease the way for hikers, such as a ladder up a rock face or a railing on a bridge, the goal of most trail work is preventing erosion.

Soil erosion is the single biggest threat to the life of a trail. If you've ever hiked up a gullied path and seen tree roots suspended in midair, you know what the effects of erosion look like. Although erosion is a natural process of soils wearing away, it becomes a problem when it prompts hikers to seek alternate routes, trampling plants and causing further damage to the trail corridor. Trails that become too badly eroded have to be relocated, and relocation is an expensive, time-consuming activity that results in additional impact on the forest.

Trail maintainers assessing an eroded stretch of trail must answer two questions: "How can I drain the water off this trail and stabilize the soil?" and "How can I convince hikers to walk on the more durable path?"

Many ways exist to drain and harden a trail—that is, to make it more durable. You've stepped in and out of countless shallow, rounded troughs that cross the trail; these dips direct downstream currents off the path. Dips reinforced with a slippery skinned log or a row of rocks are called water bars.

Step stones and bog bridges (also called puncheons) provide dry footing across persistently muddy areas while protecting soils and plants.

Log or rock steps stabilize steep trails and provide a long-lasting and relatively flat surface for footsteps. Many hikers avoid steps and climb the dirt slope beside them, causing that to erode, which also undermines the stability of the staircase. To make the steps more appealing than the hill beside them, trail maintainers plant pointy, less stable-looking rocks (called scree) alongside the staircase.

You won't look at trails the same way after you start noticing the subtle methods maintainers use to guide your footsteps and prevent erosion. That log ladder helping you up a ledge controls erosion by keeping you on solid rock rather than on erodible soil around the edge. A railing makes a bridge route the most appealing way across a ravine. Trail maintainers focus on protecting the trail and its surrounding environment, benefiting hikers in the long term, even if that occasionally means making life a little more challenging on the way up the mountain.

55 MOUNT HOR

A short hike through a lovely hardwood forest leads to lookouts with long views, including dramatic Lake Willoughby and the cliffs of Mount Pisgah.

Features

Location Sutton, VT

Rating Easy to Moderate

Distance 2.9 miles round-trip

Elevation Gain 601 feet

Estimated Time 1.5 hours

Maps USGS Sutton; Vermont Department of Forests, Parks, and Recreation: fpr.vermont.gov/sites/fpr/files/Forest_and_Forestry/State_Forests/Library/willoughby_trails_2019.pdf

GPS Coordinates 44° 42.53′ N, 72° 02.83′ W

Contact Willoughby State Forest: Vermont Department of Forests, Parks, and Recreation, District 5, Saint Johnsbury Office; 374 Emerson Falls Road, Suite 4, Saint Johnsbury, VT 05819; 802-751-0110; fpr.vermont.gov. Mount Hor: NorthWoods Stewardship Center, P.O. Box 220, East Charleston, VT 05833; 802-723-6551; northwoodscenter.org.

DIRECTIONS

From VT 5A at the southern end of Lake Willoughby, go 0.5 mile south to the height-of-land and turn right onto dirt CCC Road. After 0.5 mile, bear right at the fork and continue uphill. The parking area (space for six cars), marked by a kiosk, is on the right at 1.7 miles. (CCC Road is not maintained in winter; snowshoers should park at the bottom and add 3.4 miles to the hike.)

TRAIL DESCRIPTION

Mount Hor (2,648 feet) is one of two peaks that make up the National Natural Landmark of Willoughby Gap. Mirroring Mount Pisgah on the opposite side of the gap, Hor's cliffs rise 1,000 feet from narrow Lake Willoughby, forming a fjord-like landscape. Although the hiking is appropriate for kids 6 and older, children and dogs need to be carefully monitored at the outlook points.

Blue-blazed Herbert Hawkes Trail begins a short distance beyond the parking area. The wide path rises briefly, following an old road, and then flattens out through an airy

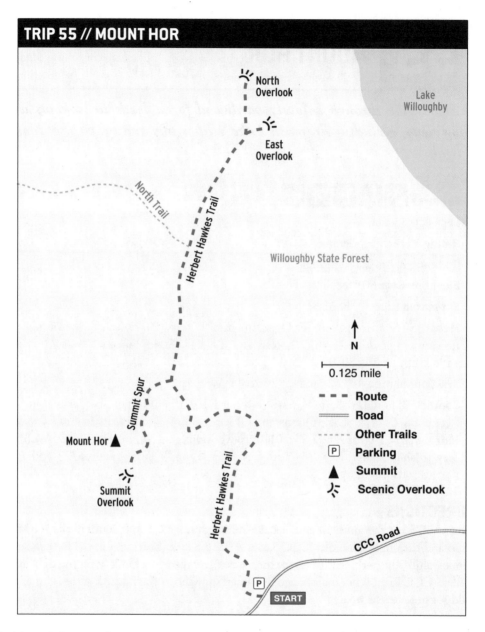

TRIP 55 // MOUNT HOR

North Overlook

East Overlook

Lake Willoughby

North Trail

Herbert Hawkes Trail

Willoughby State Forest

N

0.125 mile

- - - Route

══ Road

····· Other Trails

P Parking

▲ Summit

🔆 Scenic Overlook

Summit Spur

Mount Hor ▲

Summit Overlook

Herbert Hawkes Trail

CCC Road

P

START

hardwood forest. After 0.4 mile, Herbert Hawkes Trail turns left off the old road and climbs steadily on a narrow path. At 0.6 mile, arrive at a ridge-top T junction: to the left, the trail skirts Mount Hor's summit, offering a view southwest; to the right, it's a little more than 0.5 mile to the vistas north and east over Lake Willoughby. Go left on Summit Spur, ascending on rocks until the low curve of the summit appears above you on your right, at which point the spur path flattens and curves around it. Straight ahead, down a short slope, a hole in the forest frames a view across numerous small ponds to Norris Mountain (2,292 feet). The ponds are part of 30-acre Marl Pond and Swamp Natural Area, a northern white cedar swamp with several rare plants.

Return to the trail junction and pick up Herbert Hawkes Trail again, continuing straight along the ridgeline. The 0.6 mile to East Overlook is mostly flat, passing the junction of North Trail on your left and crossing muddy areas where you're likely to see moose prints, if not the hump-shouldered ungulate itself. A spur path leads right down a short, eroded slope to an outlook with limited views of the south cove of Lake Willoughby and the end of the Mount Pisgah cliffs. For the best views on Mount Hor, head 0.1 mile farther to North Overlook, crossing the top of the ridge and descending to an open rock ledge. Immediately in front of you, Mount Pisgah's sheer face rises from the deep lake. If you snowshoed to this point, you may see the colorful gear of ice climbers ascending the rock walls. Peregrine falcons also gather on these cliffs, where the combination of horizontal ledges that support nests (called aeries) and vertical drops for hunting dives makes this an ideal raptor habitat.

Lake Willoughby stretches 4 miles northwest from here, with the comparatively gentle slope of Goodwin Mountain (2,900 feet) rising from the water north of Mount Pisgah. The village of Westmore sits along the lake beneath Goodwin, where the shoreline curves into the mountainside.

Mount Hor sits at the heart of the approximately 8,000-acre Willoughby State Forest, which was established in 1928 with an initial 1,700 acres. The forest is managed for multiple uses, meaning some areas are conserved for ecological reasons, such as Marl Pond and

Mount Hor's viewpoints reveal a dramatic slice of Lake Willoughby and Mount Pisgah, with a less-challenging approach than most other outlooks require.

Swamp; some areas are maintained for recreation, such as the mountain summits; and some areas are designated for public timber harvest through a program that allows residents to cut wood for home heating. The forest also has a long history of work by various conservation corps programs (see "From the CCC to the VYCC: Conservation Corps in Vermont," page 249).

Return to the trail junction and go left, descending on Herbert Hawkes Trail to the parking lot the way you came up.

DID YOU KNOW?

Reaching depths of more than 320 feet, Lake Willoughby is the deepest lake located entirely within Vermont. Because it is primarily fed by underground springs, Lake Willoughby is very cold and clear.

MORE INFORMATION

Willoughby State Forest is managed by the Vermont Department of Forests, Parks, and Recreation. Mount Hor trails are maintained by the NorthWoods Stewardship Center.

NEARBY

Camping and swimming areas are at both ends of Lake Willoughby. Some dining options can be found along the lake, with more in East Burke or Lyndonville, each 20 miles south, or in Newport, 20 miles north.

56 WHEELER MOUNTAIN

Wheeler Mountain's cliff-top vistas give panoramic views of the Northeast Kingdom landscape, including the spectacular and fjord-like Lake Willoughby.

Features 🏃 🐕 ✳️

Location Sutton, VT

Rating Moderate

Distance 4.1 miles round-trip

Elevation Gain 870 feet

Estimated Time 3.5 hours

Maps USGS Sutton; Vermont Department of Forests, Parks, and Recreation: fpr.vermont.gov/sites/fpr/files/Forest_and_Forestry/State_Forests/Library/willoughby_trails_2019.pdf

GPS Coordinates 44° 43.23′ N, 72° 06.00′ W

Contact Vermont Department of Forests, Parks, and Recreation, District 5, Saint Johnsbury Office; 374 Emerson Falls Road, Suite 4, Saint Johnsbury, VT 05819; 802-751-0110; fpr.vermont.gov

DIRECTIONS

From the junction of VT 16 and US 5 in downtown Barton, head south on US 5 for 4.7 miles. Turn left onto dirt Wheeler Mountain Road (Sutton Town Road 15). Drive 1.4 miles to a large parking area on the right (space for sixteen cars).

TRAIL DESCRIPTION

The trek up Wheeler Mountain (2,371 feet) begins with a ridge ascent and culminates in a cliff-top walk with many viewpoints over the great forest of the Northeast Kingdom. The hike was historically a quick scramble onto the cliffs from directly beneath them, but in 2016 the trail was rerouted from private land into Willoughby State Forest. Before hiking, check with Audubon Vermont (vt.audubon.org) for peregrine falcon activity here. The cliffs may be closed between March 15 and August 1 to protect falcon chicks.

Wheeler Mountain Trail begins downhill from the parking area and crosses Wheeler Mountain Road. Follow blue blazes to a register box and then begin the steady climb on rocky ground, at times scrambling over and around mossy ledges and boulders. At 0.6 mile, arrive at a T junction. To the right is a view of the cliffs of Wheeler Mountain; go left to stay on Wheeler Mountain Trail and continue heading uphill.

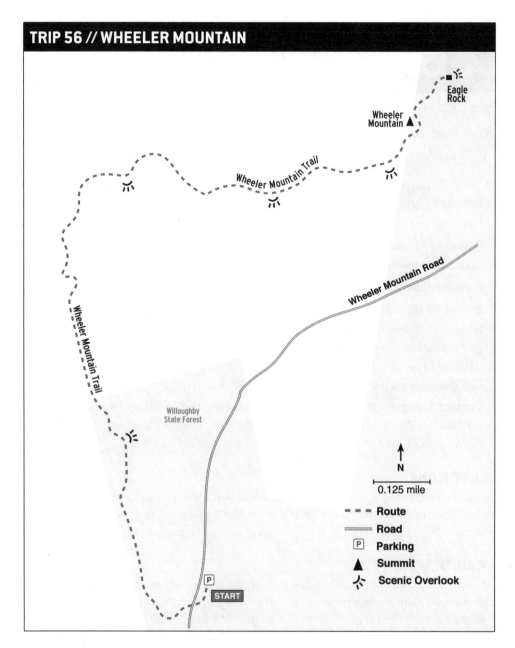

As you gain elevation, be careful traversing streams and clusters of rocks, which may have tricky, often slippery footing. Mature birches and maples shelter the undergrowth of striped maples and hobblebushes. The trail zigzags as it climbs alongside a ravine and then leads across the hillside, entering a high spruce–fir forest. At 1.2 miles, a double blue blaze marks a spur path to a limited view of Wheeler Pond, as well as the wind turbines on Granby Mountain (2,393 feet) and Libby Hill. After checking out the sights, return to

Wheeler Mountain Trail and descend 0.2 mile into a pine forest, passing the now-closed junction of the old trail. From here, meander through patches of thick forest and open rock as you approach Wheeler's cliffs, arriving at the first of many lookout points at 1.6 miles. A broad, smooth expanse of bare rock gives a magnificent view of the valley below, with Wheeler Pond and Granby Mountain in the near distance.

From here, the trail crosses exposed ledges and reenters the woods, climbing gradually. Along this top part of Wheeler Mountain, look for blazes on rocks and trees as you maneuver through forests and open areas. At 1.9 miles, Wheeler Mountain Trail emerges on open cliffs. Use extreme caution here as you scramble up a rock spine, with trees on the left and a drop on the right that affords wide views north, east, and south that get wider as you climb. From the panoramic vistas on top of the spine, Wheeler Mountain Trail heads back into a thick, mossy spruce–fir forest that edges around the summit proper. Descend gradually to the terminus of the hike at Eagle Rock, a ledge that feels like it's floating above the Northeast Kingdom landscape. Lake Willoughby shines beneath the cliffs of Mount Pisgah (Trip 54). Beyond the lake, Bald Mountain (Trip 57) is the noticeably conical peak. To the southeast, Burke Mountain (Trip 52) is also distinct in its tall solitude.

Retrace your steps to the trailhead.

DID YOU KNOW?

Peregrine falcons are still recovering from the devastating effects of DDT and other chemicals used over the past century. Vermont's peregrine population is stable but remains susceptible to human interference, particularly when hikers or rock climbers disturb the birds'

Wheeler Mountain's cliffs offer endless views as hikers follow the crest around its summit.

cliff-side aeries during nesting season. The falcons may respond to people approaching too close by sounding a loud *cack, cack, cack* alarm call or displaying aggressive flight behavior. If the birds appear agitated, retreat from the overlook.

MORE INFORMATION

Wheeler Mountain Trail is managed by the Vermont Department of Forests, Parks, and Recreation.

NEARBY

Restaurants are in Barton, 6 miles west. Crystal Lake State Park, also 6 miles west, is a good location for swimming and paddling. Closer by, Wheeler Pond has a nice loop walk around it, and the Green Mountain Club rents out two cabins on its shore. The epicenter of Vermont mountain biking is 15 miles southeast, at Kingdom Trails. The Fairbanks Museum has natural history exhibits and a planetarium in Saint Johnsbury, 26 miles south.

57 BALD MOUNTAIN (WESTMORE)

After a fun climb through a diverse forest, hikers are treated to extensive views of the Northeast Kingdom from the summit of Bald Mountain. A restored shelter makes this a great overnight excursion.

Features

Location Westmore, VT

Rating Moderate

Distance 4 miles round-trip

Elevation Gain 1,450 feet

Estimated Time 2.5 hours

Maps USGS Westmore, USGS Island Pond; Vermont Department of Forests, Parks, and Recreation: fpr.vermont.gov/sites/fpr/files/Forest_and_Forestry/Vermont_Forests/Images/WSF_summer%20kiosk%20map.pdf

GPS Coordinates 44° 45.42′ N, 72° 01.08′ W

Contact Willoughby State Forest: Vermont Department of Forests, Parks, and Recreation, District 5, Saint Johnsbury Office; 374 Emerson Falls Road, Suite 4, Saint Johnsbury, VT 05819; 802-751-0110; fpr.vermont.gov. Long Pond Trail: NorthWoods Stewardship Center, P.O. Box 220, East Charleston, VT 05833; 802-723-6551; northwoodscenter.org

DIRECTIONS

From the junction of US 5 and VT 5A in West Burke, travel north on VT 5A for 10.0 miles. Turn right on Long Pond Road and continue for 2.1 miles. The trailhead and parking area are on your left (space for twelve cars).

TRAIL DESCRIPTION

Long Pond Trail, just east of Lake Willoughby, takes hikers through an open hardwood forest at a moderate climb before ascending more steeply through a spruce–fir forest to the top of Bald Mountain (3,315 feet). The Bald Mountain fire tower provides a 360-degree vista of the surrounding mountains, lakes, and forestland, and the restored summit cabin is one of Vermont's oldest lookout stations. The hike is steep toward the end, but overall it's a moderate trek that can be enjoyed by kids 8 and older. (*Note*: Although the summit of Bald Mountain is part of Willoughby State Forest, the trail passes through private lands. Please be respectful of landowners and stay on marked trails.)

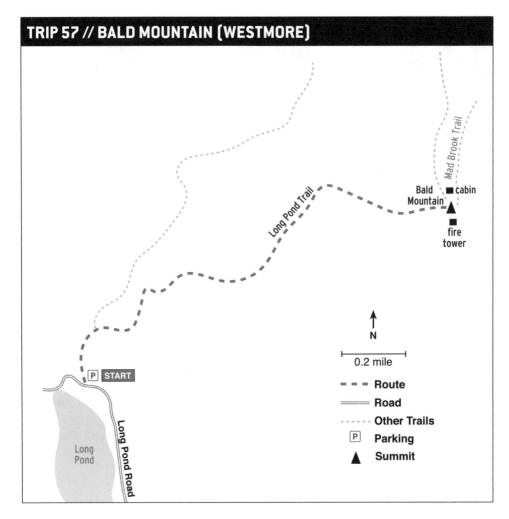

From the parking area, walk around a gate and onto a gravel logging road, bearing right at the blue-blazed Long Pond Trail junction at 0.2 mile. This flat part of the route travels through a young hardwood forest that has been recently logged. At 0.6 mile, enter a log landing with an abundance of summer wildflowers, including tall meadow rue, oxeye daisy, fox-and-cubs, and the invasive garden valerian. Long Pond Trail curves gently to the right and crosses the clearing before turning sharply left and entering the woods once again.

Sign in at the trail register and begin a moderate uphill ascent, following blue-blazed Long Pond Trail through open hardwood forest. Hop across several small streams before reaching a larger stream at the 1.0-mile mark. Well-placed stones make this an easy crossing. The trail turns sharply right here and climbs a sturdy set of steps. Steps like this not only make for easier walking but also prevent erosion on the steepest parts of the trail (see "The Psychology of Trail Maintenance," page 232).

The hardwood forest thickens, and the climb steepens. A small seasonal stream runs beside the trail, and various warblers flit about as you enter a forest of primarily spruce and

The fire tower on top of Bald Mountain provides 360-degree views of the Northeast Kingdom.

fir, with yellow birch mixed in. The trail turns left and crosses a bog bridge. At 1.8 miles, a boulder in the trail marks the final ascent to the summit. Mossy rock outcroppings and deep, craggy clefts loom along the way. Take time to explore these dark, drippy environs, and notice how the cool air settles between the rocks, which sometimes hang on to snow and ice well into summer.

The trail levels off as you approach the summit clearing at 2.1 miles. You may notice active small birds high in the spruce and fir trees flashing bright yellow crests as they energetically fly from branch to branch. These are tiny golden-crowned kinglets, whose high-pitched trills provide a lively soundtrack as you reach your destination.

The grassy summit is home to a fire tower and a lookout cabin, which is available for overnight visitors. A fire tower has stood on the summit of Bald Mountain since the early 1920s, but the current tower was built between 1938 and 1939, after a hurricane toppled numerous towers around the state (see "Standing Tall: The Legacy of Fire Towers in Vermont," page 14). Climb the fire tower for a spectacular 360-degree vista of the Northeast Kingdom and beyond. The landscape appears as an endless stretch of forested mountains, with more than a dozen lakes and ponds shining like jewels among the trees. In the south and west, you can make out Burke Mountain (Trip 52), Mount Pisgah (Trip 54), and Mount Hor (Trip 55), as well as Moose Mountain and Wheeler Mountain (Trip 56). To the north, the numerous lakes and ponds include Salem Pond, Pensioner Pond, Echo Lake, Seymour Lake, Norton Pond, and Island Pond, as well as the Nulhegan River Basin. The Green Mountains, including Mount Mansfield (Trips 45 and 46) and Camel's Hump (Trip 27), are visible in the west, and the northern White Mountains can be discerned in the east.

After descending the fire tower, orient yourself to ensure you are hiking back to the trailhead on Long Pond Trail and not on Mad Brook Trail, which is across the clearing. Return to the trailhead the way you hiked up.

DID YOU KNOW?

More than 2,000 moose live in Vermont, and the heavily forested Northeast Kingdom has the highest population in the state. Moose are excellent swimmers and frequent the region's ponds and lakes, where they can dive up to 18 feet in search of their favorite water plants. In recent years, moose populations have plummeted, partly due to a brain worm that destroys tissue in the moose's brain and spinal cord and partly due to a population explosion of winter ticks (see "Moose in Peril," page 245).

MORE INFORMATION

Willoughby State Forest is managed by the Vermont Department of Forests, Parks, and Recreation. Long Pond Trail is maintained by the NorthWoods Stewardship Center.

NEARBY

Two public beaches lie on the north and south ends of Lake Willoughby, just a short drive from the trailhead. Camping and swimming are available at Crystal Lake State Park, 11 miles west, or at Brighton State Park, 16 miles east. The Green Mountain Club rents out two rustic cabins on the shore of Wheeler Pond, 9 miles east. Kingdom Trails, 17 miles south, provide extensive mountain-biking opportunities. The nearest dining options are in Barton, 11 miles west.

MOOSE IN PERIL

Not many large animals have adapted to the Green Mountains as well as the comically majestic moose. These gangly creatures spend winters sheltering under the protective boughs of mountainside evergreens, munching twigs and using their teeth to scrape bark from balsam fir, maple, aspen, and ash trunks. In summer, they head for the leafy shade of lower-elevation forests and cool off in beaver ponds and lakes. Their long legs help them navigate deep snow and downed trees and propel them surprisingly well in the water, where they can dive up to 18 feet down in search of delicious aquatic plants.

But wooded hillsides aren't so useful to humans intent on farming, and Vermont's nineteenth-century settlers logged and cleared and slashed and burned with fervor. Forests became sheep pastures and cropland. The moose vacated, along with many other native residents, and when Vermont's legislature banned moose hunting in 1896, it was a moot point: the hump-shouldered, long-nosed beasts were nowhere to be found. As it turned out, however, farming Vermont's rocky slopes wasn't a wildly successful endeavor. Over time, forests retook abandoned pastures, beaver returned from their own hiatus and began creating swampy wetlands again, and eventually moose wandered back in from the forests of northern New Hampshire and Quebec.

You might not expect such big animals to be as quick as rabbits at reproducing, but moose excel at this activity. According to the Vermont Fish and Wildlife Department, almost all adult moose breed every year, and half of the pregnancies result in twins. Additionally, half of the yearling females breed and give birth to single calves. When the situation is ideal—that is, without natural predators, as was the case in the Green Mountains when the moose returned—moose populations can increase by as much as 25 percent per year. In 1965, there were about 25 moose in Vermont; 40 years later, in 2005, the population was a healthy 4,800 individuals.

It sounds like a success story, but a new combination of threats is quickly laying waste to the population gains of the late twentieth century. Between 2005 and 2020, Vermont's moose numbers plummeted to 2,400, well below the 3,000 animals the state considers a sustainable population. What is bringing down these mighty mammals? Several culprits: Humans with cars and rifles kill a percentage of the moose population each year. Moose also face new, tiny predators—brain worms and winter ticks. These parasites aren't particularly harmful to their traditional hosts, white-tailed deer, but are hugely destructive to moose. (Previously, moose and deer didn't mix much, but deforestation and reforestation provided landscapes that support both, and they now share habitats.) Recent warm winters have allowed ticks to flourish, with tens of thousands feeding on a single moose, causing anemia and blood loss that kills calves and weakens adults.

Even if moose survive all their current challenges, a larger problem threatens. Climate change has been hard on these creatures of the cold north. They are adept at surviving long, frigid winters but not well equipped to stand heat as the mercury rises. If forecasted temperature increases come to pass, Vermont may be mooseless once again.

58 MOOSE BOG

An easy stroll on a universally accessible trail takes nature lovers through a fragrant spruce–balsam forest and out to a boardwalk and viewing platform overlooking beautiful Moose Bog.

Features 👫 🐕 ♿ 💧 🔖

Location Ferdinand, VT

Rating Easy

Distance 1 mile round-trip

Elevation Gain 34 feet

Estimated Time 30 minutes

Maps USGS Bloomfield

GPS Coordinates 44° 45.56′ N, 71° 43.76′ W

Contact Vermont Fish and Wildlife Department, Saint Johnsbury Office, 374 Emerson Falls Road, Suite 4, Saint Johnsbury, VT 05819; 802-751-0100; vtfishandwildlife.com.

DIRECTIONS
From VT 105 in the community of Island Pond, drive east for 9.0 miles. Turn right onto South American Pond Road. The trailhead and parking area are on your right (space for five cars).

TRAIL DESCRIPTION
The secluded trail to Moose Bog takes hikers through a fragrant boreal forest on a flat, universally accessible path of crushed stone, eventually leading to a viewing platform on the edge of the bog. The treadway is 3 feet wide with a few wider spots for easy turnarounds. Benches invite visitors to rest, take in the scenery, and scout for wildlife, which may include muskrat, mink, beaver, white-tailed deer, songbirds, and the bog's eponymous moose. This short walk is suitable for all ages and abilities. (*Note*: Because Wenlock Wildlife Management Area is home to the rare ground-nesting spruce grouse, dogs must be leashed.)

As you leave the parking area and head into the woods, the first thing you notice is the fragrance of evergreens. You are entering a boreal spruce–fir forest, with its characteristic mossy hummocks and closed canopy. Velvetleaf blueberries, sheep laurel, and mountain holly are abundant, and the mossy ground is interspersed with goldthread, bunchberries, and ferns. In summer, you will immediately notice a change in temperature as you begin this enchanting outing.

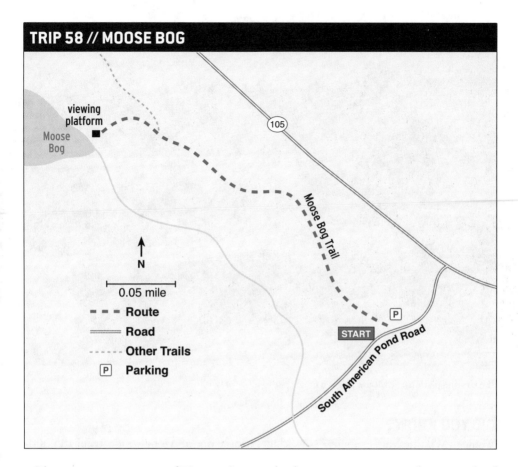

The spruce grouse, one of Vermont's rarest birds, requires extensive, dense stands of spruce trees, which are only found in small pockets of the Northeast Kingdom, including the area around Moose Bog. In winter, the spruce grouse feeds on conifer buds and needles. During summer, its diet expands to include berries, mushrooms, seeds, and insects. Numerous accounts indicate that the spruce grouse is ridiculously tame, but in Vermont, the bird is elusive and will quickly take to the trees when disturbed.

At 0.4 mile, a sign marks the path to Moose Bog. Turn left and descend two easy switchbacks to a level boardwalk that leads to a viewing platform. This sprawling black spruce bog features many opportunities for viewing wildlife, including beaver, moose, black ducks, boreal chickadees, and black-backed woodpeckers. In summer and fall, hare's-tail cottongrass is plentiful, with its characteristic white tufts that resemble both cotton and the underside of a rabbit's fluffy tail. Carnivorous pitcher plants and sundews have evolved to thrive in nutrient-poor bog habitats, relying on decomposing insects to provide them with much-needed nitrogen.

After enjoying a glimpse into this rare natural community, return to the trailhead the way you hiked in.

The viewing platform at Moose Bog is a great spot to look for wildlife.

DID YOU KNOW?

Wenlock Wildlife Management Area includes Moose Bog and is home to part of a 15,000-acre softwood basin known as the "Nulhegan Wintering Area," which is used by white-tailed deer as a critical wintering habitat. As many as 1,000 deer migrate to Nulhegan Basin each winter.

MORE INFORMATION

Moose Bog Trail is maintained by the Vermont Fish and Wildlife Department.

NEARBY

More extensive wildlife viewing can be found within Silvio O. Conte National Wildlife Refuge, just north of Moose Bog. Camp, paddle, and swim at Brighton State Park, 9 miles west. Paddle part of the Northern Forest Canoe Trail, which passes through Island Pond on its 740-mile journey from New York's Adirondacks to northern Maine. Restaurants, lodging, and shops are in the community of Island Pond, 10 miles west.

FROM THE CCC TO THE VYCC:
CONSERVATION CORPS IN VERMONT

Vermont has almost as many trails as it has citizens. OK, maybe that's an exaggeration, but think about not just the hiking trails that cobweb the entire state but also the cross-country and alpine ski trails, the mountain-bike and paddling trails, the all-terrain vehicle trails and snowmobile trails, the rail-trails and horseback-riding trails, and the birding trails and town park trails. How did one of this country's smallest states, with one of the smallest populations, come to be so covered with trails?

It's too simple to say the Civilian Conservation Corps (CCC) is responsible, but in a way it's true. The Depression-era program, part of President Franklin Delano Roosevelt's New Deal, harnessed the energies of unemployed young men to accomplish environmental conservation projects across the nation. The federal government originally allotted Vermont four CCC camps, but Perry Merrill, then the state forester, had a long list of planned projects, and he lobbied successfully for additional men and funding to complete them.

Vermont eventually hosted 30 CCC camps that supported more than 40,000 men, including more than 11,000 Vermonters, as they constructed hiking and ski trails, state park facilities, fire towers, and mountain roads. They hand-built massive earthen flood-control dams and bridges. They fought forest fires and tree diseases, and they planted thousands of trees. Their legacy is not only the physical infrastructure that enables people to actively enjoy Vermont's landscape but also the promotion of a culture of outdoor recreation and conservation that today values all manner of trails.

Another CCC legacy is its many offspring. The first and one of the most successful descendants is the Student Conservation Association (SCA), which began in 1957 with a mission to save national parks from being "loved to death" and continues in a broader capacity today. In the 1970s, the federally funded Youth Conservation Corps followed SCA's lead and employed hundreds of thousands of young Americans. When federal funding was cut in 1981, many states, including Vermont, picked up the tab to keep these programs running. The Vermont Youth Conservation Corps (VYCC) was born in 1985.

Today, VYCC is a private nonprofit organization that hires young people to complete conservation projects in the service of its mission "to teach individuals to take personal responsibility for all their actions." The NorthWoods Conservation Corps, founded separately to serve the Northeast Kingdom, hires young people as part of its mission "to help local youth become stewards of their natural and community resources."

If you come across a youth crew in brightly colored hard hats laboring on the trail, offer them some encouragement. The state's trails and recreation facilities depend on their hard work today—and on their attitudes and values in the decades to come.

59 BLUFF MOUNTAIN

Steep rock outcroppings provide exciting hiking and a bird's-eye view of Island Pond as well as the expanse of forested peaks beyond it.

Features

Location Island Pond, VT

Rating Moderate

Distance 3.3 mile-loop

Elevation Gain 1,110 feet

Estimated Time 2.5 hours

Maps USGS Island Pond, USGS Spectacle Pond; Vermont Department of Forests, Parks, and Recreation: fpr.vermont.gov/sites/fpr/files/Recreation/Activities/Library/hiking/KHT%20map_2-sided_apr2019.pdf

GPS Coordinates 44° 49.52′ N, 71° 52.57′ W

Contact NorthWoods Stewardship Center, P.O. Box 220, East Charleston, VT 05833; 802-723-6551; northwoodscenter.org

DIRECTIONS

From the junction of VT 105 and VT 114 in the middle of the community of Island Pond, go east on VT 105 for 0.2 mile and turn left onto South Street. Take the second right onto Mountain Street and drive 0.6 mile to the trailhead parking lot on the left (space for about six cars).

TRAIL DESCRIPTION

Bluff Mountain (2,450 feet) is a north–south ridge with three high points, the middle being the proper summit. The Community Trail–Lookout Trail loop climbs the steep-sided southern summit (2,380 feet) overlooking Island Pond. Lookout Trail traverses a very steep pitch with the aid of iron handles affixed to the rock. People who aren't comfortable with that level of exposure can use Bluff Mountain Community Trail to ascend and descend or to make a loop with the middle-of-the-mountain path that goes between Lookout Trail and Community Trail. If you skip the ladders and ascend via Community Trail, be sure to go past the forested summit of Bluff Mountain and continue 0.1 mile to the magnificent outlook. The steep section of Lookout Trail is best as an ascent—and best avoided altogether in wet or icy conditions. But for hikers who appreciate variety and challenge, Lookout Trail provides a fun, memorable experience.

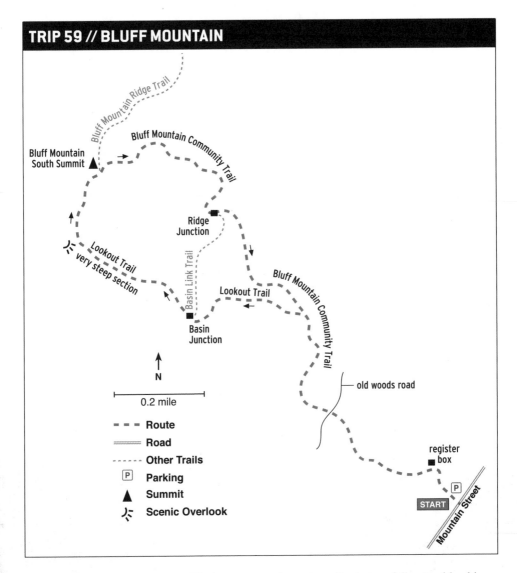

Bluff Mountain Community Trail starts in a plantation of red pine, following blue blazes uphill through tidy rows of tall trees. At 0.1 mile, a register box marks the transition into a more natural forest of maple, birch, and fir. Ferns and the glossy, dark green leaves of partridgeberry spread across the forest floor. Climbing moderately, the trail traverses a bushy swath at 0.2 mile, where blackberries and raspberries thrive. At 0.4 mile, cross an old, eroded woods road in the forest and continue snaking up the hill through a stand of big cedars. At 0.7 mile, arrive at the junction of Lookout Trail. Bluff Mountain Community Trail goes right and will be your downhill route. Go left onto yellow-blazed Lookout Trail, crossing the hillside for 0.2 mile and then descending another 0.1 mile to reach Basin Junction at 1.0 mile. Basin Link Trail heads uphill here 0.3 mile to join Bluff Mountain Community Trail, providing an alternate route to the summit that avoids the ladders of Lookout Trail.

From Basin Junction, Lookout Trail rises at a pleasant rate at first, traversing a couple of wet swaths filled with ferns and then the hillside. A rock staircase marks the beginning of the steep section of trail. Steep becomes very steep, and for the final 0.1 mile of the climb, you'll need your hands to help you ascend several sets of metal rungs attached to the ledges. At the top, an attractive view of the shining waters of Island Pond rewards your efforts. Continue a short distance up Lookout Trail to a grassy clearing with a bigger overlook and a more stable place to stand while admiring it.

Island Pond and its namesake community are the highlights of the scene. Island Pond sits in an interesting position on a watershed divide. From the pond, the Clyde River flows northwest, descending to Lake Memphremagog, which drains north into the Saint Lawrence River. Just on the other side of Island Pond, the Nulhegan River rises from Nulhegan Pond and flows the opposite direction, southeast to the Connecticut River, which drains south into Long Island Sound.

Look closely at the ridge beyond Island Pond's waters to spot the blocky Cold War–era radar building on East Mountain (3,420 feet). The summit of 3,267-foot Burke Mountain (Trip 52) curves against the sky behind the Seneca Range to the south. New Hampshire's White Mountains are in the distant south, with the pointed summit of Mount Garfield (4,500 feet) east of the big hump of Mount Lafayette (5,260 feet).

From here, follow Lookout Trail's yellow blazes across the clearing and into the woods. A rolling, mossy path leads through a boreal forest to a short spur at 1.5 miles. The south, or lower, mountain summit is at the end of the spur, on a large rock surrounded by trees. From the spur–trail junction, the blue blazes of Bluff Mountain Community Trail begin,

Bluff Mountain's outlook gives hikers a well-deserved view of Island Pond.

leading through a damp, flat-bottomed ravine at 1.7 miles and then to the Ridge Junction of Basin Link Trail at 2.1 miles. Stay left and continue downhill on Bluff Mountain Community Trail, returning to the Lookout Trail junction at 2.6 miles. Follow Bluff Mountain Community Trail out the way you hiked in.

DID YOU KNOW?

Paddlers on the Clyde River steer their boats through a tunnel under the Essex House and Tavern as they leave Island Pond.

MORE INFORMATION

Bluff Mountain's trails are maintained by the NorthWoods Stewardship Center.

NEARBY

The Northern Forest Canoe Trail's 740-mile route passes through the community of Island Pond; a kiosk with more information is in Pavilion Park, which is also a pleasant place to picnic and swim. Camp, paddle, and swim at Brighton State Park, 3.5 miles east. Restaurants, lodging, and shops are in the community of Island Pond, 1 mile south.

60 BROUSSEAU MOUNTAIN

A short, pretty climb over the summit of this small northern peak leads to dramatic cliffs and a wide vista south featuring lakes and mountains.

Features

Location Norton, VT

Rating Easy to Moderate

Distance 1.6 miles round-trip

Elevation Gain 590 feet

Estimated Time 1 hour

Maps USGS Averill

GPS Coordinates 44° 58.61′ N, 71° 44.47′ W

Contact NorthWoods Stewardship Center, P.O. Box 220, East Charleston, VT 05833; 802-723-6551; northwoodscenter.org

DIRECTIONS

From the junction of VT 114 and VT 147 in Norton, near the border-crossing station, follow VT 114 east for 3.0 miles. Turn right onto Brousseau Mountain Road and follow it 1.3 miles to its end at a gate. Park alongside the road (space for about five cars), being careful not to block the gate or driveways. (The road is not maintained in winter; depending on the conditions, snowshoers may need to park at the bottom of Brousseau Mountain Road and add 2.6 miles to the hike.)

TRAIL DESCRIPTION

Brousseau Mountain (2,723 feet), just south of the Quebec border, is off the beaten path for most hikers; consequently, its incredible views and lovely forests are often quiet. Approaching this inconspicuous forested bump from the north, you don't see the dramatic cliffs on its south face until you arrive on top of them. Peregrine falcons sometimes nest on these crags, and if they choose this spot to rear their young, the overlook may be closed to hikers between March 15 and August 1 to protect chicks; check with Audubon Vermont (vt.audubon.org) for current information. The short, steady climb is appropriate for kids 5 and older.

Go around the gate and follow the extension of Brousseau Mountain Road about 400 feet, where Brousseau Mountain Trail goes left into the woods and passes a register box just inside the treeline. Climbing this trail gradually through the thin trunks of a young forest, go by an old apple tree and brushy openings on both sides of the trail that hint at the land's

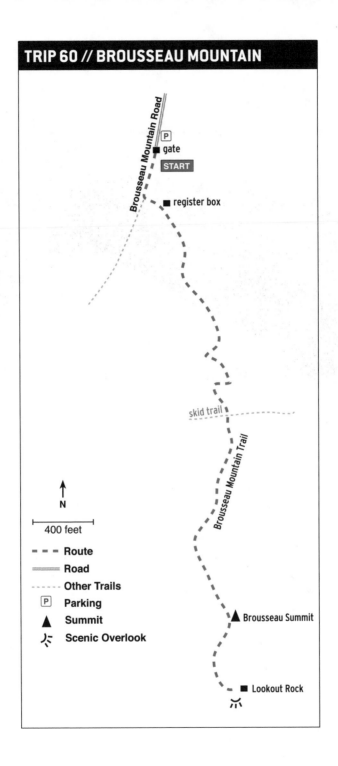

So far north it's almost in Canada, Brousseau Mountain gives hikers a view south across Little Averill Pond and the mountainous, immense forests of the Northeast Kingdom.

recent agricultural history. After traveling through a dim fir stand, the trail angles up the mountainside.

At 0.4 mile, Brousseau Mountain Trail crosses a narrow swath cut across the mountain—the remains of a skid trail used to remove logs. From here, the forest becomes more boreal: a beautiful mix of fir, spruce, mountain ash, and paper birch. These trees are older than those below, and the thick trunks are spaced far enough apart to give a view through the forest. The treadway is often solid bedrock, lined with moss, blueberries, and ferns, as Brousseau Mountain Trail makes its way back and forth and sometimes directly up the slope. Occasional rock steps and bog bridges break up the long stripes of rock trail.

The pitch lessens as you enter a tunnel of close-growing saplings near the top of the mountain. Curving left, cross the forested summit at 0.7 mile. The trail drops to the right, descending through spruce and fir for 0.1 mile before arriving at the open rocks of the lookout. Leash dogs here and keep children close by.

Little Averill Pond spreads across the valley beneath the cliffs, its inlet stream zigzagging through a marsh to the west. Sable Mountain is the little solo peak south of the pond, and the Green and Black mountains form the high ground beyond the inlet marsh. The expanse of forest beyond Little Averill Pond is largely conserved timberlands. Monadnock Mountain rises beyond ridges to the southeast, its fire tower discernible against the sky. Turbines visible on the ridges north and south of Monadnock are in New Hampshire, as are the

White Mountains spread across the southern horizon, including Mount Garfield and Mount Lafayette. Vermont's Jay Peak (Trip 51) pokes above closer ridgelines to the west.

Return downhill the way you climbed up.

DID YOU KNOW?

The border towns of Norton, Vermont, and Stanhope, Quebec, developed together, as did many other border towns in this rural area, where the lay of the land often influenced communities more than political lines did. A general store sat on the international border for years, with doors on both sides so residents of either country could enter to shop.

MORE INFORMATION

Brousseau Mountain Trail is maintained by the NorthWoods Stewardship Center.

NEARBY

Little Averill and Great Averill ponds have placid paddling around the base of Brousseau Mountain. Pack your passport to mountain bike at Hereford Mountain in East Hereford, Quebec, 19 miles northeast. Paddle, camp, and swim at Brighton State Park, 23 miles south. A general store in Norton provides some food; for more dining options, head to the community of Island Pond, 20 miles south.

APPENDIX: MOUNTAIN BIKING

The popularity of mountain biking has grown rapidly in Vermont over the past two decades and so have the number of trails specifically for bikes. The Vermont Mountain Bike Association (VMBA) is a central organizer and promoter of mountain biking, with chapter organizations heading up regional trail work. Some mountain-bike areas charge riders a fee to help defray maintenance expenses; other places are free to ride, with trail maintenance dependent on volunteers, paid memberships, and donations. Some ski areas maintain mountain-bike trails, and the many rail-trails throughout the state offer beginner-friendly off-road riding experiences.

Following is a partial list, in no particular order, of some of the best mountain biking in Vermont, with the caveat that more options exist than can be included here. More trails are added each season, all across the state. For the most up-to-date information, consult local bike shops and VMBA chapters (vmba.org).

Kingdom Trails: The award-winning Kingdom Trails in East Burke has everything from beginner-friendly farm roads to fast-flowing single-track and technical freeride trails, which include jumps, drops, and other features. With more than 100 miles of well-maintained, interconnected cross-country trails and a lift-served downhill and freeride area, this trail system is the leader in mountain biking—not just in Vermont but in the Northeast. Near Burke Mountain (Trip 52); kingdomtrails.com.

Moosalamoo National Recreation Area: The U.S. Forest Service has joined forces with VMBA and other groups to develop mountain biking in this diverse section of the northern Green Mountain National Forest. Trails range from dirt roads to technical single-track. Near Robert Frost Interpretive Trail (Trip 22) and Mount Horrid's Great Cliff (Trip 21); moosalamoo.org/biking.

Trapp Family Lodge: High on the mountain above Stowe, this iconic resort's trail system offers 40 miles and counting of double- and single-track riding that connects to a network of local trails, accommodating riders of all ability levels. Near Wiessner Woods (Trip 42), Stowe Pinnacle (Trip 44), and Sterling Pond (Trip 47); trappfamily.com.

Mad River Riders (Mad River valley): This central Vermont area has both steep technical riding and flowy, beginner-friendly single-track riding at Blueberry Lake, with advanced and intermediate trails at Sugarbush and Eurich ponds and in Chase Brook Town Forest. Near Sunset Ledge (Trip 24), Mount Abraham (Trip 25), and Burnt Rock Mountain (Trip 26); madriverriders.com.

Millstone Trails: Circumnavigating old, scenic granite quarries on the hill above Barre, more than 35 miles of trails provide tons of technical riding, as well as loops for beginner and intermediate riders. Near Spruce Mountain (Trip 29) and Owl's Head (Trip 30); millstonetrails.com.

Chittenden County: With more than 100 miles of trails in a dozen locations not far from Burlington, Chittenden County offers options for riders of all ability levels. Near Colchester Pond (Trip 34), Niquette Bay (Trip 35), and Mount Mansfield (Trips 45 and 46); fotwheel.org.

Sleepy Hollow: This inn in Huntington offers more than a dozen miles of intermediate and advanced single-track in a system that connects to a network of multiuse trails in Hinesburg Town Forest. Near Camel's Hump (Trip 27); skisleepyhollow.com.

Catamount Outdoor Family Center: These multiuse trails in Williston accommodate runners and hikers in addition to mountain bikers. Popular camps, races, and other events make the center a hub of local outdoor activity. Near Mount Mansfield (Trips 45 and 46); catamountoutdoorfamilycenter.org.

Norwich University's Shaw Outdoor Center: The hillside that historically hosted alpine ski trails is now crisscrossed with single-track bike trails; a skills park at the base helps beginning and intermediate riders get up to speed. Near Burnt Rock Mountain (Trip 26), Spruce Mountain (Trip 29), and White Rock Mountain (Trip 39); norwich.edu/shaw.

Green Mountain Trails: Twenty-five miles of multiuse single-track trails in Pittsfield, Stockbridge, and Chittenden offer all levels of riding on a variety of terrain. Near Killington Peak (Trip 16) and Deer Leap (Trip 17); gmtrails.org.

Pine Hill Park: Within Rutland, a 325-acre preserve of wooded hills and ravines hosts 17 miles of multiuse single-track trails. The majority are intermediate level, but there are beginner-friendly routes and some technical options for advanced riders. Near White Rocks Ice Beds (Trip 12), Deer Leap (Trip 17), and Helen W. Buckner Memorial Preserve (Trip 18); rutlandrec.com/pine-hill-park.

Ascutney Trails Association: The western flank of Mount Ascutney contains 35 miles of multiuse trails looping through woods and fields, accommodating all abilities. The Swoops and Loops Trail is a 3.5-mile network designed for novice riders. Near Okemo Mountain (Trip 13) and Mount Ascutney (Trip 14); ascutneytrails.com.

Slate Valley Trails: Located in southwestern Vermont, Slate Valley Trails maintains multiuse trail networks at Castleton University, Delaney Woods in Wells, and Endless Brook near Lake Saint Catherine. Near Mount Zion Major and Minor (Trip 19); slatevalleytrails.org.

Bennington Area Trail System (BATS): This network of multiuse trails encompasses the side of Mount Anthony (intermediate/advanced trails) and the property of Southwestern Vermont Medical Center (beginner trails) in Bennington. Near Bald Mountain (Trip 1); batsvt.org.

INDEX

ABOUT THE AUTHORS

Jen Lamphere Roberts is the author of the first two editions of *AMC's Best Day Hikes in Vermont* and the editor of Northern Forest Canoe Trail's debut map series and guidebook. She lives with her family in Montpelier, Vermont, where they own a gear shop, Onion River Outdoors, and spend as much time as possible with friends and dogs on the local trails and waterways.

Tara Schatz is a freelance writer and photographer who loves nothing more than exploring Vermont's hiking trails and wild places with her two dogs. She is the founder of Vermont Explored, an online travel guide to the Green Mountains, and the American road trip blog *Back Road Ramblers* (backroadramblers.com). She lives with her husband in Bennington, Vermont.

AMC BOOK UPDATES

AMC Books strives to keep our guidebooks as up-to-date as possible to help you plan safe and enjoyable adventures. If we learn after publishing a book that relevant trails have been relocated or that route or contact information has changed, we will post the updated information online. Before you hit the trail, visit outdoors.org/books-and-maps and click the link in the Book Updates section near the bottom of the page. While hiking, if you notice discrepancies with the trip descriptions or maps, or if you find any other errors in this book, please let us know by submitting them to amcbookupdates@outdoors.org or to Books Editor, c/o AMC, 10 City Square, Boston, MA 02129. We will verify all submissions and post key updates each month. AMC Books is dedicated to being a recognized leader in outdoor publishing. Thank you for your participation.

BE OUTDOORS™

Since 1876, the Appalachian Mountain Club has channeled your enthusiasm for the outdoors into everything we do and everywhere we work to protect. We're inspired by people exploring the natural world and deepening their appreciation of it.

With AMC chapters from Maine to Washington, D.C., including groups in Boston, New York City, and Philadelphia, you can enjoy activities like hiking, paddling, cycling, and skiing, and learn new outdoor skills. We offer advice, guidebooks, maps, and unique eco-lodges and huts to inspire your next outing.

Your visits, purchases, and donations also support conservation advocacy and research, youth programming, and caring for more than 1,800 miles of trails.

Join us!
outdoors.org/join

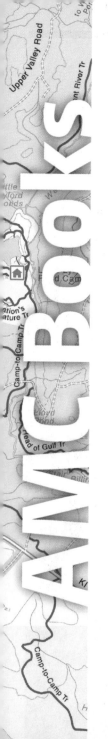

Southern New Hampshire Trail Guide, 5th Edition

Compiled and edited by Ken MacGray

This comprehensive trail guide covers New Hampshire hiking trails south of the White Mountain National Forest, including the state's beloved Lakes Region and Seacoast. Every trail description provides turn-by-turn directions, making route finding straightforward and reliable, while suggested hikes feature icons showing kid-friendly trips, scenic views, and more. Whether you're a first-time hiker or an experienced backpacker, this trail guide is a must-have.

$23.95 • 978-1-62842-115-6

AMC's Mountain Skills Manual

Christian Bisson and Jamie Hannon

This comprehensive guide tackles the essential skills every outdoor lover should master. Beginners will learn the basics, about gear, navigation, safety, and stewardship. More experienced readers can hone backpacking skills, including trip planning, efficient packing, and advanced wilderness ethics. All readers will set new goals, perfect their pace, and gain the tools to plan and enjoy their next outdoor adventure.

$21.95 • 978-1-62842-025-8 • ebook available

Quiet Water New Hampshire and Vermont, 3rd Edition

John Hayes and Alex Wilson

Great for families, anglers, canoeists, and kayakers of all abilities, this guide features 90 of the best calm water paddling trips in New Hampshire and Vermont. Explore the many ponds of Pillsbury State Park, paddle Chocorua Lake with breathtaking views, and rediscover Vermont's scenic Lake Champlain.

$19.95 • 978-1-934028-35-3 • ebook available

This Wild Land

Andrew Vietze

Almost twenty years ago, Andrew Vietze made an unexpected career change: from punk rock magazine editor to park ranger at Baxter State Park in Maine. From midnight search-and-rescue missions to trail maintenance to cleaning toilets, Baxter rangers do it all...and over the decades Vietze has seen it all. In *This Wild Land*, Vietze tells his story with humor, action, and an eye for the compelling details of life as a park ranger, making it the perfect read for outdoor and armchair adventurers alike.

$18.95 • 978-1-62842-132-3 • ebook available